Norms and Illegality

Norms and Illegality

Intimate Ethnographies and Politics

Edited by
Cristiana Panella and Walter E. Little

LEXINGTON BOOKS
Lanham • Boulder • New York • London

Published by Lexington Books
An imprint of The Rowman & Littlefield Publishing Group, Inc.
4501 Forbes Boulevard, Suite 200, Lanham, Maryland 20706
www.rowman.com

6 Tinworth Street, London SE11 5AL, United Kingdom

British Library Cataloguing in Publication Information Available

Library of Congress Cataloging-in-Publication Data

Names: Panella, Cristiana, 1968- editor. | Little, Walter E., 1963- editor.
Title: Norms and illegality : intimate ethnographies and politics / edited by Cristiana Panella and Walter E. Little.
Description: Lanham : Lexington Books, [2021] | Includes bibliographical references and index.
Identifiers: LCCN 2021006425 (print) | LCCN 2021006426 (ebook) | ISBN 9781793646309 (Cloth : acid-free paper) | ISBN 9781793646316 (ePub)
Subjects: LCSH: Social norms. | Illegality. | Ethnology—Fieldwork.
Classification: LCC GN493.3 .N68 2021 (print) | LCC GN493.3 (ebook) | DDC 306—dc23
LC record available at https://lccn.loc.gov/2021006425
LC ebook record available at https://lccn.loc.gov/2021006426

Contents

List of Figures

Preface

Cristiana Panella

In October 2012, the AfricaMuseum[1] in Tervuren hosted the international and interdisciplinary conference, "Norms in the Margins and Margins of the Norm. The Social Construction of Illegality," bringing together scholars from around the world to discuss how illegality is culturally constructed and works across multiple ethnographic contexts. In particular, the conference questioned concepts, practices, and theories of illegality from a grounded and emic perspective by addressing the interstitial interdependence between official and hidden practices. The rich ethnographic landscape described by panelists showed how official law is porous, constantly seized upon and retailored through the interaction between official and informal-versus-illegal milieus. It also illustrated how illegal values, imbricated in daily life, deeply govern social practices and self-representations of illegal actors.

Since then, it seems to me that corporeality issues, as engaged in informal and illegal practices, should shift from the empathy imbricated into embodiment to a deep reflection on the ecumene of the pathetic experience of life which goes beyond specific case studies and contingencies. Here, I take the liberty to digress with a personal experience, as it deeply influenced the conceptual frame of the conference and this book. When I conceived of an international conference on Illegality in the AfricaMuseum in 2009, I aimed to propose an ethnographic approach to balance the reification of the social practices of illegal actors which I have been observing in my main research domain, cultural heritage studies, in particular, with regard to the unofficial/illegal digging and trading in African antiquities. In the early 1990s, when I first began researching the international circuits of the Malian ancient terracotta trade, the debate on "the phenomenon of plunder" ("*le phénomène du pillage*") in European and North American universities, international organizations, and museums was in full swing.

One of the main evidences that has led my questioning many years later, from my PhD fieldwork on the local networks of the antiquities trade (1996–2000) to the present, is the contradiction between the essentialized vision of looters' bodies circulating in media and in academic discourse and the real lives of these unnamed seasonal farmer-diggers who constitute the first link of the antiquities trade chain. These actors embodied, paraphrasing Michael Herzfeld, the unpolitic values linked to loneliness, deprivation, physical endurance, and risk. At the same time, some of them were wealthy farmers able to employ digging crews and to supply antiquities in the local market, calling into question the homogeneous official discourse that presents them as delinquents and poor wretches, alike, by considering poverty and being poor as inescapable conditions. In spite of a plethora of articles in the 1980s and 1990s, the rhetoric of the "phenomenon of plunder" has relied on always the same secondhand information, unceasingly relayed in newspapers, international reports, and academic publications.

Nevertheless, who such "ugly, dirty and bad" *pilleurs* are and what they actually did to excavate and supply terracotta antiquities remained in the background, if not unknown. The social issues of the local networks of the trade grow out of research priorities that were fundamentally oriented on the archaeological evidence of plunder from traces of clandestine digs or on the white-collar crime related to international suppliers, at that time especially European and North American ones, and powerful consumers of these objects. And yet, such incorporeal narratives of illegality have been, for two decades, one of the more pervasive topics of the international debate on cultural heritage in African Archaeology, Art History and Museum Studies.

The confrontation between emic and normative representations of corporeality has been a huge aspect of my research. One of the main lessons of my field experience has been to share with "looters" the bodily perception of risk. Such an exchange was our silent pact, our deepest evidence of reciprocity and trust beyond any verbal intercourse. We were offering our bodies to one another while coping with a reciprocal strangeness with regard to cultural roots, daily life, and above all, aims. Their ugly, dirty and bad backs curved while digging in deep illegal holes that media and academic papers passed around were set in front of me and looked at me silently. In most cases, words were rare, precise; responses, gaunt. Such encounters were not conversations, but what philosopher Jean-Luc Marion would call a condition of saturation, an incumbent and unsayable excess of evidence.

Silence and waiting are usually faithful companions in field research. Waiting in silence with others is a fully bodily lived life, indeed. Such silence implies a strong ethical challenge. Ethics concerns not only the choice of contingent strategies responding to our own values but by the very fact of being exposed in a potentially dangerous event while trying to maintain communication with the source of danger and to forge trust from constraint. The challenge of my presence in my field site has been the gift of a reciprocal physical and silent exposure. Nevertheless, sometimes your body tells you that, in spite of your efforts, of your unspoken pact, trust is just too precarious. That your hope and your good will are not enough to appease distrust. That sensation of danger will become a real danger. So, you have to move away.

Considering such a strong bodily experience of risky trust, the disembodied *repetita* on looters that nourished the official discourses of academic and mediatic milieus seemed to me, simply, surrealistic. During my later fieldwork on artisanal gold miners in Southern Mali and, then, on West African petty traders of counterfeits in Rome, the gap between bodily self-representations of the hero (exposure of the body to risk while being bodily and juridically precarious), and the double register of the political representation, continued to represent cogent evidence for my research. Once again, the alternation between miserabilism and illegality of official actors concealed individual aspirations and daily life strategies.

It is undeniable that most academic research on the clandestine trade in antiquities should require long stays in the field, and current report-oriented research doesn't allow (nor need) it. That partially explains why very few works provide firsthand information on the social organization of diggers and middlemen. Nevertheless, it is not anodyne to remark on two deeper reasons for the lack of in-depth information on the local networks of the trade. The first one relates to the growing neoliberal trend of academic research that progressively gives priority to applied useful works: quick, formatted, smart, and ready-to-use. With regard to usefulness, the fact that illegality research has been mainly established and driven by archaeology and, more recently, law, criminology, and criminal sociology has implied significant consequences on conceptual and methodological approaches, as the priority conferred to proofs of evidence through statistics, georeferenced mapping, drones, and images of holes and hauls of antiques. The support of these disciplines to official entities (police, customs, museums, administration, international organizations) wouldn't be a stranger to a vision of illegal dynamics as the specular contraposed camp of official (alias legal) integrity.

The second reason, which derives from the first one, is that research on art and antiquities trades does turn around networks and actors of the market economy. Put basically, poor and illegal farmer-looters are useful to move antiquities into the circuits of international trade but useless in the economy of the international debate on antiquities networks that was and remains fundamentally reserved and targeted to Western- (ized) circuits, representations, and values. In the case of the sub-Saharan rural diggers and middlemen, the first links of the international chain are even more invisible than other categories of informal-versus-illegal farmers, as coca's farmers in Bolivia, who are endorsed by unions.

Finally, academic and popular publications on looting seem to have constituted a sort of erotic topic, a remote desire offering a fashioned danger without danger. The institutional construction of looters shows that illegality rhymes with social invisibility. That is why the invisibility question has to relate to researchers ethically. Field research on the first links of illegal/informal market chains, be they antiquities, gold, or coltan, reveals that Western official normativity of ethics and aesthetics stands thanks to an army of invisibles who are neither informed or aware of having been inserted into a moral and juridical system as a source of comparison for the construction of Western deontological values. Such a double register of opacity and transparency of official norms appears contradictory only if we do not admit that transparency discourses are based on two orders of corruption, which engage ethical and epistemological implications of the North-South conundrum. The first one is evident in the case of clandestine or, in the best cases, seasonal migrants working in European agriculture, private welfare or building. For instance, workers (mostly transnational migrants) in Italian fruit and vegetable plantations are considered outlaws. And yet, their bodies are totally transparent and visible on the roads and in the fields, also during the hottest hours of the day. If they stopped their (illegal) work, the Italian production chain would be deeply jeopardized and prices would rise out of control. The consequences of migrant labor scarcity in Italian agriculture are evident in the loss of at least 200,000 legal seasonal workers during COVID-19 lockdown in March–April 2020.[2]

In other words, clandestine migrants evolve within a system of value as they are the cause and the tool of the official discourse on illegality at the same time. As *illegals*, undocumented migrants resolve the need for workers, nourish the political emergency of clandestine migration, and participate in public initiatives against *caporalato* (undocumented recruitment and exploitation of workers without residence permit) and illegal work mixing legal, informal, and illegal status.

A further degree of corruption occurs when those who are invisible contribute to trace ethical Western landscapes that go beyond their specific condition of being illegal. For example, informal and clandestine Sub-Saharan miners constitute an enlightening example of the ambiguity which underlies Western green policies. The *Mea culpa* is driven by the popular Anthropocene analysis of global warming. The acceleration of human pollution bridges the trendy ecologism of the electric transport, underlying a deep anthropocenic social inequality. The ethical "zero-emission" slogan contributes to maintain severe pauperization and pollution of non-Western regions providing raw materials for electric cars and wind turbines, as well as to keep invisible *illegals* in precarious and dangerous life conditions. And as well as in the case of looters, such invisible *illegals* are not useful for official discourses on human ecology because humanity targeted for such ecological values lives in the most industrialized countries of the world. The daily life of Sub-Saharan miners is out of the deontological landscape of the capitalist ecologist policies, because it is simply unthinkable. Actually, moral transparency of official norms does request the hidden sacrifices of the poorest of the poor. They are the poorest not only in economic terms but especially in terms of speech and visibility, of their own vision of oikos, of what they feel as being essential to ensure their existence. It seems to me that such common destiny between *illegal* hidden lives and *legal* official frames shows how the construction of the norm and the ethical framing implies the intrinsic interdependence between opacity and transparency dynamics.

COVID-19 pandemic has not only highlighted legions of invisible ugly, dirty and bad people but it has also reminded the bloody roots of social interaction. I do intend *bloody* as the emic dimension of sociality, a bodily experience of vital needs between hope and despair. Let me mention to the drama of Celia Capira Mamani, the woman who in Arequipa ran after the former Peruvian president Vizcarra's car screaming "Mr. President, don't go!", in order to beg for a hospital bed for her husband suffering from COVID-19. This encounter embodies a pandemic sentiment of physical danger and inner idleness in a world that appears to be out of reach. Such a feeling of abandonment is an effect of the relationship between the criminalization of poverty and pain. Pain is becoming a new crime of poverty at several levels. And the high percentages of COVID-19 among low-income households and high-density neighborhoods have added new categories of pauperized outlaws coming from the middle class. That's why Cecilia Capira Mamani does disturb. Her desperate eyes behind the mask seem to transmit the contagion of her husband on the outside. Her pain is infectious because it is desperate.

Moreover, the different phases of the COVID-19 pandemic seem to represent the progressive yardsticks of the threshold of the socially tolerated pain. If one's health worsens into deep pneumonia, or a long post-infection asthenia, the suffering body is put into an illegitimate social condition not only because its productivity, social duties, and welfare efficacity are weakened, but also because the severe sickness makes the intrinsic frailty and caducity of lives realistic and absolutely trivial. The awareness that that social interaction is a fleshy exchange of emotional snapshots does explain why the pandemic could not be escaped here.

These few thoughts anticipate a vision of corporality as witness that Walt Little and I develop in the introduction: the ethical and epistemological implications of individual and social living wherever the bare body remains the only resource to signify and to act our own aspirations.[3] Silent wishes, invested every day through the consumption of fleshy bodies, request more and more to Anthropology to be a posture and a bastion of listening. Anthropology is not merely a more nuanced declination of journalism, even if the temptation to provide qualitative approaches for reading contemporary times could be envisaged as a form of engagement of the discipline. Sophisticated analysis does not help us to dismiss our skin and to detect the single heartbeat which crosses living beings and makes hope and aspiration fleshy. The anthropological attitude not only should give empirical and theoretical tools for understanding social practices, but also remind us that the really common elements of human consumption are hope and pain. And, we have to be listening too.

In this sense, Anthropology has to carry on the reiteration of the silent litanies and private prayers that mold our everyday gestures. Practices are issued by strategies and need planning, a landscape of inductive habits. Gestures, rather, encapsulate Virginia Woolf's "moments of being," and Marcel Proust's "intermittences of the hearth," the emotional consumption of the flesh. These are interstices of frailty. Anthropology does not need to constantly invent new perspectives that sometimes appear to be new only as regards contingent interests and aims. Such a search for novelties and the current trend to provide useful and ready-to-use information pushes the discipline toward contingency and the temporality of news, to be "on the piece." Instead, Anthropology should remind us of the lay sacrality infused in the ancient human daily consumption of "waste and repair," by hoping while despairing, and that such labor passes through painful and desiring bodies, including our own.

NOTES

1. In 2018, the Royal Museum of Central Africa changed its name to the AfricaMuseum.

2. The conference (October 25–27, 2012) was primarily funded by the AfricaMuseum, the Belgian Cooperation for Development, the Belgian Scientific Policy (Belspo), the Wenner-Gren Foundation, and Fédération Wallonie-Bruxelles International. It was organized by the AfricanMuseum in collaboration with the Free University Brussels and the Katholieke Universiteit Leuven. My sincere acknowledgments to AfricaMuseum Director Guido Gryseels, to Pierre Petit (ULB), and to the staff of LAMC, as well as to Filip de Boeck (KU Leuven) for having hosted, respectively, the second and the third day of sessions. My hearty thanks to Danielle De Lame, who nine years ago gave me insightful inspirations for my research and suggestions for this conference. I am grateful to Michael Herzfeld for having shared preliminary thoughts on the themes of the conference, and accompanied the first steps of the conceptual frame of this book.

3. I truly thank Walt Little for having accepted to share the coedition of the book and for having ensured the most of the editorial steps of the submission.

Introduction

Risk and Hope: Daily Life Subversions of the Norm

Cristiana Panella and Walter E. Little

Norms and Illegality: Intimate Ethnographies and Politics is a collection of ethnographic case studies that explores liminal and illegal practices from around the world in relation to forms of political control and policies that create and disrupt senses of normativity. The mutual entanglements and contradictions of what is legal and illegal, as various social actors interact in heterogeneous spaces, have given rise to debates about what is legal, illegal, and negotiable in the liminal domains in which people live and work. Beyond the confrontation between cultural and societal norms and individual expectations, what emerges from the ethnographic case studies, here, touches on the dimension of hope, as a resource in creation and productive daily experience.

Through analyses of the confrontation between different heterogeneous ethical and ethnographic frames, we address the official production of illegal subjects by the state, the creation of illegal values by liminal and illegal actors (Panella and Thomas, 2015), and the mutual entanglements of legal and illegal domains. Empirical descriptions of the social and political production of illegality show that criminalization policies are not necessarily oriented toward the erasing of crime. Instead, they maintain opaque spaces, based on arrangements and contradictions that paradoxically ensure the efficacy of control and outwardly conform to the rhetoric and ethics of global neoliberalism. Within these contexts, we aim to shed light on moral economies and frames of value entailed in systems of representation that have been set up by illegal or deviant individuals in their confrontations with the state. These often take the form of heroic accounts of risk and of honorable action, according to Michael Herzfeld (personal communication).

CORPOREALITY AS RISK AND HOPE

The contributions in this book tell the story of exposed bodies, of bodies at risk. The regime of corporeality is specific to the individual in its intrinsic contradiction and responds to temporalities offset from those of the norm. Where the norm is a starting point for action or else it intervenes the following action, the practices of corporeality (including wishes and emotions) are part of an eschatological logic, that is, an upcoming issue that is not yet completed and, sometimes, not achieved.

Up until a few decades ago, the body was the principal ethical yardstick of human societies because of the immediate perception of its consumption through physical pain and endurance, relief, sexual pleasure, hunger, and thirst. In particular, the body was ethically connoted by its own labor (from Latin *trabalium*). Originally referred to as a torture instrument, this lemma has meant, subsequently, work (in the broader sense), and sickness. It condenses the three fundamental steps of human life: birth, work (intended as consumption, *usus* of existence on its own), and the accomplishment of the biological cycle of human beings.

In the preindustrial societies, labor was an underlying compassion in which there was a literal sense of sharing feelings of pain and effort. As the tékhnē (τέχνη), then, was deeply linked to the use of the body, labor created a brotherhood between unknown destinies through the laborious and suffering flesh beyond social status. The medieval knight who engaged in the battle shared a daily life seems to be closer to that of an artisan, than a soldier would with a manager or administrator today.

Today, the body is overexposed, dissected, cloned, hibernated, scanned, but it is, nevertheless, not consciously lived in real time. It is more and more alien to the consciousness of its own gestures and to the ethical implications of the daily life *usus* of itself through the repetition of those same gestures. Changes in technology that human societies have experienced in the last 20 years, and the exponential growth and development of virtual realities and of artificial intelligence, have contributed to the progressive oblivion of the fundamentally corporeal nature of the Self. Such a disconnect of the corporeality of the Self has reinforced the perception that a lived life is perpetually still-to-become, a horizon of hope potentially unexhausted.

Perhaps even more important, the disconnection between ethical sense and corporeality is enhanced. Post-Kantian philosophy and anthropology have fully embraced a vision of ethics based on the ontologies of daily life (Holbraad and Petersen, 2017). Such approaches do stress the role of individual choice and perseverance, following an ethical project of progressive construction of the Self (Kitcher, 2011; Keane, 2016). In the weak Aristotelian relationship between individual aims and individual will (Lambek, 2015), such patient work would be based on a principle of immanence in ordinary actions and not in extraordinary events (Das, 2015). Nevertheless, the cleavage more and more marked and significant between individual aspirations and economic and juridical powers in place was such that ethical assumptions seem to not respond only to individual engagement and choice imbricated into the construction of the Self but, also, to a corporeal and emotional engagement, which in some circumstances stands as the unique powerful resource of the individual.

The social actors described in the ethnographic narratives of this book reflect these thoughts. They are not powerful puppeteers of the international weapon or drug cartels, but are informal workers, who are regarded as illegal, on the edge, and even on the margins of informal economies. They are considered illegal because they evolve in fragile and porous socioeconomic contexts in which the balance between formal, informal, and illegal is consubstantial with the precariousness of their own daily life. In other words, they do not drive ethical challenges only because they plan themselves, following a perspective of self-building. Rather, they harbor a corporeal and ethical dimension, because of the gap between the investment of their unique real resource, their body, and the materiality of an economic and juridical system that denies corporeality. Through their economic and political practices, however, the various social actors—most often vendors and workers in the informal economy—see their pain and triumphs brought to the surface, becoming political object and subject alike. These corporeal bodies are unpolitic to the extent that they are contrary to political power in place and because they are considered obsolete in the modern and effective society (Herzfeld, 2004; Panella, 2012).

Consequently, it seems to us that the dyscrasia between law and individual aspirations constitutes an ethical challenge that goes beyond the dynamics of political control and of resistance to it. Several of the ethnographic case studies in this book show the social contexts where it is difficult to access natural resources, services, infrastructures, and citizenship rights. Hope, then, becomes a primary resource of survival and determines deep dynamics of social integration and interaction, as the various examples in this book illustrate: miners in Ambondromifehy, Madagascar (Walsh), wholesale vegetable marketers in Benguet, Philippines (Milgram and Mendoza), street vendors in Antigua Guatemala (Little) and Rome, Italy (Clough Marinaro and Panella), and asylum seekers in Hong Kong (Mathews). Therefore, we consider hope and risk as resources that are directly incorporated into the creation and the experience of daily life.

The contributions of the book relate stories of exposed bodies, making a living in, often, difficult circumstances that become entwined with the fundamental work of ethnographers on the ground and with and in the lives of the people they study, befriend, irritate, and help. The choice of risk imbricated into action underlies the daily resuscitation of hope, as a ritual of survival, an initiation choice reiterated every day. And every day, hope builds its truth from its own ashes. It transforms void and absence into an issue of salvation, of providence and it repeats every day the same miracle of resuscitating itself by changing paths and tools, which can be seen in the simple acts of the vendors and workers described in this book. The repetitiveness of hope does not rhyme with the repeated application of the law but with a momentum that regenerates itself every day when people make do in the marginal spaces of the informal economy, in between legal and illegal, yet often within societal norms.

Consequently, because of its nature and function, hope is not only potential energy but, also, a propeller of the ethical achievement of individuals through the consumption of their own corporeality, which represents their primary concrete dimension beyond the purpose principle of the daily life action. Anthropological reflections on hope have been growing in recent years (Zournazi, 2002; Miyazaki, 2006; Zigon, 2009; Kleist and Jansen, 2016). These analyses have stressed the spatial and temporal dimensions of hope and how hope sketches out collective future(s), more specifically in times of crisis (Narotzky and Besnier, 2014). Nevertheless, it seems to us that few of these works directly link hope, ethics, and corporeality.

Far from being a question closed into the boundaries of philosophy, the abandonment of the in-herence, of the being adherent (from Latin *in-haerēre*) of the own body has immeasurable social, political, and ethical consequences on which Human and Social Sciences have to contend beyond the simple analysis of the body in action and in relation with regard to contingent aims. The disciplines should engage in the perspective of chorality and sacred, of a daily life offer of the body to its own consumption through huge and silent efforts and hopes. Such a vision seems to reflect the globalized contemporary daily life, where the lack of access becomes more and more visible to the civic and natural resources, ensuring survival and the construction of individuality as water, employment, or mobility for some categories of individuals have increased the self-perception of psychophysical resources as vital properties.

For instance, the court case between the Spanish NGO Open Arms that assists African migrants and Italian Home Office in the summer of 2019 is a clear example of the biopolitical challenge around the body with regard to hope. In this sense, resistance to the norm constitutes a major ethical challenge to the extent that to ban the right to hope would mean to deny the vital condition of the individual and finally to sentence social and physical death. In this perspective, a corporeal acceptation of physical and emotional risk within a life plan represents the *discrimen* between the acceptation of ethics as normatization and deontology and, then, another one for which the body is a tool of work and of claim, as well as an emotional receptacle alike.

Framing of Norms and Illegalities, Theoretical to Ethnographic

The construction of ethical constraints is essential for the official normatization of daily life, which questions individual choice while masking the contradictions between the heterogeneous spheres of value that shape it. Normatization not only instills the frontiers of the law, but it insinuates itself as an ethical conscience. Then, the individual labor of "internal contestation" of Canguilhem (Macherey, 2016), based on a structural principle of contradiction, is brought back to a linear trail through "le dressage minutieux et concret des forces utiles" (the meticulous training and concrete useful forces, Foucault, 1975, 252). The growing ethicization of daily life through the normative system goes hand in hand with a neglect of the same scale of individual ethics.

Normative systems imply a classification supposed to create a rhetorical apparatus of legitimization of an objective legal truth which intends to be also ethical. Actually, the norm has to gravitate in order to exist within a domain of opposite forces that establish it through the negative opposite. So, the application of the norm underlies an entity acting against the norm itself. What makes the assertiveness of the norm is the opacity of contradictory forces which determine its existence and application. Spheres of normativity thus imply a "cultural intimacy" (Herzfeld, 2005) in which, while some social actors recognize the paradoxes and cover-ups for what they are, all collude to produce systems that at least allow them to eke out a living while avoiding the more repressive forms of official (including state-administered) punishment, following then the well-known Italian proverb, *fatta la legge, trovato l'inganno* (every law has a loophole).

On a theoretical level, in the spirit of the Kantian concept of the beholder's "aesthetic indifference," we argue that the mere acts of producing normativity remain invisible and indistinct, that the ethical and juridical norms of official policies are effective and firm. The invisibility of legal/illegal interfaces produces ethical indifference toward the multiple spheres of contradiction while paradoxically allowing powerful actors to achieve global acceptance of their own ethical systems in the guise of collective consensus (Panella 2015).

The power relations of knowledge rely on the fact that the *indifference* that characterizes the internalization of ethical norms implies a process of confidence-building on the part of the addressees (public, consumers, users) toward the products of the normalization of supposedly illegal or unethical ways of doing and thinking. The erasure of the actual production from the display of official norms is part of what makes those norms acceptable. These dynamics also imply a crucial, material interaction between the formally recognized norms and the shadow practices that underlie them. These processes capture what Michael Herzfeld (2005) describes as "cultural intimacy," a concept that he revisits in this book.

These in-between spaces where illegalities exist and are permitted, where workers make a living, and where officials, enforcers, and consumers collude, allows governments and urban places to function, as is fleshed out in Alan Smart's theoretical contribution to this book. Building on his theory of extralegality (Smart and Zerilli, 2014), he introduces the concept of graying. Graying provides a conceptual framework for the processes by which goods, services, practices, and people slip between and in-and-out of legality and illegality, formal-to-informal economic and political sectors.

The invisibility of legal/illegal interfaces produces ethical indifference toward the multiple spheres of contradiction while paradoxically allowing powerful actors to achieve global acceptance of their own ethical systems in the guise of collective consensus. In this sense we conceive of the production of legal truth from a Foucauldian perspective as linking knowledge and power within a system of inequality. The power relations of knowledge rely on the fact that the indifference that characterizes the internalization of ethical norms implies a process of confidence-building on the part of the addressees (public, consumers, users) toward the products of such normalization of supposedly illegal or unethical ways of thinking. The erasure of the actual production from the display of official norms is part of what makes those norms acceptable.

The contributors, here, frame norms on the margin from specific ethnographic encounters, demonstrating how the construction of illegalities (and legalities) is firmly rooted in multiple, shifting contextual frames. Smart, in his chapter, explains, "The norms that lie at the margins of the state are like this: if we examine them at different points in time, we can get varying impressions of how close they are to the endpoints of black and white."

The case studies in this book provide examples of how the dynamics Smart describes play out in the everyday, on-the-ground practices in Benguet, Philippines wholesale vegetable marketplaces (Milgram), in street vending strategies in Antigua Guatemala, a UNESCO Heritage Site (Little), in artisanal sapphire mining in Ambondromifehy, Madagascar (Walsh), in extra incomes that peasant farmers make as part-time antiquities diggers in Bamako, Mali (Panella), in asylum seekers' contradictory decisions to beg or to work in Hong Kong (Mathews), and in the ways that Senegalese wholesalers and Roma street vendors navigate informal trade networks in Rome (Clough Marinaro and Panella). Taken collectively, the contributors' case studies highlight the importance of the ethnographic vantage point in revealing, as Herzfeld argues in his chapter, the ways in which people in their work, deeds, and everyday being are made into criminals, illegals, rule-breakers, security risks, and other dangerous identity labels. Exposing the damage of this kind of construction and the social and legal processes behind them is why it is important for "anthropologists to write in the first person—and explains why legal documents are rarely composed in that way" (Herzfeld, in this book). The positionality of the anthropologist is crucial in that "ethnographic perspectives . . . are particularly important because statistics—a staple in traditional studies of crime and illegality—are not only often unreliable, but can also create a false impression of the people being studied" (Rose-Greenland and Heatherington, 2014, 507).

These processes of making and, even, unmaking legal and illegal subjects can best be seen on the ground in the everyday practices of how people make a living. The embedded nature of this work plays out in the tense relationships to official laws and regulations. But it is important to think cautiously about the embeddedness of these economies in society, as Olivier de Sardan (2013) warns. He posits that the core theoretical aspects of embeddedness have been viewed from two extremes, a Marxist perspective that norms are established via relations of force and culturalist perspective that they are the result of shared past. These perspectives, however, do not need to be diametrically opposed and can be compatible (ibid. 284). He explains, "A more modern and empirically based notion of informal norms as heterogeneous, ambivalent, and dynamic could have allowed for fruitful dialogue with sociologists and anthropologists, whose very job is to go over this ground, with which economists are largely unfamiliar, in great detail" (ibid. 287). However, as Smart, Panella, and Herzfeld state in their respective theoretical positions, distinctions such as informal norms are highly problematic. To engage in a discourse of legal versus illegal and formal versus informal is to be complicit in the construction of particular kinds of subjects as normal or abnormal, legal or illegal. This dualistic or oppositional conceptualization then denies or ignores the "creative play somewhere in (and not infrequently outside) the space between the letter and the spirit of the law" (Herzfeld) where gray and graying are apt metaphors to capture the rich textures of every social, political, and economic processes (Smart). So, as all case studies here illustrate, it is not informal norms but just norms that are certainly "heterogeneous, ambivalent, and dynamic" that underlie the very relationships and ethical practices that we ethnographers engage in while conducting research on norms and illegality, where it is not simply "cultural norms in order to evaluate the appropriateness of cash payments" to collaborators, informants, and friends in one's field site (Panella).

The contributors to this book research no consensus about norms in relation to public social, economic, and political conventions. Rather, they demonstrate what Coombe described some time ago, that "regulatory frameworks in which people operate are far more nuanced than an examination of legal rules, official regulations, and sanctioned norms suggests" (1995, 806). However, where she emphasizes that "it is impossible to avoid the ambiguities and ambivalence inherent in situations where identities and communities are being reconfigured" in the "cultural politics of law and society" (1995, 834), the contributors, here, argue that ambiguity and ambivalence are the norm and part of making do in everyday life (de Certeau, 1984). The overarching position taken by all contributors can be ascribed as one based on practice theory, where attention is focused on public spaces of interaction and accessible economic, political, and social performances. This distinction is significant, because "rules, norms and concepts get their meaning, and their normative authority and force, from their embodiment in publicly accessible activity" (Rouse, 2007, 504). A practice theory approach makes understanding these norms (the creative play between the letter of the law and its spirit (Herzfeld), the shades of gray in everyday economic and political processes (Smart), and the ethical conundrums confronting anthropologists (Panella) legible because of their "emphasis upon bodily agency, intentionality, expressiveness, and affective response" and "insist that individual actions are shaped by social practices and the norms they embody, and often recognize the body as the primary target of social normalization and the exercise of power" (Rouse, 2007, 514).

ORGANIZATION OF THE BOOK

As we have tried to show above, we call specific attention to the corporeal aspects of working and living in the marginal and in-between social, economic, and political spaces. These spaces, described metaphorically and retheorized as gray spaces in most chapters, call attention to not only the specific places people live and work that cannot easily be delineated as legal or illegal, formal or informal, but extralegal and ambiguous. Hence, the book's contributors describe gray spaces with specific kinds of corporeal characteristics that come with very particular ethnographic challenges.

The fundamental ideas and concepts of this book can be traced to Cristiana Panella's (2002) book, *Les terres cuites de la discorde. Déterrement et écoulement des terres cuites anthropomorphes du Mali.* and, then, the conference "Norms in the Margins and Margins of the Norm. The Social Construction of Illegality" that Panella organized in 2012. Held in Brussels, scholars from around the world discussed and debated how illegality is culturally constructed and works across multiple societies in very different ethnographic contexts. Two of the authors in this book, Michael Herzfeld and Alan Smart, were plenary speakers.

Four significant publications emerged from the Norms and Illegality conference. First was a special issue of *PoLAR: Political and Legal Anthropology Review* 36(2), "Illegal Anthropology," edited by Rebecca Galemba and Kedron Thomas in 2013. Then, Walter E. Little and B. Lynne Milgram edited a special issue of *City & Society* 26(2), "Norms, Networks, and Informality in the Urban Global South: Unmapping Regulatory Space" in 2014. Fiona Rose-Greenland and Tracey Heatherington edited the special issue "Norms and Illegality in the Social Margins" for the *Journal of Modern Italian Studies* 19(5) that same year. Then, Cristiana Panella and Kedron Thomas edited, "Illegality" a special issue of the *Critique of Anthropology* 35(1) in 2015. These special journal issues drew inspiration from the Norms and Illegality conference, providing outlets for papers by Gordon, Little, and Milgram. Their chapters in this book are new and based on research that they continued doing on the ambiguities of illegality and extralegality.

The book is organized into two parts beginning with the chapters by Smart, Herzfeld, and Panella, who each layout the theoretical concepts that figure into the other authors' chapters. That part I, "Framing of Norms and Illegalities, Theoretical to Ethnographic," puts the emphasis on theoretical questions while the authors use examples from their years of ethnographic field research. In part II, "Ethnographies of Illegalities and the Reframing of Norms and Margins," the authors present ethnographic explorations that engage the theoretical positions that Smart, Herzfeld, and Panella introduce. The emphasis in these chapters is on presenting ethnographically rich cases that illustrate the core theoretical positions on cultural intimacy, graying, and fieldwork ethics.

In part I, "Framing of Norms and Illegalities, Theoretical to Ethnographic," in chapter 1 "Anthropological Shades of Gray: Informal Norms and Becoming (Il)legal," Alan Smart uses the color gray as a metaphor to explore "the messiness, the ambiguity, the complexity of reality as we experience it." It is a way to think through the becoming and unbecoming of legal and illegal, as well as the practice of these, rather than understand these conceptual categories as binary oppositions in high relief. Gray and grayness are developed theoretically as a way to capture the temporal aspects and ambiguous, indeterminate qualities of what is illegal and legal. A moral economy of grayness is outlined where there is no distinct line between legal and illegal and "formality and informality are not opposites, but are mutually constituted." These theoretical positions are, then, applied to an ethnographic case study that illustrates the in-between state that grayness embodies for Hong Kong squatters who live in and are allowed to live in places without the security of property rights.

In chapter 2 "Methodological Legalism" Michael Herzfeld draws on ethnographic vignettes from various places, notably Italy, Greece, and Thailand, using the concept of cultural intimacy to develop a theory that explains how norms are defied and serve to challenge authority, illustrating how breaking or bending the rules is the norm. In other words, he argues, this is "an argument for a more realistic acknowledgment of the social reality of law." He illuminates the tension between official norms and everyday acts paradoxically challenge those norms that "are thus not so much excuses for not conforming to laws as normative performances that render the solecism of hubris socially acceptable." The modern nation leans on this paradox, as do other political, religious, and other groups in the ways they conduct their daily business because adhering strictly to legality is ruinous.

In the final chapter of part I, chapter 3 "On Doing Fieldwork, Outspokenly: Ethics, Money, and Antiquities Illegal Trade," Cristiana Panella uses looting and the clandestine trade of antiquities to question why studying such phenomenon "is an uncomfortable domain of inquiry for art history, museum studies and social anthropology." An ethnographic case study among Malian art dealers, middlemen, and farmer-diggers is used to delineate the dimensions of what is perceived as an illegal network art and antiquities trade that illustrate legal/illegal are not separate domains but entwined and mutually constituted. Here, the ethics compromise theory is explained in the contexts of trader practices and researcher's methods that put the two in relation to each other via the exchange of money—legal and illegal, formal and informal bleed into each other and constitute overlapping domains, academic and antiquities networks.

Hence, social indeterminacy and unpredictability is integral to how institutions function and, in fact, produced by them in ways that bind and render legal and illegal and normal and normative (rather than formal/informal) mutually dependent on each other and negotiable. These social dynamics play out in ethnographic encounters where anthropologists face moral dilemmas when they learn of contradictions between local norms and national laws, as Herzfeld explained in his plenary address at the 2012 Norms and Illegality conference.

In part II of the book, "Ethnographies of Illegalities and the Reframing of Norms and Margins," Walter E. Little uses Antigua Guatemala as an ethnographic case study in chapter 4 "Street Economies, Illegality, and Rights in Antigua Guatemala" to explore how one's right to the city and the right to shape the city are tempered more by historical and cultural contexts than governmental regulatory complexes related to municipal regulations and national heritage preservation. The corporeality of legality–illegality relations is used to discuss and propose a theory of urban permissibility about why residents, workers, and visitors in Antigua live with, actively resist, and comply with the regulations, contributing to what are essentially gray spaces of legal/illegal/formal/informal. Street workers—food and craft vendors, cleaners-garbage collectors, shoeshine men, musicians, and watercolor artists—provide a dynamic window into the politics of regulation allowing some actors to better claim their rights to use the city and assert their local citizenship. Moreover, street workers' work in heritage sites brings out the ambiguities of legal/illegal distinctions when public space is actually practiced in economic contexts.

Isabella Clough Marinaro and Cristiana Panella in chapter 5, "Informal Economies, Illegal Subjects: Roma and Senegalese Traders in Rome" present a comparative ethnographic analysis of informal and illegal trades carried out by Senegalese and Roma street vendors in Rome by focusing on how the vendors construct their trade chains and networks and by exploring the moral economies that underlie their practices. The study highlights the different strategies by which the actors organize the production, circulation, and marketing of their merchandise, and their antithetical approaches to investment and wealth accumulation. It focuses on the socially productive nature of market exchanges in order to identify some of the means by which exclusion and inclusion come together in shadow economies. The contrasting temporalities and spatialities adopted by the two groups in their work are interwoven with their respective migration trajectories and community organization, as well as the different degrees of (il)legality of their goods and their own reification as criminal subjects in Italian society.

In chapter 6 "Repositioning the Edge: The Resilience of a Wholesale Vegetable Market in Benguet Northern Philippines" B. Lynne Milgram and Lorelei C. Mendoza, who conducted research in Benguet in the La Trinidad Vegetable Trading Post (LTVTP) in Upland Philippines, analyze the ways that wholesale marketers sustain their livelihoods through innovatively leveraging informal and "not-yet-legal" work in contrast to municipal and provincial governments. Vendors create personalized trade nodes that utilize horizontal and vertical commodity flows to ensure goods move from farmers to middle persons to buyers. Improvised tactics, complicity uses of informal and extralegal practices and networks, become urban organizing logics for those working in the wholesale market and government officials when the ends benefit wholesalers and the city. These tactics serve to counteract the ways that city officials tend to be unaccommodating to the urban poor and lower-to-middle class and push back against the elimination of undesirable remnants of traditional trade that often encompass informally negotiated and often extralegal or illegal modes of organization.

In chapter 7 "Normal Uncertainties in a Malagasy Mining Town", Andrew Walsh explores informal and artisanal, small-scale mining in Ambondromifehy, Madagascar, from the perspective of two miners and 20 years of ethnographic research to reflect on the particular relations between miners, the state, and governance that result in distinctive uncertainties enabled by the local sapphire trade and affect lives and livelihoods. It illustrates the ways a community maintains order—one not founded in the familiar certainties of state or traditional governance but in uncertainties. These uncertainties contribute to how post-boom residents established new norms in a place that never shook its reputation as a place of thievery, conspicuous consumption, and chaos to avoid. Paradoxically, although its abnormal development over the last 20 years appears unsustainable, it persists in how Malagasy state policies, projects, and representatives have figured in and relate to Ambondromifehy.

In the final case study in part II, chapter 8 "To Legally Beg or Illegally Work? Norms and Illegality among Asylum Seekers in Hong Kong," Gordon Mathews explores how asylum seekers in Hong Kong are forced by government policy into a situation in which they can either be legal or illegal. In the former scenario they live off government subsidies, effectively being beggars in violation of social norms. In the latter, they live off the work wages, conforming to social norms but can wind up in jail. For these Hong Kong asylum seekers, norms and legality are in direct contradiction, a situation used by the Hong Kong government as a means of keeping asylum seekers apart from Hong Kong life. In order to contend with their conundrum, asylum seekers employ various techniques to get work and avoid incarceration, as well as find Chinese marriage partners as a utilitarian strategy for obtaining ID cards that would allow them to work legally. However, official policy is aimed at keeping laws and norms separate for asylum seekers because it marginalizes them. They are relegated to the margins of Hong Kong society to choose between the legal, what is socially and morally disagreeable, and the illegal, what is socially and morally in line with their values. In neither scenario are they considered legitimate and, yet, the Hong Kong government and asylum seekers themselves do not want to solve this problem.

CONCLUSIONS

The ethnographic landscapes sketched out by the authors reflect the two major focus of this book: corporeality and the intrinsic imbrication legal/illegal in the construction, the application and the reception of the norm. We have proposed an acceptance of corporeality as witness of a latest revendication, of extreme engagement when every individual resource seems to be exhausted. We do consider such an engagement an ethical challenge at the extent that the display of the body to the risk becomes a political and existential act of presence. Moreover, the liminality of these informal and illegal bodies is the specular mirror of the contradictions and of the corruption's degree of the invisible norms which state their social and juridical status.

As it were, the displayed, displaced, out-of-place body is the epiphenomenon of the underground alchemical reaction between heterogeneous spheres of value, opposite, stranger for each other, and yet necessary for each other. The displayed body unveils a state of necessity, ultimately, that is of inescapability. It unveils the condition of corruption intrinsic to the normativity, and that starting from that same human dust with regard to which the norm puts itself in terms of negation, following a lax of attraction denied and yet inescapable. The purulent evidence of these out-of-place bodies, ob-scene as they stand out of the expected, agreed upon scene of a normativity which would appear as effective, does bare, on the contrary, the subsidences, the conjunctures of compromise, of failing, an abortion of linearity.

The ethnographic landscapes presented in this book raise important questions regarding the shifting status of researchers working in interstitial milieus. Specifically, Panella lays out theoretical positions on the ethics of fieldwork, explaining that illegal domains cannot be separated from the epistemological issues that such fieldwork addresses. She offers useful insights on the role of ethics (including formal ethical reviews) in the conduct of ethnographic research.

The ethnographic cases explored in the book articulate with Panella's theoretical perspectives when considering the role that liminal and illegal practices play in relation to the operation of the state. Little, Milgram and Mendoza, and Clough Marinaro and Panella, for instance, discuss forms of political control and policies in everyday vendor life that result, increasingly, in new senses of normativity. Walsh shows how sapphire miners' drive toward a dream of success results in an autarchic microsystem that cannot be qualified as illegal, in part, because it continues to be considered a place to live, that is to say to fuel its own dream, managed by a work ethic based on investment, above all physical, individual.

Norms Illegality: Intimate Ethnographies and Politics is concerned less with specific analyses that treat illegality as a given topic of discussion and something to be merely described, often, in contrast to the state (see Heyman, 1999, 2013). We are concerned less with specific examples of illegality and more with the ways in which it is practiced, is persistent, and permitted through complex collisions of politics, economies, and social actors.

One of the underlying themes of this book is informality and the informal economy, a subject recently analyzed in *The Popular Economy in Urban Latin America: Informality, Materiality, and Gender in Commerce* (Dürr and Müller, 2019). Informal economies are most often conceived of as illegal. There is a vast literature now on informal economies and these most often frame their arguments on the binary of legal–illegal, formal–informal, even when acknowledging the slippage between these poles (Fernández-Kelly and

Shefner, 2008; Roy and AlSayyad, 2004). The state or government, more generally, is the opposition to the trader or market vendor, as famously described in Clark's 1988 edited volume, *Traders Versus the State: Anthropological Approaches to Unofficial Economies*. Street vendors, often become examples par excellence of people engaged in the informal economy who, by virtue of their economic, political, and social behavior, are illegal actors (Cross and Morales, 2013; Goldstein, 2016; Hansen, Little, and Milgram, 2013; Mendiola García, 2017). Even in the production of clothing, the lines between legal and illegal are blurred (Antrosio and Colloredo-Mansfeld, 2015; Thomas, 2016) with unauthorized copies of designer brands and sport logos being sold in street markets.

Although there is a good deal of debate about legalizing drugs, prostitution, and migrants and plenty of arguments against it, they are more easily delineated as illegal and the authorities more prone to curtailing, prosecuting, and incarcerating those involved with them. The case studies, here, present the work of those who perform it in the open and are part of everyday life of getting on with the business of maintaining local economies and governments.

The ambiguities or grayness we describe above and in our chapters have theoretical roots in Heyman and Smart's (1999) essay, "States and Illegal Practices: An Overview." This ambiguous space has been explored by Yiftachel (2009, 2012) who uses the metaphor gray spaces to capture the urban places, neighborhoods that exist and help cities function while technically being illegal. It is his concept that Smart, in our book, reworks his and Heyman's earlier framing of gray, as well as Yiftachel's concept into a cultural process, graying, that helps capture the phenomena described in our book. These ambiguities of legality (or illegality) are, likewise, noted in the work of Aguiar (2011, 2012, 2013) and others (Galemba, 2017) who study smugglers and contraband in Latin America.

Indeed, several of the chapters here relate to vendors, marketers, traders of various types, but we do not treat them as intrinsically illegal but caught in economic and political conundrums within which they persist in their livelihoods and allowed to do so by the government and the local community at large. These workers—vendors but, also various others—who are described in our book are doing what Smart and Zerilli (2014) characterize as extralegal work, rather than illegal work. This emphasizes the particular ways in which something or some person's trade or service they provide is in a process of being legally made and unmade or illegally permitted and prohibited. The illegalities our book describes are not fixed as illegal but part of far more ambiguous and flexible processes that theoretical conceptualizations like extralegality and cultural intimacy capture and help us understand the everyday workings of norms.

REFERENCES

Aguiar, José Carlos G. "Smugglers, *Fayuqueros, Piratas*: Transitory Commodities and Illegality in the Trade of Pirated CDs in Mexico." *PoLAR: Political and Legal Anthropology Review* 36, no. 2 (2013): 249–265.

Aguiar, José Carlos G. "Cities on Edge: Smuggling and Neoliberal Policies at the Iguazú Triangle." *Singapore Journal of Tropical Geography* 33, no. 2 (2012): 171–183.

Aguiar, José Carlos G. "The Ambivalent Relation Between State and Illegal Actors: Piracy Retail in Mexico." *Etnográfica: Revista do Centro de Estudos de Antropologia Social* 15, no. 1 (2011): 109–128.

Antrosio, Jason, and Rudi Colloredo-Mansfeld. *Fast, Easy, and In Cash. Artisan Hardship and Hope in the Global Economy*. Chicago: University of Chicago Press, 2015.

Clark, Gracia, ed. *Traders Versus the State: Anthropological Approaches to Unofficial Economies*. Boulder, CO: Westview Press, 1988.

Coombe, Rosemary J. "The Cultural Life of Things: Anthropological Approaches to Law and Society in Conditions of Globalization." *American University International Law Review* 10, no. 2 (1995): 791–835.

Cross, John and Alfonso Morales, eds. *Street Entrepreneurs: People, Place, and Politics in Local and Global Perspective*. London: Routledge, 2013.

Dürr, Eveline, and Juliane Müller, eds. *The Popular Economy in Urban Latin America: Informality, Materiality, and Gender in Commerce*. Lanham, MD: Lexington Books, 2019.

Fernández-Kelly, Patricia, and Jon Shefner, eds. *Out of the Shadows: Political Action and the Informal Economy in Latin America*. University Park, PA: Penn State University Press, 2008.

Foucault, Michel. *Surveiller et punir—Naissance de la prison*. Paris: Gallimard, 1975.

Galemba, Rebecca B. *Contraband Corridor. Making a Living of the Mexico-Guatemala Border*. Stanford: Stanford University Press, 2017.

Galemba, Rebecca, and Kedron Thomas, eds. "Special Issue: Illegal Anthropology." *PoLAR: Political and Legal Anthropology Review* 36, no. 2 (2013): 211–307.

Goldstein, Daniel M. *Owners of the Sidewalk: Security and Survival in the Informal City*. Durham: Duke University Press, 2016.

Hansen, Karen Tranberg, Walter E. Little, and B. Lynne Milgram, eds. *Street Economies in the Urban Global South*. Santa Fe, NM: SAR Press, 2013.

Herzfeld, Michael. *Cultural Intimacy: Social Poetics in the Nation-State*. New York: Routledge, 2005.

Herzfeld, Michael. *The Body Impolitic: Artisans and Artifice in the Global Hierarchy of Value*. Chicago: University of Chicago, 2004.

Heyman, Josiah McC. "The Study of Illegality and Legality. Which Way Forward?" *PoLAR: Political and Legal Anthropological Review* 36, no. 2 (2013): 304–307.

Heyman, Josiah McC., ed. *States and Illegal Practices*. Oxford; New York: Berg, 1999.

Heyman, Josiah McC, and Alan Smart. "States and Illegal Practices: An Overview." In *States and Illegal Practices: An Overview*, edited by Josiah McC Heyman, 1–24. Oxford: Berg, 1999.

Heywood, P.M., ed. *Routledge Handbook of Political Corruption*. London; New York: Routledge, 2015.

Holbraad, M., and M.A. Pedersen. *The Ontological Turn: An Anthropological Exposition*. Cambridge: Cambridge University Press, 2017.

Keane, Webb. "Ethics Without Guarantees." *HUA: Journal of Ethnographic Theory* 6, no. 1 (2016): 485–492.

Kitcher, Philip. *The Ethical Project*. New Haven: Harvard University Press, 2011.

Kleist, Nauja, and Stef Jansen, eds. "Special Issue: 'Hope Over Time: Crisis, Immobility and Future-Making'." *History and Anthropology* 27, no. 4 (2016): 373–467.

Lambek, Michael. *The Ethical Condition. Essays on Action, Person, and Value*. Chicago: University of Chicago Press, 2015.

Little, Walter E., and B. Lynne Milgram, eds. "Special Issue: 'Norms, Networks, and Informality in the Urban Global South: Unmapping Regulatory Space'." *City & Society* 26, no. 2 (2014): 150–238.

Macherey, P. "Canguilhem et l'idée de milieu." Exposé présenté au colloque "Georges Canguilhem. Science, technique, politique: perspectives actuelles" (Liège, 22 avril 2016), accessed August 6, 2018, https://philolarge.hypotheses.org/1737.

Mendiola García, Sandra. *Street Democracy: Vendors, Violence, and Public Space in Late-Twentieth-Century Mexico*. Lincoln: University of Nebraska Press, 2017.

Miyazaki, Hirokazu. *The Method of Hope: Anthropology, Philosophy, and Fijian Knowledge*. Redwood City: Stanford University Press, 2004.

Narotzky, Susana, and Niko Besnier. "Crisis, Value, and Hope: Rethinking the Economy. An Introduction to Supplement 9." *Current Anthropology* 55, Supplement 9 (2014): S4–S16.

Olivier de Sardan, Jean-Pierre. "Embeddedness and Informal Norms: Institutionalisms and Anthropology." *Critique of Anthropology* 33, no. 3 (2013): 280–299.

Panella, Cristiana. "Lost in translation. Unprovenanced objects and opacity/transparency agenda of museum policies', *ANUAC (Rivista della Società Italiana di Antropologia Culturale)*, 4, no. 1 (2015): 66-87.

Panella, Cristiana. "Introduction: Lives in Motion, Indeed. Interdisciplinary Perspectives on Social Change in Honor of Danielle de Lame." In *Lives in Motion, Indeed. Interdisciplinary Perspectives on Social Change in Honor of Danielle de Lame*, edited by Cristiana Panella, 5–31. Tervuren: Koninklijk Museum voor Midden-Afrika, 2012.

Panella, Cristiana. *Les terres cuites de la discorde. Déterrement et écoulement des terres cuites anthropomorphes du Mali. Les réseaux locaux*. Leiden: CNWS Publications, 2002.

Panella, Cristiana, and Kedron Thomas, eds. "Special Issue: 'Illegality'." *Critique of Anthropology* 35, no. 1 (2015): 3–113.

Rose-Greenland, Fiona, and Tracey Heatherington, eds. "Special Issue: 'Norms and Illegality in the Social Margins'." *Journal of Modern Italian Studies* 19, no. 5 (2014a): 505–582.

Rose-Greenland, Fiona, and Tracey Heatherington. "Introduction Norms and Illegality in the Social Margins." *Journal of Modern Italian Studies* 19, no. 5 (2014b): 505–513.

Rouse, Joseph. "Practice Theory." Division I Faculty Publications. Paper 43, accessed November 11, 2020, http://wesscholar.wesleyan.edu/div1facpubs/43.

Roy, Ananya, and Nezar AlSayyad, eds. *Urban Informality: Transnational Perspectives from the Middle East, Latin America, and South Asia*. Lanham, MD: Lexington Books, 2004.

Smart, Alan, and Filippo Zerilli. "Extralegality." In *A Companion to Urban Anthropology*, edited by Donald Nonini, 222–238. Malden, MA: Wiley Blackwell, 2014.

Thomas, Kedron. *Regulating Style: Intellectual Property Law and the Business of Fashion in Guatemala*. Berkeley: University of California Press, 2016.

Yiftachel, Oren. "Critical Theory and 'Gray Space': Mobilization of the Colonized." In *Cities for People Not for Profit: Critical Urban Theory and the Right to the City*, edited by Neil Brenner, Peter Marcuse and Margit Mayer, 24–41. London and New York: Routledge, 2012.

Yiftachel, Oren. "Theoretical Notes on 'Gray Cities': The Coming of Urban Apartheid." *Planning Theory* 8, no. 1 (2009): 88–100.

Zigon, Jarrett. "Hope Dies Last: Two Aspects of Hope in Contemporary Moscow." *Anthropological Theory* 9, no. 3 (2009): 253–271.

Zournazi, Mary. *Hope. New Philosophies for Change*. Sydney: Lawrence & Wishart, 2002.

Part I

FRAMING OF NORMS AND ILLEGALITIES, THEORETICAL TO ETHNOGRAPHIC

Chapter 1

Anthropological Shades of Gray

Informal Norms and Becoming (Il)legal

Alan Smart

Gray has negative connotations in Western popular culture. Gray is drab, boring, as in the 1956 movie "The Man in the Gray Flannel Suit." Or it is compromised, in the dubious and dangerous, liminal, no-man's land between black and white, good and evil. Primary colors are seen as more vibrant and attractive. If monochrome is needed, then the absolutes of black or white are preferred. Even those who turn to "the Dark Side" prefer clarity of affiliation rather than the muddle of the middle.

In this chapter, I consider the advantages of giving more attention to gray, particularly as it relates to anthropological contributions to norms on the margin of the state and within the state. Gray is a particularly appropriate banner for such work. It may be murky, but it also represents the full complexity of everyday life, rather than the abstractions and absolutes of black and white. Gray is not just the product of the mingling of black and white. If you mix all the colors in paint, you end up with some shade of gray. Gray, then, can serve as a metaphor for the messiness, the ambiguity, the complexity of reality as we experience it, and as the people we research with experience it, not the tempting but unworldly purity of primary colors. Grayness also helps us to bring temporality into our analysis of legality and illegality, focusing attention on how practices become legal or illegal, often from an earlier stage of indeterminacy.

An image that I have in mind is an old piece of technology, the grayscale used for chemically developing black and white photographs, when they weren't just digital bits and bytes. There is a progression from blank to black, with shades of gray in between, but how graya particular part of the grayscale ends up depends on how long you let it develop. The norms that lie at the margins of the state are like this: if we examine them at different points in time, we can get varying impressions of how close they are to the endpoints of black and white. We only know how dark or light things will end up *once* the process has run its course. These diverse trajectories taken by shades of gray -are my second issue.

An example that illustrates both issues, gray as messy and as emerging in time, comes from Bernard Edelman's social history of photography (Edelman 1979). In France, during photography's nineteenth-century infancy, claims of property rights in photographic images were denied by courts. The grounds for denial included the argument that the camera "did not involve any creative activity of the subject and was a mere mechanical reproduction of reality" (Hirst 1979, 14). Reality was common property, in the public domain, so images of it could not be copyrighted, the French courts ruled. However, shortly thereafter capitalists became interested in the possibilities of photography as cinema (Edelman 1979, 53). Once photography became a significant sector of capitalist production, and not just a craft activity, the absence of property rights became a serious constraint and legal challenges resulted. Edelman (1979) shows that under pressure from the cinema industry, the legal system reinterpreted photography and found a way to justify the ownership of photographic reproduction through fascinating legal gymnastics.

The resolution of this problem, by reinterpreting and modifying property law, facilitated cinema's growth. How it was accomplished was constrained by the *form* of law, rather than by simply adopting rules that are useful for the most powerful actors. The appropriate reinterpretation had to be demonstrated to be compatible with prevailing notions of property law. The need to achieve such reinterpretations through the law and its precedents leave the outcome potentially open, an illustration of the essential indeterminacy of law insisted upon by critical legal theorists. Even if the interests of important new industries are generally supported, precisely how this legal support is accomplished can vary, affecting consequent organization and industrial dynamics, as is apparent in the different approaches being taken to the legalization of marijuana in various jurisdictions.

Other goods have qualities, whether physical or moral evaluations, which make the ascription and distribution of property rights to them problematic. Such anomalous objects of exchange require legislative and judicial resolution of what can be owned, and what rights ownership conveys in such cases. Examples of such anomalous categories include labor contracts (Kay and Mott 1982), slaves (Kopytoff 1982), seeds (Kloppenburg 1988), intellectual property (Edelman 1979), body organs and fetal material (Scheper-Hughes 2001), contraband and squatter dwellings (Smart 1985), and the products of biotechnology (Fleising and Smart 1993). These have all been, in the past or at present, involved in what Smart and Zerilli (2014) call the domain of the not-yet-(il)legal.

In what follows, I discuss some possible paths through what might be called the moral economy of grayness, which includes opposed trends to lightening and darkening. Another way of thinking about this is as an *ethicoscape*, with textures of interwoven colors of moral valuation.

There are a variety of useful precedents for my discussion. They tend, though, to only provide initial openings onto a sprawling landscape of ambiguity, compromise, control, and cooptation, driven by contested narratives and arguments about anomalous practices and goods. Kopytoff's critique of economists for taking the existence of commodities for granted is apropos here. He suggests that:

> the production of commodities is also a cultural and cognitive process: commodities must be not only produced materially as things, but also culturally marked as being a certain kind of thing . . . shifts and differences in whether and when a thing is a commodity reveal a moral economy that stands behind the objective economy of visible transactions. (Kopytoff 1986, 64)

In capitalist societies, the process of commodification is only complete when transactions of things are legally recognized and state protection is extended to the owner of such things. There are *commodities* which are not (yet) legally ownable, such as illegal drugs, humans, and sexual services, but their illegality constrains and distorts the economic production and distribution of such goods. Legal protection is not available so corporations may be subject to risks for moving into these fields prior to legal clarification. Full commodification and the development of a conventional industry producing and distributing goods generally requires legal recognition and protection, although some are attracted by the promise of greater gains in situations of greater risk.

The issues are not only moral, but also conceptual. Edmund Leach (1979, 61) suggests that:

> The more sharply we define our boundaries, the more conscious we become of the dirt that has ambiguously got onto the wrong side of the frontier. Boundaries become dirty by definition and we devote a great deal of effort to keeping them clean, just so that we can preserve confidence in our category system.

Scientific and technological development is constantly throwing up such "conceptual dirt," throwing into question the most fundamental of the boundaries that we create in our societies. As Mary Douglas (1966, 36) indicates, anomalies, inhabiting gray zones of the law and moralities, reflect what we cannot interpret, or for which interpretations have not yet been fixed. Economic and political contestation can also keep them in such gray zones. Things that are not-yet-(il)legal present interpretive challenges which various parties may dispute. Resolution of these interpretive challenges can have considerable impact upon subsequent economic and social development. How do people decide whether to make the "not-yet-(il) legal" white or black, legal or illegal? How does a gray thing or practice become clearly black or white? Even after it does, it may begin to lose its pure state, and start to gray once again. We could trace historical geographies of shades of gray around the human planet, pulsing, ebbing, and flowing to a vast palette of influences from religious fundamentalism to trade deals (Smart and Smart 2016).

The legitimacy of law depends on belief that laws constrain the decisions of legal authorities, at least to some degree. The contest for the legitimacy of law must be pursued through the medium of legal discourse, not explicitly through a discourse of interests and negotiation. When we use the law to pursue our interests, the legitimacy of law is reinforced. If we are to be convinced of law's authority as something other than naked power, it should be accorded respect by those using it, and outcomes sought *through* the medium of legal discourse. The efficacy of instrumental manipulation of law, then, relies on some degree of legitimacy of that resource for success through its manipulation. What Sally Falk Moore refers to as processes of situational adjustment, how people maneuver around the rules without necessarily rejecting the rules, have inherent limits in the countervailing processes of reglementation or rule imposition (Moore 1978). Legal sources influence outcomes by the very nature of the medium through which desired outcomes are sought. As Rosemary Coombe (1989, 93) notes, on occasion, a legal situation:

> arises in which there is no easy fit [with prevailing categories], the activity of bringing structure to bear is a struggle, and in the course of this struggle, received structures undergo modest but real transformations. The nature of these transformations is certainly circumscribed by the boundaries in which the play of analogy takes place, but they are in no way predetermined.

A good current example of an emerging set of gray grey property concerns robotics and prosthetic extensions of human capacities. In 2012, the European Commission funded a Science in Society project entitled "RoboLaw: Regulating Emerging Robotic Technologies in Europe: Robotics facing Law and Ethics." The main objective of the project, to investigate the ways in which emerging technologies in the field of (bio-) robotics (e.g., bionics, neural interfaces, and nanotechnologies) will influence the content, meaning, and setting of the law, reveals the kind of situation I am interested in. The RoboLaw project addresses the ways in which robotics and human enhancement generate regulatory issues. The project focuses on areas of regulation "in need of adjustment or revision." These have only become more contested as the field's technologies and capacities expand (Smart and Smart 2017a).[1]

An article about the project in *The Economist* noted an urgent need for rules to manage new technologies like prosthetics and implants:

> If you are dependent on a robotic wheelchair for mobility, for example, does the wheelchair count as part of your body? Linda MacDonald Glenn, an American lawyer and bioethicist, thinks it does. Ms Glenn . . . persuaded an initially sceptical insurance firm that a "mobility assistance device" damaged by airline staff was more than her client's personal property, it was an extension of his physical body. . . . Similarly, Neil Harbisson, a colour-blind artist who wears an "eyeborg"—a device that enables him to "hear" colours—successfully argued with British authorities that he should be allowed to wear the device in his passport picture, on the basis that it is part of his body. These are just early examples of the sorts of legal problems to come. (*The Economist* ["You, robot?" September 1, 2012: TQ5])

Emerging regulatory regimes for robotics have not yet raised issues with the high profile of genetic engineering, but the potential for autonomous military robots, among other issues related to new technologies such as self-driving cars (Pink et al. 2020), is likely to put the issue more firmly onto the public agenda.

The challenge of incorporating innovative but anomalous objects of exchange into conventional political economies requires reinterpretation of what can be owned, how it can be owned, and what rights are accorded by ownership. Legal discourses and texts are resources used in legal contests. In being used they structure and constrain the battlefield, but are also subject to reinterpretation through the play of analogy, metaphor, and precedent.

The situation is even more complicated: once a government and its legal system decide that something gray grey should be categorized unequivocally as black or white, citizens of that country, or other countries, may not agree. The anger over the depiction of Muhammad in cartoons in Denmark and elsewhere clearly illustrates this, but so does the widespread practice of paying cash to avoid sales taxes. A survey in Canada found that 55% of respondents would opt to pay cash to avoid sales taxes. Only 30% thought it wrong to avoid tax in this way, while 17% of those aged 18–34 didn't see it as wrong.

In earlier work with Josiah Heyman on states and illegal practices (Heyman and Smart 1999), we offered a brief sketch of the legal fabric of grayness:

> The line between "legal" and "illegal" is held to be clear and definitive within a given state . . . Yet the actual practice is ambiguous and subject to resourceful manipulation. Legality and illegality are thus simultaneously black and white, and shades of gray.

The metaphor of grayness continued to emerge in subsequent research, reflecting the conflict between legitimation practices used by states and by their subjects. I never, though, took the metaphor as seriously as it deserves, given its ubiquity in discussions of the practical moralities on the margins of the state. One of my goals for this chapter is to give the figure of speech its due in more precise analysis.

In van Schendel and Abraham's *Illicit Flows and Criminal Things* (van Schendel and Abraham 2005), the authors argue that we need to resist "seeing like a state." The "definitional problems associated with international crime show how important it is to relativize the state as 'just' another form of modern political authority so as to avoid using the state's own dominant categories for our analysis" (2005, 6). Tracing illicit flows highlights the contingency of illegality. What "determines legality and illegality at different points of the commodity chain is the particular regulatory scale the object finds itself in . . . we find it useful to distinguish between political (legal and illegal) and social (licit and illicit) origins of regulatory authority" (2005, 17). Commodities, such as *qat* or coca leaves, and practices, such as sex work, can be legal but illicit on one side of a national border while illegal and licit on the other. Social boundaries have comparable effects. By transposing grayness onto their analysis, it is clear that two cells of their matrix are gray for very different reasons: one shade is legal but illicit in the eyes of people, while the other is illegal but licit.

Gray practices can be fundamental to allowing governments to function. It is hard to imagine government agencies getting much done without informal work-arounds to cope with the inflexibilities of formal procedures (Herzfeld in this book). Formality and informality are not opposites, but are mutually constituted; neither is possible without the other (Koster and Smart 2019). "In Russia informal practices such as "gray piar" (a Russian transliteration of the abbreviation PR) simultaneously "compensate for the defects of political institutions . . . but also exploit these institutions for the advantage of vested interests (Ledeneva 2006, 30)." Gray PR is distinguished from both white PR (legal and ethical) and black PR (illegal and unethical). A key point is that gray PR takes two different forms: legal but unethical as well as illegal but ethical. The latter could include illegal acts necessary to expose corruption among the powerful, for example.

Another way of considering grayness is in terms of what Holocaust survivor Primo Levi described as the "gray zones" of Auschwitz's complicated internal structure which "created moral ambiguity and compromise in ways large and small." Levi felt that the prevalence of "gray, ambiguous persons, ready to compromise" (Levi 1988, 49) was "more the rule than the exception in any time or place," but in concentration camps the proportion swelled because "survival depended on finding or taking some advantage that made nearly all survivors—Levi included himself—'the rightful owners of a quota of guilt'" (Petropoulos and Roth 2005, xvii). Levi's gray zones differ from many other usages of the term. Rather than emphasizing the legal/illegal distinction, even if combined with recognition of the potential for social legitimacy of illegal practices and objects, black and white are inverted through a very different distinction. For Levi, Auschwitz was a "gray zone, poorly defined, where the two camps of masters and servants both diverge and converge" (Levi 1988, 42). It is a "zone of ambiguity which radiates out from regimes based on terror and obsequiousness" (Levi 1988, 58). The white band is defined by moral rejection of compromise with the dark evil of the masters, almost impossible to maintain in such atrocious conditions. In this version, whiteness is a rejection of the power of a state rather than conformity with formal legality. It is only if we, and war crimes commissions, adopt external interpretations of what kinds of use of power can be *right* that we can reconcile this zone of the black with other analyses of grayness such as that used by van Schendel and Abraham.

In a very different context, Michel Anteby (2005, 90) finds that in the unauthorized use of company materials to make artifacts that are taken home, the gray zone is "clearly bound at both ends" but "contains multiple shades of meaning, and by extension, layered moralities." Although explicitly drawing on Levi's ideas, he doesn't appear to recognize the conflict between master/servant versus legal/illegal as polar opposites in the gray zones, instead treating them more in line with van Schendel and Abraham's legal/licit distinction. The strength of Anteby's work is its demonstration of the contingency and complexity of establishing a practice as legitimate despite being illegal. He builds on a genealogy in the sociology of deviance that accounts for the conditions in which people feel justified in stretching or breaking rules. The two versions of gray zones might be reconciled by treating them as mapping white and black onto right and wrong, but obviously the situations in which authorities can be assumed to be unequivocally wrong are contested and far from clear at the moment of questionable action. More positively, he provides a detailed examination of the complex interactional practices in moral gray zones, the boundaries of which "were constantly patrolled" so that "non-normative behaviours within gray zones were rapidly identified" (2005, 149). Anteby argues that skillful performance reinforces occupational identities: "Gray zones offer repeated tests of the participants' moralities. They also provide numerous opportunities for inclusion and exclusion" (2005, 167). The utilities for both workers and managers mean that there are "probably few organizations and occupations that are entirely exempt from gray zones" (2005, 151).

The accounts of gray zones that I have considered so far neglect the spatial dimensions that are implicit in the idea of a "zone," for example, when policing illicit cross-border activities (Feldman 2019). Oren Yiftachel (2009) has worked specifically on this aspect, theorizing "gray spaces" as territories that only partially incorporate people into a city. They exclude residents from full, or any, urban citizenship. He describes *gray space from above* when elites break the rules, or have the rules changed to fit the nonconforming uses of their mansions, golf courses, or development projects (Alterman and Calor 2020). Illegality is not only a tactic of the marginalized. Browne (2004) demonstrates the commonplace nature of informal transactions among Martinique's middle class. Wedel (2009) documents the informality and illegality of the shadow elite, moving fluidly between government and private contracting. Gray spaces from above often tend to whitening, the "tendency of the system to *launder* gray spaces."

Gray spaces from below include places of proletarian informality and illegality, ghettoes, slums, and camps. Authorities frequently respond to "the problem of marginalized gray space by destruction, expulsion or elimination," trajectories of blackening (Yiftachel 2009, 92). Important gray zones emerge in conflicts between what is formally legal and informally legitimate, or vice versa, and in some contexts may characterize the majority of a city's practices and spaces. Confinement of socially legitimate practices by prohibition fosters the expansion of informality and illegality.

In my previous work, a key concept related to grayness is *toleration*, particularly for illegal buildings. Toleration is a situation where illegal conditions are allowed to persist, but without change in the official or formal situation. Letting squatter structures (see Figure 1.1) and their occupants stay is presented by the authorities as a concession, rather than acknowledgment of rights. To avoid appearing to recognize property rights, until 1984 in Hong Kong it was the structures that were registered and tolerated, not the occupants. The persistence of practices that are declared illegal by governments has not received sufficient theoretical attention in urban studies, although it is of course the subject of huge amounts of empirical and policy-oriented study (Smart and Aguilera 2020). Unable to rely on secrecy, the continued existence of squatter areas has to be understood in the context of the techniques, intentions, and limitations of administrative control over the urban fabric. Illegal settlements that persist over long periods of time eventually generate some coordination over the use of space, whether as the product of direct governmental intervention or the self-regulation of the residents. Usually, it is a complex amalgam of both kinds of attempts to control what happens in these unruly spaces. Markets certainly do develop for these illegal structures, but the markets are *distorted* by the absence of formal support for them, creating a kind of property vacuum (Câmpeanu 1986; Smart 1986). Governmental officials and programs certainly have an impact on the zones of illegality, but usually not the kind of impact envisioned. Past struggles may generate

Figure 1.1 Diamond Hill Squatter Area, 1999. *Source*: Photo by Alan Smart.

tacit compromises between residents and administration, sometimes explicit arrangements like that of routinized toleration, or semiformality (Cross 1998). Toleration usually satisfies nobody, but can be surprisingly stable for temporary resolution of the problems created for governments by their inability or unwillingness to restructure an area into conventional and legal spaces. Illegal structures in Hong Kong were often not immediately destroyed upon discovery, once people had moved in with some furniture. They were generally allowed to remain for the time being, but without thereby acknowledging any rights to the builders or inhabitants. Toleration is related to governmental and public acknowledgment of the legitimate needs of people to occupy some space, but not of their rights to be in any particular place. As Anteby (2005, 158) points out, tolerance in moral gray zones allows management to maintain discretion and a degree of control.

In the remainder of this chapter, I explore how beliefs about the future of gray areas affect their development. Two short cases from my research will illustrate these issues, unauthorized housing in Hong Kong, and the creation of a real estate market in China. A key feature of current urban planning policy affecting the poorer cities of the world has been the policy of formalizing the informal sector, for example, by giving occupants of illegal/irregular/spontaneous housing (choose your preferred label) title to their home (*The Economist* 2020). Hernando de Soto's proposal that turning informal property into legal property is the best way to create prosperity for the poor has received a great deal of attention in development agencies, NGOs, and think-tanks (Gilbert 2012). Kregg Hetherington (2011) found that *campesinos* in Paraguay, where de Soto's ideas had been very influential, saw land titles as a tool of privatization, a documentary trap that allowed land to be taken away from them after they had put so much work into it. Similarly, one risk of such policies is that former squatter settlements might be gentrified, the residents displaced, and the supply of affordable housing diminished even further (Smart and Smart 2013).

Even without squatter titling, there are complex relations between the markets for illegal housing and conventional real estate markets (Smart 1985, 2001, 2003, 2006, 2010). The nature of the linkage between the two housing markets, however, is strongly influenced by the probable ultimate state of an irregular settlement. Where regularization is likely, market forces will tend toward price convergence between informal and formal housing of similar amenities. Investment in improvements becomes a better bet, so that middle-class individuals are more likely to move in. If eradication is recognized as the inevitable fate, though, as in Hong Kong, the conditions of compensation for displaced residents will have the greatest effect on the illegal housing market. Where the outcome is "in the balance" or dependent on political developments, collective mobilization to influence decision-makers may be more likely. The relative darkness of the gray markets for irregular housing is thus influenced by their expectations for eventual legalization. Housing improvements are more likely to occur if residents think that it is only a matter of time before their settlement has de facto if not de jure security (Varley 1998, 2002).

Persisting squatter settlements, unless actively defended from clearance, are either formally or informally tolerated. Toleration accepts their presence until the government decides that the land is needed, but does not provide any legal rights, although ex gratia compensation in the form of rehousing and monetary considerations may be provided (Tanasescu, Chui, and Smart 2010). Why did the Hong Kong Government simultaneously tolerate, and refuse to regularize, squatter areas throughout the postwar era? The explanation lies in the colonial restructuring of space to accommodate the reintroduction of control and government revenues.[2] In Hong Kong, revenues generated by land and real estate have always been extremely important, both for the government and for large companies. Archival research reveals that a central concern has always been to avoid doing anything that might give the legal appearance of squatter's rights, including allowing squatter to improve their housing. A great deal of government effort has gone into keeping squatters unequivocally in the black zone, rejecting any appearance of gradually lightening grayness, as has been common in many parts of the Global South. Hong Kong's resistance to whitening, and success in blackening and largely eradicating squatter settlements, required constant effort to maintain this status while battling their spatial expansion. Control requires both spatial and temporal confinement (Smart and Smart 2017b).

Toleration allows residents of illegal settlements to remain in their unconventional shelter "for the time being," without providing security of property rights or entitlements. Although squatter residents whose structure was registered have frequently received rehousing, this was a result of policy which could be changed rather than legal rights. Toleration, in a way, allows the administration to have its cake and eat it too, allowing some people to provide housing for themselves without allowing a permanent loss of the space from governmental control.

The process of creating markets for real estate in early reform China, particularly during the 1980s, shows similar dynamics in a different context. Illegal building must be seen in the context of contestation over the classification of gray practices (Zhu 2002). There were widespread expectations that local practices for developing land would eventually become "white" as had other economic projects which "pushed the envelope" of acceptable practice under the reforms (Smart 2000). Some practices, such as secondary market exchange of allocated land, eventually became legal, while others eventually became a black market. The system of property rights in land has become more routinized, particularly since the Land Administration Law of 1998 (Xie, Parsa, and Redding 2002). The Maoist system of land allocation (*huabo*) was supplemented with a system of "conveyance" (*churang*) where commercial users obtain additional rights of transfer to other users (Ho and Lin 2001, 9). The potential profits in shifting land from one track to the other prompted rent-seeking behavior (Zhu 2002).

Not all use of black market or gray practices results from individual greed. Most illegal land use resulted from the activities of rural collectives and state organizations. This may benefit individuals, but is often intended for economic development by the local unit. Many regulations put in place to control land use were seen by rural officials as stripping them of prerogatives that they de facto held. The illegalization of previously accepted actions is clear in relation to new building by villagers. Cultivated land converted to rural housing accounted for 33% of all farmland conversion from 1985 to 1988 but dropped to 8% by 1993 (Ho and Lin 2001, 19). Rural governments and individuals tried to increase their share of the profits from commercialization by not going through required procedures (Zhu 2002). Official expropriation procedures generally give the villagers insufficient resources to compensate for loss of their livelihood. Often little from the fees paid goes to the actual users of the land. Illegality often results, as those "who have lost their cultivated land attempt to make use of their residential land—their only resource—to support themselves. This induces them to construct illegally" (Tang and Chung 2002, 49).

The conversion of agricultural land has created massive new wealth but increasingly villagers get less of it (Zhou 2009, 125). Outright predatory land seizure seems to have been less blatant and extreme in the first reform decade than after 1992. The reason is that many capitalist practices that were gray, or even black, in the 1980s and early 1990s have become white, at least in official terms. Local officials do not have to be as concerned about the moral evaluations of local residents as they did in the early reform era (Smart 2010).

How can we explain this shift toward predatory local government in the period since 1992? Scalar shifts are key. Control over land conversion has moved from local governments to higher levels more distant from local voice and influence (Lin 2009). Forceful "production of property rights over suburban land, not ambiguous delineation of property rights, . . . resulted in the resentment, social discontents, conflicts, and violence" (Lin 2009, 32). It is not only that capitalist practices are more routinely accepted in China since Deng's 1992 southern tour, but that recentralization since the late 1980s has also moved key decisions over land farther away from local citizens so that their informal voices have been muted. In the silences created by this rescaling, predatory government has increased, and protests against the injustices of land expropriation have emerged in many places. The simultaneous processes of becoming legal and illegal have disenfranchised villagers, taking from them most legal ways to profit from the creation of wealth through land.

CONCLUDING COMMENTS

It is not just legal status itself that determines the quality and character of a structure, or of its inhabitants, but people's expectations about how that legal status will influence (or fail to influence) the future of the structure and its surroundings. As Sally Falk Moore (1987, 727) perceptively noted, "Conjectures about the future thus become an implicit part of the understanding of the present," and this is perhaps never more the case than in gray zones and the processes implicated in becoming (il)legal. In certain contexts, authorities take these expectations into consideration in planning their regulatory policies, for example, by accepting their inability to prevent new illegal building and putting in place a framework by which its operations are influenced by enabling policies that channel it into particular forms and places. The trajectories of irregular settlements are thus subject to dialectical influence between residents, authorities, and the wider population of potential illegal builders. Their expectations about future trajectories, about the development of the gray scale, influence that very developmental dynamic.

What I have tried to do here is to use a close examination of how scholars, including myself, have used the metaphor of grayness to explore the norms in the margins and margins of the norms. Greyness is often presented as a common-sense term, situated in the middle ground, or the overlapping margins, between plural legalities and moralities. By complicating this taken-for-granted metaphor, it becomes possible, or perhaps necessary, to explore in greater detail the shifting boundaries between whites, blacks, and grays, and the complicated and shifting multicolored palette of processes and perceptions that produces the shades of gray. Graying is something that many of us in this book know far too much about on a personal basis, but which we could benefit from thinking about more deeply at a theoretical level.

NOTES

1. http://www.robolaw.eu/index.htm#RoboLaw. Overview, accessed September 16, 2012.
2. As I write this, I am midway through a book on the formalization of informality in colonial Hong Kong that complicates this explanation, and explores alternatives to decide which explanation is both plausible and has sufficient empirical support.

REFERENCES

Alterman, R., and I. Calor. "Between Informal and Illegal in the Global North: Planning Law, Enforcement and Justifiable Noncompliance." In *Comparative Approaches to Informal Housing Around the Globe*, edited by U. Grashoff, 150–185. London: UCL Press, 2020.

Anteby, Michael. *Moral Gray Zones: Side Productions, Identity, and Regulation in an Aeronautic Plant.* Princeton, NJ: Princeton University Press, 2005.

Browne, Katherine E. *Creole Economics: Caribbean Cunning under the French Flag.* Austin, TX: University of Texas Press, 2004.

Câmpeanu, Pavel. *The Origins of Stalinism: From Leninist Revolution to Stalinist Society*. Armonk, NY: M.E. Sharpe, 1986.

Coombe, Rosemary. "Room for Manoeuver: Toward a Theory of Practice in Critical Legal Studies." *Law & Social Inquiry* 14, no. 1 (1989): 69–121.

Cross, John C. *Informal Politics: Street Vendors and the State in Mexico City.* Stanford: Stanford University Press, 1998.

Douglas, Mary. *Purity and Danger: An Analysis of the Concepts of Pollution and Taboo.* New York: Pantheon, 1966.

Economist, The. "Parcels, Plots and Power." September 12, 2020: 37–39.

Edelman, Bernard. *Ownership of the Image: Elements for a Marxist Theory of Law.* New York: Routledge, 1979.

Feldman, Gregory. *The Gray Zone: Sovereignty, Human Smuggling, and Undercover Police Investigation in Europe*. Stanford: Stanford University Press, 2019.

Fleising, Usher, and Alan Smart. "The Development of Property Rights in Biotechnology." *Culture, Medicine and Psychiatry* 17 (1993): 43–57.

Gilbert, Alan. "De Soto's The Mystery of Capital: Reflections on the Book's Public Impact." *International Development Planning Review* 34, no. 3 (2012): v–xviii.

Hetherington, Kregg. *Guerrilla Auditors: The Politics of Transparency in Neoliberal Paraguay*. Durham: Duke University Press, 2011.

Heyman, Josiah McC, and Alan Smart. "States and Illegal Practices: An Overview." In *States and Illegal Practices: An Overview*, edited by Josiah McC Heyman, 1–24. Oxford: Berg, 1999.

Hirst, Paul. *On Law and Ideology*. Atlantic Highlands, NJ: Humanities Press, 1979.

Ho, Samuel P.S., and George C.S. Lin. "China's Evolving Land System." Center for Chinese Research Discussion Paper 01-1. Vancouver, BC: Centre for Chinese Research, 2001.

Kay, Geoffrey, and James Mott. *Political Order and the Law of Labour*. New York: Macmillan Press, 1982.

Kloppenburg, Jack Ralph. *First the Seed: The Political Economy of Plant Biotechnology*. Madison, WI: University of Wisconsin Press, 1988.

Kopytoff, Igor. "The Cultural Biography of Things: Commoditization as Process." In *The Social Life of Things: Commodities in Cultural Perspective*, edited by Arjun Appadurai, 64–92. Cambridge, UK: Cambridge University Press, 1982.

Koster, Martijn, and Alan Smart. "Performing In/Formality beyond the Dichotomy: An Introduction." *Anthropologica* 61, no. 1 (2019): 20–24.

Leach, Edmund. *Culture and Communication*. Cambridge, UK: Cambridge University Press, 1979.

Ledeneva, Alena V. *How Russia Really Works: The Informal Practices that Shaped Post-Soviet Politics and Business*. Ithaca: Cornell University Press, 2006.

Levi, Primo. *The Drowned and the Saved*. New York: Summit Books, 1988.

Lin, George C. S. *Developing China: Land, Politics and Social Conditions*. London: Routledge, 2009.

Moore, Sally Falk. "Explaining the Present: Theoretical Dilemmas in Processual Ethnography." *American Ethnologist* 14, no. 4 (1987): 727–736.

Moore, Sally Falk. *Law as Process: An Anthropological Approach*. London: Routledge & Kegan Paul, 1978.

Petropoulos, Jonathan, and John K. Roth. "Prologue: The Gray Zones of the Holocaust." In *Gray Zones: Ambiguity and Compromise in the Holocaust and Its Aftermath*, edited by Jonathan Petropoulos and John K. Roth, xv–xxii. New York: Berghahn, 2005.

Pink, Sarah., K. Osz, K. Raats, T. Lindgren, and V. Fors. "Design Anthropology for Emerging technologies: Trust and Sharing in Autonomous Driving Futures." *Design Studies* 69 (2020): S0142694X20300247. https://doi.org/10/ggxp6b.

Scheper-Hughes, Nancy. "Commodity Fetishism in Organs Trafficking." *Body & Society* 7, no. 2–3 (2001): 31–62.

Smart, Alan. "The Strength of Property Rights, Prospects for the Disadvantaged, and Constraints on the Actions of the Politically Powerful in Hong Kong and China."

In *Marginalization in Urban China: Comparative Perspectives*, edited by Fulong Wu and Chris Webster, 90–111. London: Palgrave Macmillan, 2010.
Smart, Alan. *The Shek Kip Mei Myth: Squatters, Fires and Colonial Rule in Hong Kong, 1950–63*. Hong Kong: Hong Kong University Press, 2006.
Smart, Alan. "Impeded Self-Help: Toleration and the Proscription of Housing Consolidation in Hong Kong's Squatter Areas." *Habitat International* 27 (2003): 205–225.
Smart, Alan. "Unruly Places: Urban Governance and the Persistence of Illegality in Hong Kong's Urban Squatter Areas." *American Anthropologist* 103, no. 1 (2001): 30–44.
Smart, Alan. "The Emergence of Local Capitalisms in China: Overseas Chinese Investment and Patterns of Development." In *China's Regions, Polity and Economy: A Study of Spatial Transformation in the Post-reform Era*, edited by Si-Ming Li and Wing-Shing Tang, 65–95. Hong Kong: Chinese University Press, 2000.
Smart, Alan. "Invisible Real Estate: Investigations into the Squatter Property Market." *International Journal of Urban and Regional Research* 10, no. 1 (1986): 29–45.
Smart, Alan. "The Squatter Property Market in Hong Kong." *Critique of Anthropology* 5 no. 3 (1985): 23–40.
Smart, Alan and Thomas Aguilera. "Towards a Political Economy of Toleration of Illegality: Comparing Tolerated Squatting in Hong Kong and Paris." In *Comparative Approaches to Informal Housing Around the Globe*, edited by U. Grashoff, 39–65. London: UCL Press, 2020.
Smart, Alan and Josephine Smart. *Posthumanism: Anthropological Insights*. Toronto: University of Toronto Press, 2017a.
Smart, Alan and Josephine Smart. "Formalization as Confinement in Colonial Hong Kong." *International Sociology* 32, no. 4 (2017b): 437–453.
Smart, Alan, and Josephine Smart. "Tangled Up in Food: The Moral Economy of Food Politics in the Transpacific Region." In *Transpacific Americas: Encounters and Engagements Between the Americas and the South Pacific*, edited by Eveline Dürr and Philipp Schorch, 150–166. New York: Routledge, 2016.
Smart, Alan, and Josephine Smart. "Formalizing Hong Kong: Explaining Governmental Efforts to Eradicate and Control Urban Informality." *Social Transformations in Chinese Societies* 9, no. 1 (2013): 55–78.
Smart, Alan, and Filippo Zerilli. "Extralegality." In *A Companion to Urban Anthropology*, edited by Donald M. Nonini, 222–238. Malden, MA: Wiley-Blackwell, 2014.
Tanasescu, Alina, Ernest Chui, and Alan Smart. "Tops and Bottoms: State Tolerance of Illegal Housing in Hong Kong and Calgary." *Habitat International* 34, no. 4 (2010): 478–484.
Tang, Wing-Shing, and Him Chung. 2002. "Rural-Urban Transition in China: Illegal Land Use and Construction." *Asia Pacific Viewpoint* 43, no. 1 (2002): 43–62.
van Schendel, Willem, and Itty Abraham. *Illicit Flows and Criminal Things: States, Borders, and the Other Side of Globalization*. Bloomington: Indiana University Press, 2005.

Varley, Ann. "Private or Public: Debating the Meaning of Tenure Legalization." *International Journal of Urban and Regional Research* 26, no. 3 (2002): 449–462.
Varley, Ann. "The Political Uses of Illegality: Evidence from Urban Mexico." In *Illegal Cities*, edited by Edesio Fernandes and Ann Varley, 172–190. London: Zed Books, 1998.
Wedel, Janine. *Shadow Elite: How the World's New Power Brokers Undermine Democracy, Government, and the Free Market*. New York: Basic Books, 2009.
Xie, Qingshu, A.R. Ghanbari Parsa, and Barry Redding. "The Emergence of the Urban Land Market in China: Evolution, Structure, Constraints and Perspectives." *Urban Studies* 39, no. 8 (2002): 1375–1398.
Yiftachel, Oren. "Theoretical Notes on 'Gray Cities': The Coming of Urban Apartheid." *Planning Theory* 8, no. 1 (2009): 88–100.
Zhou, Feizhou. "Creating Wealth: Land Seizure, Local Government, and Farmers." In *Creating Wealth and Poverty in Postsocialist China*, edited by Deborah Davis and Feng Wang, 112–125. Stanford, CA: Stanford University Press, 2009.
Zhu, Jieming. "Urban Development under Ambiguous Property Rights: A Case of China's Transition Economy." *International Journal of Urban and Regional Research* 26, no. 1 (2002): 41–57.

Chapter 2

Methodological Legalism

Michael Herzfeld

LEGALISM, ESSENTIALISM, AND FORMALITY

When we ask ourselves whether an intended action *is legal* or not, we assume that legality is ultimately a fixed quality and that the answer to our question therefore already exists.[1] We essentialize legality. Most nation-state governments assume legality to be a matter that rests on textual evidence; even where it is contested on the basis of existing precedent, textual acts constitute its authority. Legality thus easily appears to be a refraction of larger essentialisms; therein lies its capacity both to reinforce and to draw upon the authority of those reified entities, among which culture, nationhood, and the state are particularly important in the present-day geopolitical context. Legalism thus corresponds in jurisprudence to what Stolcke (1995) has called "cultural fundamentalism" in the realm of national identity politics. It is hardly a coincidence that cultural fundamentalists also tend to be extremely legalistic in their arguments for the fixity, as they see it, of ethnic identities. The concept of *extralegality* advanced by Smart and Zerilli (2014) was a useful early attack on the seemingly absolute standing of *legality* and on its objectivist treatment as outside, and immune to, social process and semantic instability—on, in a word, *legalism*.

From an ethnographic perspective, however, the act of essentializing legality itself emerges as clearly tactical or strategic (which of the two is in turn also determined by the intentions behind the act).[2] It is an act of interpretation that we represent as grounded in incontrovertible fact. If that were not the case, so that laws did not require interpretation but only obedience to a state structure claiming to represent eternal cultural verities, decisions about appropriate action in a wide range of social life would become blessedly simple; crooks would be unable to plead exonerating circumstances; and lawyers would be out of business. (Anthropologists would probably be out of business too; but that, I fear, will strike most readers as considerably less consequential.)

Nicholas De Genova and his associates (2017) have worked from the realization that migrants are not illegal; migrants are *illegalized*. The same can be said of most categories to which the label *illegal* is affixed. It is, consistently with the thrust of this volume, a recognition of the agency operated by those with officially constituted power. By extension, moreover, other alleged abstract properties attributed to entire social groups and actions—such as marginality, criminality, and security—turn out to be the results of processes for which we then use more appropriately processual names: marginalization, criminalization, securitization. These revealing neologisms together remind us that powerful human actors operate the processes in question, usually against other human actors operating on very different ethical assumptions. It is this realization of the significance of agency that constitutes a major reason for anthropologists to write in the first person, and explains why legal documents are rarely composed in that way. Language offers useful clues to the evasions of responsibility that are apparently essential to the smooth working of social life, even, or especially, in those bureaucratic contexts where we usually assume that the attribution of responsibility, whether for good outcomes or bad, is simply a matter of fact.

Legality, moreover, is one element in a larger area of interpretability.[3] This is the domain of *formality*. In at least five major areas of human activity—language, law, economics, habitation, and religion[4]—a perverse binarism has taken the form of an assumption that establishment systems set an absolute standard of formality; everything else is informal by definition. We read of informal speech (or slang), informal economic practices, informal settlements, informal rules, informal rituals and folk religion. Yet in each of these arenas, scholars describing social phenomena in such terms often also reveal, intentionally or otherwise, the fundamental political dualism that underlies all these apparent realities. That dualism posits a systemic organizational and conceptual structure (the linguists' *langue*) against which everyday practice (the equivalent of *parole*) always looks inadequate. Yet practice usually has the last laugh.

In a dualistic conception of social life, ordinary people are either incapable of managing the rules without help or are criminally involved in breaking them. That perspective would perhaps pass muster were it not for one inconvenient circumstance: that bureaucrats and experts are themselves human beings. So, too, are politicians, of whom Bailey (1988: 1–10) wrote that they could not even afford to be literally honest in what they say. Their injured protestations of innocence, like the disclaimers I will discuss below, are understood by their constituents as a shared mask for various forms of collusion, as are the seemingly irrational antics of some leaders who instead perform outrageous violations of conventional political conduct (see, e.g., Dematteo 2007).

The work of all three groups—politicians, experts, and bureaucrats—involves creative play somewhere in (and not infrequently outside) the space between the letter and the spirit of the law, a space that employs as much self-exonerating casuistry as the pleadings of the most abject malefactor or corrupt cleric. The play lies in the continual adjustment of existing rules—or, more precisely, in the retrofitting of rules to reality. An illegally constructed house becomes part of a new master plan; a grammatical rule is treated as common usage and declared acceptable by *Webster's Dictionary* and the *Oxford Dictionary*, while punctuation is rejigged by the *Chicago Manual of Style*. Yet such retrofitting is a historical act, taking place in real time. It also encounters resistance, as those of my students who have cheerfully split clusters of infinitives find to their cost, and as—more seriously—people who are too bold in erecting new structures in the middle of a carefully zoned historic district similarly discover when irritated neighbors denounce them. Notice how I have phrased this description: I have deliberately mixed the trivial with the consequential to show how wide a range of activities are subject to this binarism; triviality and *serietà*—let me tactically revert to the useful abstractions of Italian here!—are themselves subject to its either-or logic.

Laws, like the syntax of a language, are often honored in the breach—a sure sign both that they exist as a feared reality in human experience *and* that they are as selectively malleable in practice as a naughty child's excuses. Like all social performances, or what I prefer to call "social poetics" (Herzfeld 2016a: 165–79), infractions are about demonstrating mastery. As in linguistic performative utterances (see Austin 1975), one must go far enough along the road of nonconformity to display the mastery, and especially the ability to bend the rules—perhaps lastingly—into new shapes. Those who go too far, however, are more likely to fall flat on their faces. People are more impressed by the stylish rogue than by the dully obedient citizen, but they—perhaps tactically—profess themselves horrified when the rogue pushes their own moral limits too far (or threatens by that action to disclose their own very similar misdemeanors).

In this chapter, I propose that we abandon, once and for all, the pretense—a clear instance of "methodological legalism"[5]—that the formal–informal dichotomy serves any useful purpose other than as a term of abuse. Other people's practices are *informal*, ours are not; the very notion of this binary reproduces the logic of colonialism, especially as expressed through town planning that set up *rational* European quarters as a deliberate contrast with the apparent chaos of "native" housing (see Rabinow 1989). While some anthropologists have bravely attempted to rescue the idea of informality from official opprobrium (see especially Milgram 2019), and have pointed to the origin of some of these distinctions in colonial practice (e.g., Smart and Smart 2017), the social reality is such that the use of the terminology itself risks inadvertently signaling a preemptive surrender to official classification.

REALISM AND PRACTICE

The bureaucratic nation-state has inherited much of the authority of the colonial powers. Its ability to relegate already marginalized citizens to the bleak exile of informality parades as the rule of law, common sense, hygiene, and security—all favorite excuses for the structural violence of hierarchy. There *is* a binary distinction that people make in their everyday social lives, but it is not between the formal and the informal; it is between the rules as they are articulated and the practices that people represent as following those rules even when, from a literal perspective, they do not. In between, there are all the innumerable minor infractions of popular morality that either are not, or are not yet, classified as illegal, but that those who commit them feel social pressure to excuse (Karstedt and Farrall 2006). There is, it seems, a continuum of actions across a wide spectrum of legality, the edges of which are nowhere near as clear as legal positivists would wish.

This is not an argument for dispensing with law. It is, however, an argument for a more realistic acknowledgment of the social reality of law—or, rather, of *laws*, of specific speech acts that create reality and that, in the context of that same reality, can, under the right felicity conditions, be challenged. Hiding the specificity of legal pronouncements behind the abstraction of law is counterproductive. What defines the right felicity conditions for declaring an act illegal will always in turn be a question of social reality; it is an empirical matter.[6] We can see this most clearly when those who are charged with enforcing legality seem both willing to stretch it and creative in their ways of doing so.

Let me illustrate with a pair of simple anecdotes about encounters I experienced in my youth. When I was 14 years old, I received a lesson in sociality that may well have been the trigger of a lifelong career in social anthropology and, ultimately, my dawning appreciation of that zone of true sociality that I have come to call "cultural intimacy." I had just learned a little Italian, and we were vacationing in Italy. My father told me to ask a city policeman (*vigile*) for permission to park the car briefly in front of a hotel on the grandiose Via Veneto in Rome so that we could unload the baggage. "It's not permitted—but it is permitted (*Non è permesso—ma è permesso*)," replied the *vigile*, perhaps amused by this presumptuous English adolescent speaking in what was undoubtedly an atrocious Italian accent. His use of a lofty, abstract grammatical construction allowed him to cloak the contingency of his pronouncement as a general principle, and the deception would stick for long enough to allow my father to unload our baggage and then park the car in a "legal" location.

This official's kindliness was a more benign improvisation than that of a Greek policeman who stopped me on an Athens street during the junta (1967–1974) years because I had dared to cross the road where there was no line indicating that pedestrians might do so. With the very young, very serious Greek policeman, who questioned me in a tone of offended authority, I resorted to deadpanning: I had not known that I should not cross where there was no line; no, I could not produce an identity card (carrying one was compulsory for Greek citizens at that time); no, I did not have my passport with me because it was one of those old British ones, too big to fit into the pocket of my trousers. At that point, baffled and perhaps wondering whether tangling with a British citizen would be favorably viewed by his superiors, he puffed himself up and solemnly informed me that he could have hauled me off to the police station but instead was going to let me go this time—"because I liked your sincerity!" He then stalked off, his precarious dignity saved. As we know, sincerity is a social attribution, not the product of an impossible feat of mind-reading (see Handler 1986: 3). While I cannot be sure that the policeman was concerned with his dignity, in a world of agonistic masculinity that would not be an unreasonable proposition. As a performance designed to protect his reputation, the youthful officer's display of self-importance was at least consistent with a decision to let me off the hook—perhaps thereby himself committing an illegal act, but one that potentially saved him and his superiors from potential trouble.

Both these incidents show how officials must always be prepared to improvise. Nothing in their training really prepares them for the slightly offbeat realities that are the commonest form of social encounter. The Roman policemen's response was a small act of collusion, a surface manifestation of the many ways in which Italian police find themselves implicated in socially acceptable arrangements that technically violate the law. Allowing one foreigner to park a car illegally for a few minutes was less troublesome than looking like an unfeeling brute, and it would have seemed trivial when placed against the larger picture. Rome policemen have locally been so famous for their "corruption"—another of those social attributions masquerading as incontrovertible fact—that in more recent years the national state apparatus has forbidden them to patrol except under the surveillance of at least one of the several national-level police forces.[7]

Both policemen's responses were reflections of rules that had been codified but not written down. (Legalism demands textual materiality.) They could both be reasonably sure that, even had their superiors caught them in their respective technical violations, those superiors would normally have preferred to look the other way. The rules that govern such moments are well understood, as they are by civilians. If one intends to bribe an official, for example, the bribe should be wrapped in a local newspaper (this not only shows the recipient that the donor knows these rules but also indicates that the rules are indeed local). The same predictability guides interpretations of the unctuously polite gesticulations and expressions of friendship from a *mafioso* who is in fact demanding compliance, as well as everyday assumptions that it is more *civil* (*civile*) to break the law than to hand over some hapless undocumented immigrant or even a petty thief to the punitive authority of the police. These are (social) rules, and people know them and to a large extent follow them. What is informal about that?

As for so-called informal settlements (see, e.g., Huchzermayer and Karam 2006), they are usually governed of necessity by procedural and hierarchical structures that offer a minimal basis for bare survival. Labeling settlements as informal—as in the case of the Turkish *gecekondu*, the name of which means literally "landed overnight" on account of its surreptitious and rapid construction under cover of nightfall, for example—sets them up as targets; it does not change the reality of their capacity for self-governance. Such communities are often governed by a home-grown leadership, which demands and enforces adherence to a clearly codified set of rules. That these rules are not always written down does not make them less formal; indeed, the evidence of religious texts suggests that orality sometimes induces a greater fear of revision than would be the case with written scripts (where the rationale for change can also be inscribed).

CLAIMING AND DISCLAIMING

It is because all regulation is social that actors often excuse themselves for *obeying* the law. We are used to excuses for disobedience, but excuses can be made toward any source of disapproval—and what could be stronger than social or peer group pressure? A schoolchild who reports another child's misdeeds to a teacher will have a lot of explaining to do to other peers aware of the situation. One might expect that the teacher, by contrast, would not need an explanation, and might indeed congratulate the sneak. In many pedagogical traditions, however, and notably in the so-called public school culture of upper-class England, teachers actively discourage sneaking, viewing it as a poor preparation for the tough realities of social life. Standing up for oneself is considered more virtuous than running to the teacher to report being bullied, as I discovered for myself during my high-school years. A boy who complained to his teacher was as likely to have to explain why he was doing so rather than defending himself even, if necessary, with violence. This is not very different from the situation of the craft apprentices I studied in Crete. Those youths are more likely to be kicked out if they are too obedient and passive than when they "steal with their eyes" and thereby demonstrate their ability to survive in an agonistic male-dominated society (see Herzfeld 2004). Obedience and passivity require explanation; disobedience and "cunning" (*poniria*), technically acts of defiance against authority, do not, in social practice, require such self-exoneration. Everyone understands.

These dynamics often include a complicit and collusive reading of disclaimers (see Bauman 1977: 21–22)—the formulaic denial of one's own excellence (virtue, social worth, or other claim to merit). Disclaimers are, in social practice, the opposite of what they appear to be; they are, in a word, claims. When Cretan villagers told me that they were "illiterate," they were not expecting me to agree, and they never hesitated to proclaim the superiority of their practical knowledge to the highly abstract learning found in the classroom. The disclaimer of literacy is not, in any case, literal; Greece has a low illiteracy rate. This particular disclaimer is a rhetorical claim, understood as such by any insider, to a socially embedded and morally superior form of knowledge.

Disclaimers represent a specific form of what Malinowski (1936: 313) called *phatic communion*: they establish a right to mutual intimacy, and failure to understand them marks an interlocutor as an outsider. (Ethnographers necessarily learn them quickly since failure to do so can lead to a wide range of solecisms. When I innocently followed the example of villagers on the island of Nisiros who labeled as "barbaric" the habit of throwing exploding fireworks at others' feet during Easter celebrations, I was forced to grovel in apology.[8]) Disclaimers are thus shibboleths and, as such, useful for regulating access to cultural intimacy. They are also performatives (Austin 1975): they perform the *phatic labor* (Elyachar 2010; Sopranzetti 2017) of communicating social competence. We cannot possibly know what others think, we insist, but we assume that such disclaimers mean exactly the opposite of what they literally say. In short, disclaimers model the paradox of legalism, which would not exist were it not for the fact that "everyone knows" that laws are always and without exception a matter of interpretation.

When one of my Roman friends, during a film shoot, wanted to claim an empathic reading of Pope John Paul II's emotions on his first papal encounter with the people of Rome, he made a self-dismissive gesture as he declared, "I could also be wrong (*posso anche sbagliare*)," making it clear that he thought no such thing—or so *I* claim, perhaps meretriciously implying that his intentions were transparent to me.[9] Claims to transparency are, like disclaimers, recognizable devices of self-proclaimed deception, and it is precisely their obviousness to those who are in the know—the speaker's cultural intimates—that makes them so useful to corrupt politicians (see especially Morris 2004). They provide the assurance of knowing that one's intimates will know that they mean the opposite of what they literally say. They are like ironic politeness formulae, used to exclude others in ways that also make it impossible to protest against the violence they perform because, after all, who could possibly object to being treated politely?[10] It may be more pertinent for my present purposes to ask who would want to get rid of such useful devices, which, precisely because they convey the opposite of what everyone understands them to mean, make further argument pointless and create a cultural safe zone for one's intimates.

All these disclaimers are about social norms rather than institutional regulations. They are thus not so much excuses for not conforming to laws as normative performances that render the solecism of hubris socially acceptable. To legally constituted authority, by contrast, we answer, not with disclaimers, but with excuses (Austin 1971); in these cases, self-exoneration follows a formally established procedure, and our excuses—as conventional as disclaimers—merely foreshadow what will become our advocates' logic in the courtroom, thereby revealing the semantic lability of the law.

Disclaimers and excuses do nevertheless share a basic feature of conventionality: they are not about what people believe, but about what is socially acceptable. More specifically, they remind interlocutors that what is being said is not necessarily literally credible (in the case of excuses) or even potentially so (in the case of disclaimers). They model a deception that is obvious to those who know the game. When musicians and actors deprecate their own performances, they do not expect anyone to take their disclaimers literally. The disclaimers are liens on cultural intimacy that announce an agreed collusion, one that also marks as outsiders those who fail to apprehend the intended irony.

In the same way, officers of the law and bureaucrats more generally are well aware of the importance of seeing claims to innocence as performances that may actually *create* both innocence and complicity. They use such devices themselves: "It is not permitted . . . but it is permitted." Conversely, an accused person's direct claim to being law-abiding is likely to be met with incredulity, not necessarily because the speaker is already known to be dishonest, but because the speaker's interlocutors would expect some sort of disclaimer: "I know how it looks, officer, but..." In other words, a special kind of casuistry is needed for situations if a citizen wants to obey the law. Furthermore, citizens who for any reason wish to obey the law when others are pressing them to break it must produce an excuse for what would otherwise be a solecism. Nothing could more clearly show that society, too, has its rules.In extreme cases, such as the Cretan village where one of my informants sententiously informed a police officer that "we have two laws here" to explain why the officer should respect local norms while in the village, these rules are rendered explicit when they are brought into direct confrontation with the laws of the state (see Figure 2.1).[11]

Performance, Casuistry, and Deception

Failure to realize the importance of an effective performance, or to distinguish between the literal and the ironic, can have unpleasant consequences. Until a few years ago, Greek law required all real estate contracts to show both an estimated valuation and the tax office's assessment. An American citizen of Greek extraction, schooled in the United States to react in horror to what he saw as Greek duplicity, refused his local lawyer's entreaties to declare only half the value of the land he was purchasing, only to be charged double tax on the grounds that no one would ever declare the correct amount. It took considerable effort, when the case came to court, to persuade the judge that he had been telling the truth, and it was only the lawyer's insistence that the American was an ignorant and socially unskilled foreigner that did the trick. Moreover, the American was fortunate in that he did not have the same surname as the seller. The deal took place in a town on Crete where, implicitly but without ambivalence, patrilineal kinship still played a large role in channeling loyalties, so that, as I discovered on reading through many such contracts, those who were buying from members of the same surname group (i.e., patrilineal clan) would be assessed for tax on *four* times the estimated value. Clan identities have no legal standing in Greece, and indeed are associated

Figure 2.1 Signs of a Standoff: "We have Two Laws" (Crete, 2017). *Source*: Photo by Michael Herzfeld.

with local illegality (such as vendettas), but they are a systemic part of the local social reality in western and central Crete and the bureaucrats, who are drawn from the same general social milieu, are absolutely cognizant of this circumstance.[12]

Formality, again, is not a helpful concept here. From a local perspective, intimate social and cultural relations are governed by conventions every bit as identifiable to all insiders as the laws of the land, and indeed quite often a good deal more so. Bureaucrats may collude with local people because of some gradually earned mutual empathy, as happened in China with a village that did not want to allow planners to route a national road through its venerable cemetery; in an officially atheist state, such sentimental attachments would have no legal basis, but the bureaucrats in this case shared the affective universe of the local citizens (Steinmüller 2013: 217–20). In other situations in the same country, bureaucrats might instead interpret the law to allow them an exploitative relation with local people, a situation often exacerbated by differences of status or wealth (see, e.g., Osburg 2018; Wu 2016), and exacerbated by a sense of "disconnect between representation and reality" that "is presumed to be the organic product of a society in which everyone (including leaders) 'lack belief' and thus feel that they have the license to manipulate representations to advance their own interests" (Osburg 2016: 48).

Religious officials, too, are adept at creating case-specific exceptions that suit their immediate social circumstances; this is what the term *casuistry* means. For example, Catholic priests who in nineteenth-century Rome sidestepped the ecclesiastical ban on usury by arguing that they were saving their debtors from a worse fate at the hands of much more extortionate loan sharks were pleading an exceptionalism that may well have rested on a reasonable social contract. In that case, priests, debtors, and church authorities will have connived at interpreting the absolute ban on usury, but the ban itself remained, textually speaking, absolute. A religious system that operates the confessional as a safety valve against the intolerable pressures of accumulated guilt for sins committed for arguably benign reasons is not unlike the secular reconciliation devices to be found in some vendetta-prone societies, including that of western Crete, that create conditions under which forgiveness has practical advantages (such as the creation of alliances and the avoidance of ongoing mayhem). It is a socially realistic device that does not disturb the categorical rigidity of the rules. The example of the moneylending priests is embedded in a larger social reality, in which even the more egregious loan sharks are sometimes considered a benign alternative to banks sanctioned by the state and increasingly implicated in the neoliberal structures of the economy—banks, moreover, whose local managers are removed every three years because, so residents claim (and with good evidence if the media are to be believed), by that point in their incumbency they are already sealing under-the-table deals whereby usurers relieve them of the burden of making high-risk loans in exchange for immunity from prosecution for their illegal activities. Local shopkeepers and artisans are anxious to keep the usurers in business precisely because the banks consistently refuse their requests for loans, while the usurers rarely kill defaulters because they wish to maintain a reputation as friendly souls who are simply trying to help.[13] At the most inclusive level, the banks themselves are participants in these arrangements; since they can claim that the law does not allow them to lend to citizens unable to produce collateral in the form of real estate, they facilitate a social flow that benefits the artisans and shopkeepers as well as the usurers and, at the invisible far end of the feeding chain, the bank managers themselves. There is nothing informal about these arrangements except the absence of legal writ; the participants all know the consequences of defying the rules as well as the casuistic logic that keeps them operative.

Laws carry institutional and literal force; social norms define and follow the contours of intimacy. This is a radical difference, and it is also the difference that separates abstraction from performance. Neither is *inherently* formal or informal; both can be stretched precisely because the rigid signifier is the most effective disguise for the manipulable signified. But establishing which rules will prevail is always a question of context—of asking which actors, in a given context, are assumed to have the right to determine what the rules mean and what conclusions can be drawn about particular cases. As James C. Scott (1998: 328–33) has pointed out, moreover, citizens are also aware that the state itself would collapse under the strain of internally conflicting regulations if every bureaucrat applied each law literally to every situation (see also Glaeser 2004; Smart and Smart 2017: 438).

A polity, religious community, or even local group that conducts its daily business according to strict legality is a formula for disaster. But the institution retains the right to clamp down on infractions at any time, usually for highly contingent reasons and when infraction exceeds practicality. In other words, the indeterminacy of social life is not an inversion of the way institutions function. To the contrary, it is produced *by* the institutions, whose power often indeed resides in the unpredictability of their own future actions. Like all meaning systems, including language, the significations of law and bureaucracy are arbitrary, and their effects, intentionally or otherwise, may not correspond with stated intentions.

Let me illustrate with an example of this duplicitous formalism. If today, as Noelle Molé (2010) has cogently argued, neoliberalism uses the condition of precariousness as a means of imposing docility on workers fearful of rocking the boat and losing their jobs, that massive and destructive condition is in harsh reality the globalized and intensified condition of indeterminacy that defines all social experience, corralled and redirected as an instrument of large-scale governance. Rules contradict each other, serving the convenience of those who exercise power but displaying far less consistency in application than they do textually. On one occasion with which I am familiar, outraged that a colleague had been mistreated by a moderately important university, some scholars collectively protested in writing to the administration. The response included a declaration that the administrators could not discuss a personnel matter with third parties. Then, however, the letter-writers discovered that the administrators had sent the letter, unredacted, to the alleged victim. When they protested that the administrators were violating the very confidentiality they had invoked, the administrators responded by claiming that they were legally obliged to share all documents about an employee with that individual. Their lofty response illustrates the indeterminacy of what are ostensibly inflexible rules as well as the opportunism with which those exercising power can wield this indeterminacy in the name of "fairness."

FROM RISK TO RULE: THE NEOLIBERAL MOMENT

Here, the role of risk, hitherto a key component of the social poetics typical of what Robert Paine (1989) once called "high-wire cultures" (see also Malaby 2003), is shifted from the ceaseless negotiation between institutional authority and individual performance to a situation in which institutional authority takes over the tactical devices of individual action and turns them into long-term strategies disguised as law and order, or as institutional morality. As Andrea Muehlebach (2012) has shown, neoliberalism—like *mafia* (see, e.g., di Bella 2008)—is a highly moralistic ideology, not least when it takes over the running of universities and other institutions supposed to be free of profit-making motives and constraints.

And yet even here there is space for rebellion. Indeed, the growth of the neoliberal economy has been accompanied by a concomitant dismissal as informal of activities hitherto considered to be the responsibility of the state and necessitated by its increasing evacuation from social life (e.g., Cabot 2016; Rakopoulos 2014). In a world in which the major economic forces appear to be increasingly uncontrolled by any systemic application of law, it is local operators who now don the rhetoric and symbolism of formality. What is more, they can also challenge the weakened national state and its subdivisions (regions, municipalities, etc.) by disputing their legitimacy to represent the people. Many of the new solidarity movements are about precisely that.

Transactional interactions ranging from the mutual respect of police and animal thieves on Crete to the carefully orchestrated relations between ostensibly respectable bank managers and equally disreputable usurers in Italian cities share a strong sense of engagement in a rule-governed universe. There is nothing informal here, if by informal we mean an absence of procedure. On the contrary, such arrangements depend on procedural codes that govern connivance between persons or groups of persons who might reasonably be expected to have diametrically opposed interests. Without a good measure of codification, neither side to such transactions would consent to engage in the first place. The procedures themselves resemble all other codes inasmuch as they are themselves liable to violation as well as to gradual change, but no more so, at least in principle, than the laws of the state. Using the language of formality merely cedes conceptual authority to the state.

Attributions of informality are especially damaging to small local communities, notably those embedded in large cities. Such communities are often older and better established than the political and bureaucratic bodies that so describe them. In the small Bangkok community of Pom Mahakan, a community characterized by the municipal authorities as a nest of squatters and as totally outside the law, the residents' view was that it was the authorities who were the "invaders" of their space, while they were its legitimate occupants. Their rhetoric is a precise mirror image of that used by the authorities. The residents certainly deployed forms of legalism themselves, and they also acknowledged that in a technical sense they were now occupying the land illegally. But by citing moral rights, they created an institutional framework quite their own, one that in some respects modeled and reproduced in miniature the structure and logic of the royal nation-state. And they were assiduous in their emphasis on the disjuncture between the official values of the state and what they describe as the un-Thai and un-Buddhist lack of compassion displayed by the bureaucrats. As the community president remarked to me, the residents largely respected the institutional order of things (*rabob*) but they did not respect the people who staffed it or the values they represented. With the military coups of 2006 and especially of 2014, the community's luck ran out. Already weakened by fighting the legalism (and literalism) of a court that declared that private homes could not be permitted in a space designated as a public park, and by the reluctance of any Thai court to stand up for judicial fairness against the authority of the current elite (see McCargo 2019), they were forced to leave and their homes, including some fine examples of vernacular Thai architecture, were ruthlessly destroyed.[14]

Nonetheless, the challenge that they effectively posed to the authorities for a quarter of a century constituted a persuasive denial of informality. Managed by an elected managing committee, they arranged a roster of guards mounted on the encircling wall, nets across the canal during any time of heightened fear, whistles to sound the alarm, and a PA system that rallied the residents and reminds them of their emergency training. These are forms of civil defense that speak to the practicalities of survival. In response to an increasing concern with how the community was represented in the larger Thai society, they mounted a concerted campaign to build a "current" (*kra-sae*) of support against the prevailing bureaucratic regime. That they also had their own cozy relations with some of the state's representatives, notably the police, was itself a deliberate survival strategy. Such a strategy did not work under thinly disguised totalitarianism in part because the regime had its own self-interested reasons for marginalizing the existing police corps in relation to military power. Thailand's drift to authoritarian rule was certainly bad news for the community, not because the new authorities are necessarily more even-handed in their application of the law, but because it is much easier for an authoritarian state to obfuscate the evidence of its own special arrangements, using the trappings of formality to disguise and retrospectively justify its decisions.

To see this in a larger, comparative frame, we might think of the Israeli settlements that have gone up around Jerusalem in defiance of international outrage. It is not my purpose here to argue the rights and wrongs of such state-driven actions (although readers may guess my perspective from the angle of approach), but simply to argue that what constitutes them as formal is a simple performative utterance—a "verdictive," in Austin's (1975) terminology—by a law court that, on behalf of the state, declares them to be so, and, at the same time, declares Palestinian settlements in the same area to be illegal. Of course, there is a body of law to which the court must appeal; it is bound by the requirements of legality. But there is something inherently circular in such a conceptual arrangement. The *informality* of those other settlements is an attributed quality, and does not look so informal from the perspective of the inhabitants, who must live by a set of rules in order to make their existence even bearable, and also as a basis of their appeals to the international community.

Formality is thus not an objective quality; it is an attributed one. It almost appears as though what we mean by an "informal" settlement is one that is at risk of being uprooted. Normativity is constituted by those who make and enforce the laws, and it is, ironically, in their hands that the laws seem to acquire their greatest degree of interpretative lability. In an enormous range of countries, from Israel/Palestine to South Africa (see Huchzemayer and Karam 2006), and notably including India, Pakistan, and much of southeast Asia as well as significant parts of East and West Africa and Latin America, we find the same dynamic: settlements whose solidity can vanish at the drop of a judge's gavel, internally regulated by norms that often seem to violate the very notion of legality from the perspective of the state but that are observed with great seriousness by the inhabitants of these fragile socio-spatial entities. The terminology of formality and informality would seem to undermine rather than increase understanding of how norms and rules are applied, or, at the very least, render analysis complicit in the official vision of state power.

It is the ostensibly most rigidly systemic arrangements—be they moral codes, official laws, or bureaucratic procedures—that allow for the greatest degree of subversion of their own systematicity. Moreover, this point is directly linked to institutions' seemingly paradoxical dependency on the spaces of cultural intimacy. We can imagine the legal superstructure as a thick wall shielding the wielders of power from close inspection of what they do; the thicker the wall—the more formalistic the legal language and symbolism—the easier it is to make the kinds of arrangements that permit the formal institutions of state and municipality to do their work rather than founder on the logjam of excessive pedantry. Cris Shore (2000: 82–119) amusingly reports on how he caught out some British financial officers of the European Union in Brussels, people who were assumed to be of impeccable bureaucratic probity, admitting to fixing various procedures in order to keep things moving along. They presumably could not have done so without the combination of a highly formalized official role and the stereotype of British official adherence to the substance of correct procedure. (And it is probably no coincidence, now that we have mentioned that stereotype, that it was in Britain that the work-to-rule, that ultimate *reductio ad absurdum* of bureaucratic pedantry and literal-minded adherence to the rules, seems to have been invented.)

The consequences of this observation are far-reaching. Even if we revert for a moment to the *traditional* concerns of social anthropology with remote communities and highly formalized moralities (such as the alleged "honor and shame" systems associated with the circum-Mediterranean lands), we see a similar principle at work. The rhetoric of chastity in rural Greece, for example, evidently rose in intensity in direct proportion to the frequency with which its literal meanings were subverted; good performers of demure innocence could get away with far more than those who were already considered rather disreputable (Herzfeld 1983). Again, the highest incidence of a type of miniature shrine to the Virgin Mary in Rome—medallions that served as loci of worship—was locally understood to be, not indices of deep piety (although the parish priest made strenuous efforts to redirect their use in such terms), but evidence of the greatest need, in the two low-life areas of central Rome for much of its history, for intercession by the Virgin with her severe Son on behalf of the assorted miscreants who made up much of these districts' populations (Herzfeld 2009: 104; Ricci 1999: 38–44; Scaraffia 1990). When religion meets patronage—and there is a convincing case to be made that patronage is structured by religious ideas about the cosmology of power (Boissevain 1969: 78)—we have the perfect combination for erecting that shield of piety to protect those eminently practical and thoroughly scurrilous arrangements that mark the "art of fixing things" (*l'arte dell'arrangiarsi*).

This seems too cynical a view of the world, some will say. But it is hardly less cynical to ignore the deep systematicity of the rules and norms that govern the daily lives of precisely those who live outside the self-constituting jurisdiction of institutions, or to overlook the ways in which legal principles have been invoked to protect the powerful from the legal consequences of their illegal actions. One need only think of the ways in which the principles of subsidiarity have been used to shield the perpetrators of pedophilia in the Catholic Church and other religious institutions, for example, or the casuistic refusal of a parish priest to intervene in evictions of the poor and weak on the grounds that doctrine forbade him to interfere in another priest's struggle with his conscience (Herzfeld 2009: 94–95). Recognizing the empirical evidence for such patterns of routinized infraction is not cynical; it calls the bluff of the truly cynical. And it recognizes that creative reinterpretations of the law are not the exclusive preserve of the those who have been dismissed or ignored as informal. Indeed, the sheep thieves of the Cretan highlands would argue that when in the past they could rely on the word of honor, or at most an oath sworn on a holy icon, they had no need of the state's version of the law (Herzfeld 2016a: 139–64). For them, it is bureaucratic modernity that has subverted trust and introduced cynical calculation into human relations. (Again one can think of religious parallels—as, for example, the cynical manipulation of the confessional for advance absolution from one's sins.)

So what from the outside, or the top, looks like illegality, it appears, is from the inside a matter of business as usual. This moral system may sometimes look like a mirror inversion of official morality—of legality—and it is in this regard, feeling the opprobrium that attaches to an excess of virtue, that people sometimes feel obliged to excuse themselves for acting according to the rules. When the law interferes with everyday sociality, and especially when it insists on what looks like conformity for conformity's sake, acting legally can appear antisocial. The Cretan shepherd who refuses the challenge of a raid by reciprocating in kind would have a lot of explaining to do if he is to avoid becoming the target of his fellow-villagers' mockery. One villager who was confronted by the murderer of a brother he had never even known was told that if he failed to take the man's life his own existence would become unbearable. In such extreme situations, it is doubtless whether an adequate excuse could even be found.

But in more trivial situations, excuses may be more acceptable—for the one who does not join in a drunken party, who buckles up in his car, or who observes the speed limit, for example, or who refuses to attend a right-wing political rally without wearing a mask against the 2020 pandemic virus. Such actions appear to be a rejection of cultural intimacy inasmuch as they appear to endorse official embarrassment over the persistence of undesirable habits. Socially, a brush with the law is often more appealing than conformity with its dictates. To be sure, not all the marks of cultural intimacy are actively illegal. Speaking a dialect that differs markedly from the official national language, for example, is not (usually, at least) illegal. But it defies the image of encompassing conformity—the methodological legalism—that the state wishes to impose, and, insofar as a local dialect is often regarded by its speakers as less a language form than the embodiment of a way of life, it is redolent with the small peccadilloes that define that collectively intimate space. In the Cretan case the link is explicit: the language of theft is uniquely and recognizably local. In the case of *romanesco*, the dialect of Rome, idiomatic variations on everyday expressions convey a sense of complicity—as, for example, when a slight pronunciation shift turns a simple inquiry as to where someone is going into the verbal equivalent of a wink (Herzfeld 2009: 27). Cockney rhyming slang, which seems to have evolved in part as a means of evading the unwanted attentions of the police, similarly encapsulates an etymology of minor sin (see, e.g., Lillo 2018: 689). Such linguistic traces are treated with affection even when they no longer represent the dominant speech form; another, common example is the persistence of Yiddish words in English and German speech, hinting at social values and attitudes that are either below the official radar screen or are actually associated with some degree of resistance to authority—or, as Friedman (2020) has argued, with an embarrassing triviality that language activists are now seeking to combat.

I have deliberately drawn the paper to an end with what some would regard as the minor dimensions of language use because it is precisely the ways in which the attitudes in question are sedimented in everyday communication that assures us of their centrality to the normal procedures of everyday life. These devices are just as codified, and just as procedural, as the rules that govern the application of official norms, hence the absurdity of treating them as informal.

There is another lesson to be learned from ethnography as well. The rhetoric and terminology of propriety provide a mask that skilled actors use to conceal their violations of that same propriety. All formal systems have the same capacity to be used as subversive devices. In other words, as we move from rules to process, or from structure to practice, we find that the very essence of formality as a concept lies in its usefulness as a means of assuaging official anxieties while permitting a socially more comfortable course of action. What works for ideals of chastity and masculinity also works, *a fortiori*, for bureaucracy. Bureaucratic skill lies in precisely that ability to present an arbitrary decision as the purest instantiation of normativity. Thus, we should not be surprised that the most holier-than-thou bureaucrats in the European Union should turn out to be the most successful manipulators of the system, just as we should not be surprised at the number of preachers and priests who have been caught, almost literally, with their pants down. Power gives control over the representation of one's actions in terms of rules one has the authority to enforce.

The circularity of power, thus revealed, suggests that the study of law and its violations should be radically recast. Instead of describing moral systems as though the social actors who use them did not in reality also create their significance, we should—as is consistent with the already well-established shift in anthropology from "reference" to "use" in the study of meaning (Crick 1976)—start with the social actions and relations of power that determine who treats what as formal or informal. For too long, methodological legalism has employed the terminology of formality and informality to conceal the agency that state and other official actors share with the vast majority of human beings. It is time to see as materially consequential the symbolic, linguistic, and legal denial of recognition that reinforces the already toxic inequalities of our world.

NOTES

1. I wish to acknowledge the kindly patience of our editors, Cristiana Panella and Walter Little, as well as Cristiana's original invitation to the conference. Some elements of this analysis were further developed in a stimulating workshop on "humbuggery" convened by Giovanni Da Col on the island of Capri in September 2017.

2. Spivak (1989) is credited with first coining the term "strategic essentialism." I prefer, however, to retain de Certeau's (1984) useful distinction between strategy and tactics; for reasons that should become clear in this chapter, contesting legality is a preserve of both.

3. Such abstract names nouns stretch conventional English-language usage. Some languages—Italian is an excellent example—seem much more tolerant of abstraction, producing words like *progettualità* ("projectuality") and *agentività* ("the quality of [social] agency) that raise abstraction far beyond "projection" and "agency." Others are more reluctant. In the French translation of my book *Cultural Intimacy* (Herzfeld 2016a, 2007), the translator's original neologism (*agentivité*) was deemed inappropriate and replaced, at my suggestion, by the more cumbersome but also more explicit *capacité d'agir*).

4. On religion, see especially Stewart 1989.

5. I model this term on the concept of "methodological nationalism" (Wimmer and Glick Schiller 2002) and its predecessor in social theory, "methodological individualism"; it could also be called "methodological statism," which would perhaps make the relationship between this stance and the properties of the bureaucratic nation-state more apparent but would exclude other lawmaking entities.

6. It is for this reason that I have argued (Herzfeld 2018) that good anthropology is a realist discipline but not an objectivist one—a crucial distinction that is often ignored or misunderstood.

7. For a more complete description, see Herzfeld (2009: 234–44).

8. This event occurred in 1974, when Greeks were still deeply worried about whether the military regime would return to power and were watching neighboring Turkey's military adventurism with alarm; in that context, a term that specifically mean "non-Greek" in the ancient cultures of which modern Greece ideologically claimed to be the unsullied continuation carried potentially offensive implications in Greek that the equivalent English word lacks.

9. *Monti Moments: Men's Memories in the Heart of Rome*, filmed and produced by Michael Herzfeld (Berkeley Media LLC, 2007).

10. Of course, we do not actually know for certain what others think (Needham 1972; Robbins and Rumsey 2008). But the performance of any disclaimer is predicated on the assumption that insiders will at least know that the speaker does not wish to be taken literally. Genuinely modest performers are likely to be suspected of hypocrisy, a suspicion that too ardent a denial will only tighten around them.

11. In a forthcoming, extended treatment of the forms and consequences of traditionalism (Herzfeld 2021), I explore these implications in ethnographic and comparative contexts. In the local dialect, the statement was a pun, as the same word (*nomous*) was used for both "laws" and "shoulders."

12. For more details on these cases, see Herzfeld (1991: 147–52).

13. For a fuller account of this connivance, see Herzfeld (2009: 172–76).

14. This sad story is told in more detail in Herzfeld (2021); see also, on the earlier phases, Herzfeld (2016b).

REFERENCES

Austin, J.L. *How To Do Things With Words*. 2nd edition, edited by J.O. Urmson and Marina Sbisà. Cambridge, MA: Harvard University Press, [1962] 1975.

Austin, J.L. "A Plea for Excuses." In *Philosophy and Linguistics*, edited by Colin Lyas, 79–101. London: Macmillan, [1956–57] 1971.

Bailey, F.G. *Humbuggery and Manipulation: The Art of Leadership*. Ithaca: Cornell University Press, 1988.

Bauman, Richard. *Verbal Art as Performance*. Rowley, MA: Newbury House, 1977.

Boissevain, Jeremy. *Hal-Farrug: A Village in Malta*. New York: Holt, Rinehart and Winston, 1969.

Cabot, Heath. "Contagious" Solidarity: Reconfiguring Care and Citizenship in Greece's Social Clinics." *Social Anthropology* 24 (2016): 152–166.

Crick, Malcolm. *Explorations in Language and Meaning: Towards a Semantic Anthropology*. New York: John Wiley/Halsted, 1976.

de Certeau, Michel. *The Practice of Everyday Life*. Berkeley: University of California Press, 1984.

De Genova, Nicholas, ed. *The Borders of "Europe": Autonomy of Migration, Tactics of Bordering*. Durham, NC: Duke University Press, 2017.

Dematteo, Lynda. *L'idiotie en politique. Subversion et néo-populisme en Italie*. Paris: Fondation Maison des Sciences de l'Homme, 2007.

Di Bella, Maria Pia. *Dire ou taire en Sicile*. Paris: Éditions du Félin, 2008.

Elyachar, Julia. "Phatic Labor, Infrastructure, and the Question of Empowerment in Cairo." *American Ethnologist* 37, no. 3 (2010): 452–464.

Friedman, Joshua B. "Serious Jews: Cultural Intimacy and the Politics of Yiddish." *Cultural Dynamics* 32, no. 3 (2020): 151–169.

Glaeser, Andreas. "Monolithic Intentionality, Belonging, and the Production of State Paranoia: A View through Stasi onto the Late GDR." In *Off Stage/On Display: Intimacy and Ethnography in the Age of Public Culture*, edited by Andrew Shryock, 244–276. Stanford: Stanford University Press, 2004.

Handler, Richard. "Authenticity." *Anthropology Today* 2, no. 1 (1986): 2–4.

Herzfeld, Michael. *Subversive Archaism: Troubling Traditionalists and the Politics of National Heritage*. Durham, NC: Duke University Press, 2021.

Herzfeld, Michael. "Anthropological Realism in a Scientistic Age." *Anthropological Theory* 118, no. 1 (2018): 129–150.

Herzfeld, Michael. *Cultural Intimacy: Social Poetics and the Real Life of States, Societies, and Institutions*. 3rd edition. New York: Routledge, 2016a.

Herzfeld, Michael. *Siege of the Spirits: Community and Polity in Bangkok*. Chicago: University of Chicago Press, 2016b.

Herzfeld, Michael. *Evicted from Eternity: The Restructuring of Modern Rome*. Chicago: University of Chicago Press, 2009.

Herzfeld, Michael. *Intimité culturelle: Poétique de l'État nation*. Translation of Herzfeld 2005 by Anne-Hélène Kerbiriou. Québéc: Presses Universitaires de l'Université Laval, 2007.

Herzfeld, Michael. *Cultural Intimacy: Social Poetics in the Nation-State*. New York: Routledge, 2005.

Herzfeld, Michael. *The Body Impolitic: Artisans and Artifice in the Global Hierarchy of Value*. Chicago: University of Chicago Press, 2004.

Herzfeld, Michael. "The Absent Presence: Discourses of Crypto-Colonialism." *South Atlantic Quarterly* 101, no. 4 (2002): 899–926.

Herzfeld, Michael. *The Social Production of Indifference: Exploring the Symbolic Roots of Western Bureaucracy*. Oxford: Berg (paperback, University of Chicago Press, 1993), 1992.

Herzfeld, Michael. *A Place in History: Social and Monumental Time in a Cretan Town*. Princeton: Princeton University Press, 1991.

Herzfeld, Michael. "Semantic Slippage and Moral Fall: The Rhetoric of Chastity in Rural Greece." *Journal of Modern Greek Studies* 1, no. 1 (1983): 161–172.

Huchzermayer, Marie, and Aly Karam, eds. *Informal Settlements: A Perpetual Challenge?* Cape Town: University of Cape Town Press, 2006.

Karstedt, Susanne, and Stephen Farrall. 2006. "The Moral Economy of Everyday Crime: Markets, Consumers and Citizens." *British Journal of Criminology* 46, no. 6 (2006): 1011–1036.

Lillo, Antonio. "Etymological Myths and Compound Etymologies in Rhyming Slang." *English Studies* 99, no 6 (2018): 688–703.
Malaby, Thomas. *Gambling Life: Dealing in Contingency in a Greek City*. Urbana: University of Illinois Press, 2003.
Malinowski, Bronislaw. "The Problem of Meaning in Primitive Languages." In *The Meaning of Meaning*, edited by C.K. Ogden and I.A. Richards, 296–336. London: Kegan Paul, Supplement I, [1923] 1936.
McCargo, Duncan. *Fighting for Virtue: Justice and Politics in Thailand*. Ithaca: Cornell University Press, 2019.
Milgram, B. Lynne. "Gift-Commodity Entanglements: Repositioning (In)formality in a Transnational Philippine Market Trade." *Anthropologica* 61 (2019): 51–63.
Molé, Noelle J. "Precarious Subjects: Anticipating Neoliberalism in Northern Italy's Workplace." *American Anthropologist* 112, no. 1 (2010): 38–53.
Morris, Rosalind. "Intimacy and Corruption in Thailand's Age of Transparency." In *Off Stage/On Display: Intimacy and Ethnography in the Age of Public Culture*, edited by Andrew Shryock, 225–243. Stanford: Stanford University Press, 2004.
Muehlebach, Andrea. *The Moral Neoliberal: Welfare and Citizenship in Italy*. Chicago: Chicago University Press, 2012.
Needham, Rodney. *Belief, Language, and Experience*. Chicago: University of Chicago Press, 1972.
Osburg, John. "Making Business Personal: Corruption, Anti-corruption, and Elite Networks in Post-Mao China." *Current Anthropology* 59, Supplement 18 (2018): S149–S159.
Osburg, John. "Morality and Cynicism in a 'Grey' World." In *Irony, Cynicism, and the Chinese State*, edited by Hans Steinmüller and Susanne Brandtstädter, 47–62. Abingdon: Routledge, 2016.
Paine, Robert. "High-Wire Culture: Comparing Two Agonistic Systems of Self-Esteem." *Man* (n.s.) 24, no. 4 (1989): 328–39.
Rabinow, Paul. *French Modern: Norms and Forms of the Social Environment*. Cambridge, MA: MIT Press, 1989.
Rakopoulos, Theodoros. "The Crisis Seen from Below, Within and Against: From Solidarity Economy to Food Distribution Cooperatives in Greece." *Dialectical Anthropology* 38, no 2 (2014): 189–207.
Ricci, Antonello. "Gli occhi, le luci, le immagini: le madonnelle. Spazio del sacro e pratiche devozionali delle edicole religiose." In *La sacra Città: Itinerari antropologico-religiosi nella Roma di fine Millennio*, edited by Luigi Lombardi Satriani, 33–73. Rome: Meltemi, 1999.
Robbins, Joel, and Alan Rumsey. "Introduction: Cultural and Linguistic Anthropology and the Opacity of Other Minds." *Anthropological Quarterly* 81, no. 2 (2008): 407–420.
Scaraffia, Lucetta. "Immagini sacre e città." In *Edicole sacre romane: un segno romano da recuperare*, edited by Luisa Cardilli, 19–24. Rome: Fratelli Palombi, 1990.
Scott, James C. *Seeing Like a State: How Certain Schemes to Improve the Human Condition Have Failed*. New Haven: Yale University Press, 1998.

Shore, Cris. *Building Europe: The Cultural Politics of European Integration.* London: Routledge, 2000.
Smart, Alan, and Josephine Smart. "Formalism as Confinement in Colonial Hong Kong." *International Sociology* 32, no. 4 (2017): 437–453.
Smart, Alan, and Filippo Zerilli. "Extralegality." In *Companion to Urban Anthropology*, edited by Donald M. Nonini, 222–238. Chichester: Wiley Blackwell, 2014.
Sopranzetti, Claudio. *Owners of the Map: Motorcycle Taxi Drivers, Mobility, and Politics in Bangkok.* Berkeley: University of California Press, 2017.
Spivak, Gayatri. 1989. "In a Word. Interview with Ellen Rooney." *Differences* 1, no. 2 (1989): 124–156.
Steinmüller, Hans. *Communities of Complicity: Everyday Ethics in Rural China.* Oxford: Berghahn, 2013.
Stewart, Charles. "Hegemony or Rationality? The Position of the Supernatural in Modern Greece." *Journal of Modern Greek Studies* 7, no. 1 (1989): 77–104.
Stolcke, Verena. 1995. "Talking Culture: New Boundaries, New Rhetorics of Exclusion in Europe." *Current Anthropology* 36, no. 1 (1995): 1–24.
Wimmer, Andreas, and Nina Glick Schiller. 2002. "Methodological Nationalism and Beyond: Nation-State Building, Migration and the Social Sciences." *Global Networks* 2, no. 4 (2002): 301–134.
Wu, Jinting. *Fabricating an Educational Miracle: Compulsory Schooling Meets Ethnic Rural Development in Southwest China.* Albany: State University of New York Press, 2016.

Chapter 3

On Doing Fieldwork, Outspokenly

Ethics, Money, and Antiquities Illegal Trade

Cristiana Panella

My concern in this chapter is to bring a wider perspective to ethics matters by considering money encounters with local actors in my fieldwork experience and, then, describe the balance of silence/speech that characterizes the market of objects and of words following a perspective of exchange relationships.[1] Specifically, I will utilize a approach to exchange dynamics by questioning the function of money in relation to the trust between researchers and informants. Marcel Mauss opened the way for crucial reflection not only on the function of objects in social organization and the production of difference but also on the role of the symbolic and imaginary in the production of value. Two aspects of Mauss's theory of the gift are pertinent to my conceptual approach: the role of object/information within the social organization of exchange between the actors at stake, and the ethical implications of exchange in the moral economy of heterogeneous value systems. From a Maussian perspective these dynamics imply the equivalence between art objects and persons as social agents through heterogeneous spheres of ethical frames. In this way the principle of exchange imbues the dynamics of object/information reception to the extent that the objects and information correspond to gradients of ethical and market values, or in other words, to *transactional agents*. As argued by James Leach (Leach 2010), a Tardean emphasis on microinteractions allows us to consider the research situation is itself such an encounter among a chain of interactions where ethics and values are co-constitutive features.[2]

INCONVENIENT TOPICS: THE SOCIAL LIFE OF PLUNDERED THINGS

Over the last 20 years, social scientists have approached informal and illegal contexts focusing on interfaces between shadow and official networks as well as on the role of the State in managing frontiers of legality (Bayart, Ellis, and Hibou 1997; Heyman 1999; Comaroff and Comaroff 2006). A second set of studies has oriented on the role of informal and liminal actors as vectors of squeezing in citizenship claims and economic resistance to the State (MacGaffey and Baguenzissa 2000; van Schendel and Abraham 2005; Mathews, Lins Ribeiro and Alba Vega 2012; Smart and Zerilli 2014; Panella and Thomas 2015; Pardo 2017). A third set, mainly developed in the wake of the international debate on cultural heritage, has concerned studies in "art crime" (Meyer 1973; Conklin 1994; Palmer 1998). Under the behalf of UNESCO's international organizations for safeguarding of cultural property, as ICOM, ICCROM, and ICOMOS,[3] scholars concentrated on top-bottom approach based on an object-oriented vision of cultural heritage: preservation, collection, display, restitution (Merryman 1994; Leyten 1995; Brodie and Renfrew 2005; Hoffmann 2006; Charney 2009). In this frame, the fight against clandestine trade in antiquities represented a worldwide spearhead of a deontological discourse on cultural heritage opposed to the *nasty* transactions underlying the illegal art market.[4]

Unquestionably, archaeologists have constituted the main flywheel of the "looting question" (Herscher 1983; Tubb 1995; Brodie, Doole and Watson 2000), particularly with regard to Mali (Togola and Raimbault 1989; Dembélé and van der Waals 1991; Schmidt and McIntosh 1996; Bedaux and Rowlands 2001). In the last years, this trend was strongly reinforced by lawyers and criminologists (Mackenzie 2005, 2019; Tijhuis 2006; Manacorda and Chappell 2011; Ulph and Smith 2012).[5] Similarly, an institutional approach to "the phenomenon of plunder" started to be put into discussion through a growing analysis from the ground (Staley 1993; Matsuda 1998, 2005; Paredes Maury 1999; Panella 2002; Hollowell 2006) that contributed to fill the gap between the material-oriented vision of classical archaeology and a more sensitive approach to the social contexts of "looting." (Vitelli 1996; Scarre and Scarre 2006; Field, Gnecco and Watkins 2017).

In spite of a growing interest in the illegal contexts of the clandestine practices of the African art market, this still represents an uncomfortable domain of inquiry for art history, museum studies, and social anthropology. The strong link between stylistic studies and market overvaluation in the making of African art (Errington 1998) implied stylistic fixity and "authenticity" as an integral part of market value. The social life of African objects, already displayed in the swing of international exhibitions during the 1930s (Corbey 2000; de l'Estoile 2007), had, thus, been obscured by the art market itself to the advantage of an aesthetic formal identity based on fixity and authenticity (Arnoldi, Geary and Hardin 1996). Such a silent choice implied a direct proportional relationship between opacity of outflow practices and museums' deontology (Panella 2015). Art historians and anthropologists have mainly been oriented toward the dynamics of cultural brokerage in tourist art (Graburn 1976; Jules-Rosette 1984; Kasfir and Förster 2013), and in contemporary African art (Enwezor and Okeke-Agulu 2009; Fillitz 2018) by minimizing clandestine/illegal practices imbricated into the trade (Steiner 1994; Stoller 2003). By contrast, several large public-oriented publications present a well-crafted and glimmering storytelling on looting (Atwood 2004; Watson and Todeschini 2007).

DOING FIELDWORK IN AFRICAN ANTIQUITIES TRADE: SOME METHODOLOGICAL CONCERNS

On January 15, 1996, I began my fieldwork in Bamako.[6] During my research, I introduced myself as a student and not as a researcher. The role of student had a tacit mechanism of sponsorship/learning that allowed me to enter the world of *antiquaires* without raising too much mistrust. From these first interviews, I had almost daily meetings with a group of five dealers who knew each other well, but I visited them individually.[7]

> On an iron trunk lay a pile of Sotheby's sales catalogs. Some had the pages corners folded, where there were pictures of objects of the same typology as those offered in the store. Above, bronze miniature keyring statuettes scattered like bowling pins, Dogon oil lamps, and a Touareg box in red leather. In one corner, two young apprentices, perched on a stool, were dusting two Dan masks. A huge Maninka door was leaning against a wall, carved in wood: granaries, lizards, and asterisks floated like snowflakes. I followed my host inside, into the living room, and sat down in the chair he had indicated to me with a wave of his hand. A girl came in with a decanter of ginger juice; she put it on the table, and she slipped behind the door without a sound. Shortly after, two girls came forward with two salad bowls covered with a dish on which was placed a small enamel pan. The first bowl contained rice in sauce; the second, a millet porridge enriched with curdled milk.
>
> "You know . . ." he said as he stirred the rice with a carved silver ladle, "this work you do, there . . . we are art dealers, we're one family, Africa to Asia, via Japan and the United States . . . go, take a handful of rice, but watch yourself,

it burns . . . the traffic of art objects . . . this fanfare of cultural heritage, it is a sub-question . . . the more you cry, the more you can act silently, you know what I mean? . . . Come, I'll show you something."

It was a carved wooden bust of a young girl. The nose was long and prominent, the eyes large and slanted, the head covered with a braided headdress to the nape of the neck and pendant earrings. "I have not figured out where it came from, it's amazing, is it not? But she's so beautiful that it doesn't matter."

(Field notes, Bamako, January 1996)

AN ELASTIC TEXTURE: THE NETWORK BY RELATIONAL CLUSTERS

As well as other contexts considered informal (Peraldi 2001), illegal, or criminal (Eilstrup-Sangiovanni and Jones 2008), the antiquities supply chain is organized in groups that are, in turn, constituted by links governed by fixed or variable hierarchies (Panella 2010; Campbell 2013) similar to drug social organization.[8] One of the major issues in the hierarchical relationships governing illegal networks is the management of information. Contrary to the cross-sectional information that links the relational networks of the "economy of the bazaar" (Geertz 1978; Trager 1981), the art market is ruled by a range of actors in power (*chefs d'équipe*, local intermediaries, dealers) who hold the monopoly of information through the compartmentalization of links in the market chain. Thus, like a set of Russian dolls, the links of the chain are interdependent but not intercommunicating, so that each link in the chain receives from the dominant players only the information that is essential to the completion of specific tasks. The fragmentation of the overall vision of the chain, through the compartmentalization of its links, ensures that the dominant actors maintain status quo power, governed by the internalization of hierarchies and the economic dependence of rural suppliers. Because of the hierarchical organization of the links, the structural short circuit of the ganglia that ensure the isolation of the actors of the sector is thus opposed to the "structural holes" as theorized by Ronald Burt, which he defines as spaces separated between equivalent contacts within the relational network (Burt 1992). For example, the relationships of trust and kinship in the business community of Senegalese large diamond families (Bredeloup 2007) can be considered exchanges between equivalent actors. On the other hand, if we take the case of the farmer-diggers of the Southern regions of Mali, they are structurally isolated in a relationship of trust because of their exclusion from urban and international flow patterns and their reliance on rural middlemen and urban merchants. Thus, a *chef d'équipe* from the Baniko region described the closed circuit of supply:

> Komakodo was unavoidable because we are from the same background, it is difficult to offer the goods to someone else. The problem in Bamako is that if you do not agree with the first buyer, all the others will offer you even less. When Komakodo sets his price and you refuse, you will not be able to sell the piece elsewhere. (Panella 2010: 234, trans. from French by the author)

The relational meshwork of the network flows of works of art implies relationships of trust and reciprocity under influence, as well as clientelist logics (Medard 1992; Gregoire and Labazée 1993; Warms 1994) governed by dual reports of the redistribution of benefits and penalties. The mesh of the network can, thus, present an intermittent density, following the opportunities and the evolution of the contacts and articulating itself by relational clusters rather than by groups. Thus, starting from a core matrix, welded by *strong ties*, such as kinship ties, these actors develop opportunistic contacts based on *weak ties*, that is to say contingent and time bound, functioning in maintaining and consolidating the dense network in an arrangement that is neither constant nor homogeneous.[9] This structure is also characteristic of other actors involved in rapid consumption dynamics without accumulation (hot money), such as hunters of shrimp (Godefroit 2001), gold (Grätz 2004), diamonds (Boeck 2001), or sapphires (Walsh 2003).

POWER: PERFORMANCE AND SILENCE

The management of interviews is a sensitive element of the investigation in an illegal and informal context. The performance of the interview is, in fact, closely related to the status of speech.[10] In rural Bamana and Maninka, this emanates from the hierarchical relations that govern society. Speaking is only formally requested at official meetings or celebrations, where interlineage or intergenerational power struggles emerge through dual confrontation (Cisse 1973). The word has a power of action and performance and can be translated into heavy mockery but also punishment, curse, or even death (Dieterlen 1981; Kedzierska-Manzon 2008).

Among the Mossi and the Dogon of Yatenga and Séno, in Burkina Faso and Mali, language and power are closely linked. In the Dogon and Moore languages, speech is the materialization of a prohibition and thus becomes an "instance of secrecy" as well as a stigma (Martinelli 1998). It is in this sense that one can speak of efficiency of speech. Complementary to speech, silence is the materialization of secrecy (Cissé 1973; Camara 1992; Diawara 2003). William Beeman has analyzed the role of silence in music through the concept of figure-ground, hollow/full optical effect. This derives from the scansion of the same motif, reiterating the application of the binomial silence/non-silence to other oppositional contexts, such as ritual/non-ritual, supposedly to draw, by their contrast, the underlying power stakes that underlie social confrontation (Beeman 2006). Similarly, as a conventional tool of action for a society (Gable 1997; Zerubavel 2006), silence is a revealing phoneme of contrasting elements intertwined in social confrontation (Achino-Loeb 2006) such as the avoidance of respect, the ostentatious authority marks of seniors and the strategies of resistance of the cadets in power. The weight of the *given word* is even more important, if we consider that in our field sites there is little or no possible recourse to statistics, and this is because of the extreme mobility of the networks, their opacity, and a structural interface between official, informal, and illegal domains (Ellis and MacGaffey 1997).

Similarly, the collection of interviews considered to be exhaustive is rare. In the clusters of the underground network, the increase in the number of informants does not necessarily lead to a more precise frame of the network, given the limited number of actors who have the monopoly of the sector as a whole. In many cases, for security or circumstance reasons, my meetings with some informants were limited to one time and a few hours of interviews. This short period makes it possible to check certain crucial points in the chain, such as the number of intermediaries and their respective tasks, the change in prices during the flow stages, the final destination of the goods. In other words, the ganglion structure of clandestine networks is mirrored in a survey method which accords itself to a fragmented and intermittent temporality reproducing, finally, a one-shot approach (Peraldi 2001), which is the basis of weak network contacts. Temporalities of the field research on looting seem to be almost systematized with regard to Robert Aunger's fieldwork methodology as he recommends repeated interviews with the same informant and a comparative perspective in order to esteem the degree of reliability of information (Aunger 2004).

IN MONEY, WE TRUST: ETHICS OF COMPROMISE

The "qualitative turn" that has characterized fieldwork theorization since the turn of the 1980s (Crapanzano 1980; Clifford and Marcus 1986; Battaglia 1999; Rabinow and Marcus 2008) has given prominence to the emotional and bodily dimensions of the researcher. Moreover, theoretical issues of "scapes" (Appadurai 1996) have been developed for the first time on contemporary shifting contexts and new orientations of anthropological theory. In particular, reflexive works registered the researcher's precariousness in relation to slippery and contradictory landscapes, such as civil wars and political control (Green 1999), which questioned the balance of power between researchers and local actors (De Soto and Dudwick 2000; Sriram, King, Mertus, Martin-Ortega and Herman 2009).

Specifically, in the current rethinking fieldwork these realities constrain anthropologists from examining ethics of collecting knowledge (observation and participation to clandestine transactions, accusations of spying, emotions), consequences of trust relationships, reciprocity, interpretations of suffering (Bouillon, Fresia and Tallio 2005), management of danger and fear (Lee 1993; Nordstrom and Robben 1996; Kovats-Bernat 2002). Sociological research on addiction and deviance provided consistent literature on ethical limits of shifting fieldwork, putting into discussion, for instance, the principle of informed consent in dangerous settings (Ferrel and Hamm 1998; Calvey 2008).

Nevertheless, the overused production on methodology in qualitative research and ethics (Punch 1986; Meskell and Pels 2005; van den Hoonard and van den Hoonard 2013) seems to lack analysis of the uncomfortable backstage steps tailoring the field patchwork of illegal trade as modalities of the approach to informants are usually not explained. Works on looting and on "art crime" are at the forefront in this trend. Academic writing on illegal art trade is problematically devoid of in-depth information on the social organization of the first links of the trade chain. Consequently, the same old data have been discussed for decades via conferences, workshops, magazines, and academic publications leading to a global pedigreezation of the public discourse on looting (Panella 2012), also due to the appeal of studying a sexy topic without risk.

One of the most striking gaps in methodological concerns in the fieldwork of illegality is the nature of transactions between researcher and informants. The information market has never been, to my knowledge, a specific object of in-depth analysis. In *Money: Ethnographic Encounters*, Stefan Senders and Allison Truitt present a range of case-studies where money represents a huge epistemological challenge (Senders and Truitt 2007). In particular, they state that money put into question the patient construction of empathy driven by the researcher toward local actors as well as, the status of the researcher on the field, by considering that money pollutes "the domain of pure humanity" (ibid. 6) which is supposed to underlie intimacy relations. Nevertheless, in spite of the several concerns raised by the authors of the chapters with regard to ethics and identity (for instance, the economic cleavage between local actors and the automatic overlapping between the researcher and her/his status as White-and-Wealthy source of cash), the ethnographical portraits presented in the volume seem to be not concerned by a concrete and direct relationship between money and information nor on the riskiness of the economic value of information, which constituted an inescapable element of conditionality of my PhD fieldwork research (Panella 2002: 60–70).

The question arises, then, to what extent is possible to undertake fieldwork in clandestine/illegal trade networks and to get firsthand information for free. At which extent researchers avoid mentioning money exchanges as a crucial part of the fieldwork.[11]

The market role of trust in informal networking has been registered in anthropological analysis (Grätz 2004). When, however, market ethics concern the exchange between researcher and local actors, one is stuck to a glass ceiling. Most of academic works on illegality relate ethical issues to the consequences of publication over local informants. Beyond the questioning of the unequal relationship of the field (discrepancy between the economic status of the researcher and his informants, economic profitability of the data), the payment of the information is usually mentioned in relation to the remuneration for services rendered (research assistants, translators, guides, informants for one-off information). The American Anthropological Association as well speaks about informants' pay: "The AAA has never specifically provided guidelines on the level of remuneration (beyond informants fees) that is appropriate through time to study populations, and how that remuneration should be linked to the overall earnings to a researcher as a result of his/her focus on a particular population."[12] Regarding remuneration (wages for labor, remunerations for interviews or demonstrations), the version of the AAA Code of ethics approved in November 2012 refers to International Labor Office.[13] Stanford University suggests that young linguistics researchers follow local cultural norms in order to evaluate the appropriateness of cash payments.[14] The anthropologist H. Russell Bernard, for his part, considers that information should be paid whenever it appears appropriate because of the added value that information would gain once it has been channeled into Western networks of knowledge (Bernard 1994).

Integrating speech as a commercial object and especially presenting this logic as an integral part of the anthropological inquiry process is problematic. Certainly, the growing normalization of public sphere, along with cultural heritage institutions[15] and academic dynamics of valuation (Lamont 2012), discourages research topics that underlie an osmotic interdependence between researchers and illegal domains. Nevertheless, I would tend to explain the refusal to consider money as a crucial conjuncture of the field also by the fact that this is not envisaged in direct association with the emotional sphere of the exchange. In other words, money encounters are not considered ethically sustainable.

The reflective literature has offered many readings of emotions in the field (Kleinman and Kopp 2009) including sexuality management (Golde 1986) to issues of harassment and rape (Moreno 1995; Kloß 2017). Because of the psychic trauma to which the researcher is confronted, the weight of the constraints of the field, which would limit its power of action and ultimately weaken not only the control of his choices but also the very perception of it/itself (Pollard 2009), the emotional dimension of the field search is a "clean" sphere, is not supposed to be able to be judged according to the same regime of values that underlie the pecuniary exchange (Casagrande 1960; Samarin 1967).

Samarin (1967) and Crapanzano note that paying informants represents a sort of identity marker: ("they had a job") as well as an understanding of the researcher's wishes (Crapanzano 1985: 146). The admission of a commercial trust would call into question, however, the ability of the researcher to forge privileged relations with his informants as well as the assertiveness of the anthropological text. Declaring having paid for information beyond the psychological threshold of retribution or *prix de cola* (which means to leave "a little something" as a thank you). appears to be a capitulation to the difficulty of conducting an independent field search. In other words, the objectifying force of money would imply that any other argumentation justifies the exchange's affective and intellectual engagement in terms of the exchange would simply have no meaning in relation to the interests of the actors in place.

MONEY: AN OVERALL RATIO OF EXCHANGE?

In Malian antiquities market relationships, where the principle of exclusivity and secrecy govern both social relations and the sale of objects, transactions are based on dyadic relationships of trust. Trust would be particularly relevant in a context of ignorance or uncertainty regarding actions unknown to the agent (Gambetta 1988) while unknown would thus produce a situation of certainty at the moment when one would try to control it and this floating would allow the development of confidence (Möllering 2001).

In the case of the fragmented context of the antiquities trade, two factors stand out: the researcher's dependence on the trajectories traced by his local referents and the volatile nature of the *given word*. It is the informant who weaves, filters, and selects the contacts according to a selection to which the researcher, especially at the beginning of the research, must often bend. The researcher's margins of autonomy and movement are thus restricted because of the ignorance of the network and the exclusivity principle that governs transactions with its informants. This premise is essential to understand the evolution of power relations on the ground.

An anthropological approach to money relations, thus, implies the passage from a conception of the payment of informants as retribution for services rendered to an ethical ratio of the trading nature of the exchange. In this case, the researcher/informant reports would imply the confrontation between heterogeneous spheres of value that would determine market parameters without, however, constituting in themselves economic referents.

The relational power of money has been analyzed on several occasions (Parry and Bloch 1989; Simmel 1990; Graeber 2001; Guyer 2004; Maurer 2006; Gudeman 2009; Hart 2010). Money is persuasive in that it involves a structural interdependence between abstraction and personal representations, objectification and subjectivity. Thus, it determines the ethics of exchange from a preexisting moral order that would ensure the sustainability of individual competition in the short term (Maurer 2006) while constituting a discrete relationship of trust. The monetary element in the field is not, therefore, a reward or a counter-gift but, rather, it takes place in an immanent logic of engagement where money is the precondition for building trust between peers. It is in this logic that the relationship of trust and the establishment of the rules of collaboration are credible only in the mutual understanding and acceptance of the economic nature of the relationship. In the case of my fieldwork, I have entered a highly monetarized exchange register, not only because of the commercial nature of the transactions, but, also, the auction conducted by a myriad of satellite domains such as journalism (weekly newspapers and fashion, design, magazines), value chain networks (art dealers, brokers, collectors), and even tourism (travel agencies, local guides, hotel staff).

Of course, not all market players are asking for money. In the case of my field experience, the core group that has sponsored me since the early stages of my research has never asked me for money, at least openly. I have rarely asked direct questions. The continuous comings and goings of shuttles, intermediaries, and art traders in these merchants' homes enabled me to follow useful conversations as well as to understand, through gestures and repeated words, the hierarchical roles of the network. Nevertheless, buying from time to time "ordinary" items (contemporary production) was considered a reasonable compromise. A fair distance was needed between the appreciation of the objects, to which the merchants have an emotional attachment, and my choice not to buy terracotta, and this in an environment where the border between participant observation and active participation is unclear. I will come back to this aspect to show the implications of my approach.

How Much? Objects, Words, and the Market Value of Invisibility

The dyadic structure of trust that governs the commercial transaction of objects is reproduced in the arena of the purchase and sale of information from the same auction process for the sale of decontextualized objects. Within certain limits, pricing is a conversion of interest between demand and supply. Especially the commodity is rare (presented or perceived as such), especially its purchase value increases. Goods have a traceability established within official parameters (production costs, wholesale prices, distribution monopolies, contraction of markets).

In the case of contraband goods, clandestine transactions follow the wake of official slots, which provide a reference ceiling for price fluctuations and govern the word economy in parallel networks. The case of the flow of gasoline is an example (Guyer 2004; Titeca 2006). On the other hand, in the case of completely illegal flows, pricing is more nuanced. In the case of drugs, local dealers estimate the oscillations of the purchase-sale prices according to the standards of confidence of the clandestine market. The price depends on the risk factors and the number of passages in the chain (number of local dealers, distance from the place of order, payment deadlines). Another variant is the place of sale. Patricia Adler notes, for example, that in the 1980s marijuana was higher in the southern parts of Mexico than in the north; it would have been the same inside the United States (Adler 1985). This element is obviously not specific to drug networks but characterizes the relationship between supply and purchasing power governing the flow of goods.

In the antiquities market, there are some differences. First, the place of sale is not an essential variant. The same object with pedigree sold in the United States, Europe, or Japan will likely vary within a similar price range, due to a greater homogeneity of purchasing power compared to drugs. On the other hand, a difference will occur from one circle to the other of the flow channel. The selling price of a local intermediary to an urban antiquities dealer can be X times lower than the price offered by the same dealer to a European or North American buyer. Similarly, the sales price between European and North American merchants will be X times higher than the selling price proposed in the local sectors. Moreover, the ascendency of the archaism infused by archaeological objects reinforces the sensible experience of the object rather than its use value. While in the drug market trust is the quality of the powder, in the case of archaeological objects the expectations that determine the relationship of trust are indebted, beyond sensory factors (texture, patina, color, shape), an aesthetic and moral landscape indebted to the system of representations of the object. Malian farmers-diggers, for example, consider money as the materialization of the physical and psychological effort engaged in prospecting and excavation. The search for objects in the bush by the farmer-diggers could be considered as a symbolic manifestation of physical work, first of all agricultural work, which considers physical suffering and risk as essential values of peasant ethics in Francophone West Africa (Lemaire 2009).[16]

The unseizability of the value of information plays a fundamental role in choosing, as the AAA Code of Ethics suggests, "who it is appropriate to remunerate." How should this choice be made? On what basis should actors engaged in illegal activities be paid? The dimensions of presence and absence, speech and silence, and visibility and invisibility are crucial not only in relation to the flow of objects but also to the practices, aesthetic, and commercial creation of these.[17] Finally, it is the flips of the same coin that shape each other. Like powerholders, such as blacksmiths (McNaughton 1993; Brett-Smith 1994), the invisible thing exerts an influence by being inaccessible. Its value is therefore amplified by desire in absence. Following this logic, because of the dyadic structure of trusted trading relationships in a sales transaction, the same object seen by two potential buyers undergoes the same devaluation process as a newly purchased car that is resold the next day, due to the loss of the aura of uniqueness of the work of art. This is because each disclosed object represents, in itself, the *ex-machina* materialization of an expected event at the end of the initiatory journey represented by the transaction. In other words, in the name of the pact of exclusivity between the merchant and the buyer, one stages the discovery of the "unique" piece whose epiphany is supposed to occur only once and for one only spectator.

In the case of information, the opacity of flow networks (the social and spatial organization of supply, quantitative and typological statistical data, hierarchies) and the invisibility of the ultimate referents of the social control of the merchant chain structure the confrontation between researcher and local referents (art dealers, shuttles, middlemen, diggers, fakers) constitutes a register influenced not only by the hidden nature of the object of exchange but also, like commercial transactions, by the absence of common value-of-use parameters. The non-visibility of the information object (links in the chain, goods, etc.), thus, enables the knowledge holders to create, apart from any shared reference parameters, value assignment relays through the fragmentation of information. The element common to the two objects of research, ancient objects and information, is thus a refracted dimension of time that, finally, erases the contemporaneity between acts of production and product. A typical exchange would be, "I understand you're going to last ten days here. After, you'll come back . . . Well, make your price pure all . . . I mean, if you come back in a month, I'll be there; if you come back next year, I'll be there too, all the time! Make your money for the time you need, did you understand?" (Panella 2002: 65, translation from French by the author).

Mastery of temporalities is an essential element of the commodity production of the object/information. Like transactions for the sale of objects, this occurs in a dyadic logic of exclusivity able to weave a relationship of dependency through the dilution of the waiting time of the researcher while reiterating a declaration of availability in the purpose of securing future financial contributions. These mechanisms of the construction of dependence, which are, moreover, specific to other market contexts, such as the used car market (Beauving 2013), reveal the link between desire and invisibility. Thus, just as for objects, the price of information is modeled through fuzzy and constraining poles of value at a time, because of the physical absence of the object of the information. The content of desire becomes itself an object. The economic value of the latter does not coincide with its value in general but stems from a sum of values. That is to say, flows of interaction between gain and sacrifice, engines of desire. This value occurs within a mutual exchange (Simmel 1990).

These voids that punctuate the production of information are similar to the *et cetera* that constitute the process of construction of trust described by Niklas Luhmann (1973). It always underlies a representation of complexity that is not represented in detail where the factual experience is linked to other unrealized possibilities. These perceptions give sense to the object (work of art or daily life things) and constitute its meanings (Kemp 1998). In the case of interviews, the *et cetera* correspond to the unspoken and the forgotten of the discourse. According to Andras Zempléni, the management of the secret "to let escape, to pierce, to filter, to flee . . ." is part of a process of regulation of the tension and, hence, preservation of the latter. The relationship between the holder of the secret and the recipient is not limited to the choice between silence and utterance.

> I call *secrètement* [. . .] all the more or less involuntary or organized processes by which the holders or the depositories A and B exhibit fragments of the secret [. . .] in front of its addressees (C and D) without revealing it. (Zempléni 1996: 24; trans. by author)

Compared to ancient objects, this shift, exploited both by the art market and by museums, leads to the archaization of the past following the hiatus between functional and commercial life of the object. In the case of information, this gap occurs between the acts of the production of the flow of objects and the communication of these same acts that constitute the social life of the *objets trouvés*. In both cases, it is a process of objectification aimed at the creation of a market value, and this is because of the presumed intrinsic value of the object/information.

In the absence of reference parameters, the investigation of the disposal of works of art is also detached from the investigation of corruption. It is characterized by a structural interface between official parameters and unofficial short-circuiting (Amselle 1992; Blundo and Olivier de Sardan 2006; Médard 2006; Reeves 2013) where the remuneration, rather related to the toll, aims at the access to administrative services (authorizations research, operating permit, transit authorization, buffers, paper control). On the other hand, in the case of information related to value chain networks, the term toll would be inappropriate since the invisibility of a legal boundary to be crossed leads to a confrontation between researcher and local actors without shared standards of departure.

Money and Danger

Although the terrain of the antiquities trade is not renewable to a real "ethnography of violence" (Nordstrom and Robben 1996; Ghassem-Fachandi 2009), it is potentially violent, suddenly violent, or likely to become violent, according to the changes of the hierarchical equilibrium within the network, the misunderstanding of situations of danger, or the materialization of the danger after the publication of the data.[18] The lack of self-representation of local actors as a social category and, consequently, the usefulness of the researcher as spokesman for local interests, weakens the decision-making power of the latter. Certain categories of invisible actors consider the researcher as a means of social and/or political visibility.[19] For example, when I asked a colleague, who conducted his research in an informal and illegal environment in the Great Lakes region (Central Africa), the question of the payment of information, he explained to me that he did not pay his informants in money but, rather, in intercessional approaches to the national authorities in order to get advantages for his informants.[20] In other cases, these marginal actors do not seek the support of the researcher. The farmer-diggers, for example, would not constitute a recognized critical mass because of the individual and/or punctual character of their activity and the lack of recognition by the State and the donors. These actors fear their local bosses first and then the national authorities. In general, interviews with farmer-diggers were governed by an intermediary who exercised almost total control over the content of the responses and the payment of the meetings. Therefore, having no voice in relation to the cultural policies of the state, nor their network of activity, in which they are only isolated ganglia, farmer-diggers have no interest in making themselves visible.

To this general element are added contingent risk factors. One factor concerns the fragmented nature of rural links. The "cover" of urban antiquities dealers is important to permit first contact with local intermediaries. Usually, I moved in the countryside from an urban relay (a dealer or an intermediary) that facilitated contact with its referents. However, once there, unplanned actors can be part of the management of interviews and they can govern the balance of power and hierarchy within the stakeholder group. Often, these satellite actors had no relation with the urban dealers who had sponsored the meeting but, rather, they were related to the rural referent of the latter for reasons of kinship or business. Often, during the first interview, the local referent is accompanied by people who are not involved in the conversation but who are involved in the search and/or the flow of the parts. Possible interventions from them occur at the end of the interview, after they have formed an opinion of the researcher, and can be added a second circle of external interlocutors, such notables as village councilors and religious authorities.

In the countryside, where the researcher is no longer covered by the sphere of influence of his core group, a second risk factor is the prolonged permanence in the same village as well as the reiteration of the interviews because of the lack of knowledge of the links within the informant group. Satimbé's approach, my main reference for the region of Mopti, is an example of the exponential progression of danger (see Figure 3.1). In the most isolated pockets of the Inland Niger Delta, exposed to the vagaries of the Niger floods, the cessation of the terracotta trade could lead to a real state of poverty. Nevertheless, the automatic binomial poverty-equal-looting would not reflect the social dynamics in place. In the Baniko region, for instance, the digs of ancient sites are done in parallel to cotton culture; moreover, some healthy farmers invest a part of their gains in digging teams (Panella 2010).

In this context, the misunderstanding of the presence of the researcher can be dangerous. If she/he is not there to buy objects, which is quickly proved, it is automatically deduced that she/he was sent by authorities for the purposes of control, interrogation, or arrest. During my investigations, I always refused to buy terracotta. In occasional interviews with rural intermediaries met only once, this choice represented a dangerous misunderstanding. In the understanding of these isolated actors of the value network, the fact of not buying implied a negative judgment of their activity and fueled the suspicion that I was a relay of the authorities of Bamako. These examples demonstrate that manner of approaching through snowball sampling (Biernacky and Waldorf 1981), proposed for research in an illegal context (Ellis and MacGaffey 1996), rather than favoring the selection of a reliable number of informants, can, on the contrary, multiply the risk situations.

A third factor of risk is the multiplication of languages over the arbitration stages with rural informants. In the case of Satimbé, the proceedings with his entourage took place in Bamanankan, Fula, and Songhay. Thus, several filters coexisted: preliminary discussions of the presentation in Fulani between Dolo ("boss" of Satimbé), the team leader Dabo (whose mother tongue was Songhay), and the villagers. The translation of Dolo from Fula to Bamanankan and the translation in French from my transcript (retrospectively)[21] summarizes as much as possible the content of the interviews. Given these events, an adviser to the village chief, according to Dolo's translation, said that seeing Satimbé follow strangers with his backpack would have fueled the rumor that he was going to submit to a second arrest and this would have destabilized the village. It was necessary to return to the village a second time so that he let Satimbé go with us (Panella 2002).

Figure 3.1 Weekly Market in Djenne, Mali. *Source*: Photo by Cristiana Panella, 1996.

Despite his availability, Dolo kept some gray areas during our interviews with Satimbé. His translations from Fulani to Bamanankan omitted that the notables of the village were fiercely opposed to Satimbé following us. Dolo and Satimbé had been linked for years to these villagers. This double-dealing was reiterated during the interviews with old Satimbé. His main purpose was to dilute the detailed information, especially that concerning the referents of their network. This was reflected in interventions of contrast in order to interrupt Satimbé: jokes, anecdotes, or phrases of circumstance and away from its detailed descriptions. The goal of Dolo was, finally, to make a credible substitute that could satisfy us without compromising vis-à-vis the power referents of his network.

Consequently, the fluidity of the "strong" and "weak" ties that make up the management of illegal network communication can upset the confidence pact between the researcher and his informants, as a result of a change of hierarchy within the links or a recovery of activity by former players in the sector. The outcome of our collaboration, in February 2001, with Dolo and Satimbé is an example:

> This last encounter with these two key informants proved to be a fiasco. As soon as Dolo arrived at home and the warm greetings that followed, we realized that he was no longer the same person who had welcomed us the previous year: he had now resumed his contacts in Bamako.[22] He was in the circuit again. Satimbé looked tired and, during the interviews, seemed to have been indoctrinated by his landlord: he now gave only short answers, without details, drawn from his memories, that so much enriched us during our previous interviews [. . .]. After three days, we decided to leave, pushed, among other things, by an unpleasant impression of danger. (Panella 2002: 194)

A FEW NAIVE QUESTIONS ON MONEY AND ETHICS

I have tried to show that by its polyhedral symbolic charge money can be considered a "total social fact." On the one hand, it puts on the same plane objects and individuals; on the other hand, it levels the balance of power between researcher and informant by modulating its value through the lagged temporalities of information management. From this perspective, it would be possible to envisage money as a tool of governmentality of social inequality.

Compared to the first links in the chain, the farmer-diggers, the unequal confrontation results in a lack of access to the heritage discourse as well as to information about them and, in the case of market networks, to the exponential growth of the resale price of the objects. Thus, a semantic gap between the excavation practices and the self-representations by their actors was consolidated and the construction by the official powers of illegal objects/subjects modeled by the sounding board of the media machine of elsewhere. The case of looting holes (see Figure 3.2) is just one example, becoming in the 1990s one of the *corpora delicti* that labeled the "phenomenon of plunder" and the "intrinsically" illegal essence of the digs. These traces materialize, according to the representations of the farmer-diggers, memory of risk and phisical endurance (Panella 2015). The reports of money, thus, seem to place researchers and informants on an equal access plan (money versus information) in a field governed by inegalitarian economic and representational balances.

Compared to these multiple exchange registers, my final reflections are attached to the state in being of a rickety ontology. My first question concerns the thread of this chapter. Is money, by its very nature, the bone of contention par excellence or would it simply be the easiest target to classify within a range of ambiguous exchanges? In other words, one might wonder whether it was ethically acceptable to try to gain the trust of farmers in order to obtain information about objects that constitute their source of sustenance. And this while refusing to buy these same objects because of transactions considered illegal by an elite unknown and distant from the survival daily life of these farmers. Again, if it was ethically acceptable to hide this embarrassment by buying trinkets that are considered legal or by bringing small gifts, fragile screens of an awkward compromise. Moreover, would the payment of information be ethically more viable in the case of investigations aimed at unmasking a traffic network?[23] Would it be honorable to betray the trust of those who have been able to access sensitive information that exposes them to peer judgment and, in some cases, unfortunate consequences? It goes without saying that the first impression of farmer-diggers is the fear of being arrested following the disclosure of the information given to the researcher.

Finally, who does care?

A question which seems to me to be crucial concerns the real usefulness of detailed information on the rural networks of the antiquities trade in the context of the technical and intellectual management of heritage policies. In other words, which official actors of such grounded research topics are really interested in?[24] The same question could be broadened to the relevance of the clandestine art trade as a *sustainable* topic of social sciences, in particular social anthropology. The qualitative method required in the illegal networked field as I tried to sketch it seems not to find its place in the current report approach which reduces social complexity to normative grids answering a principle of traceability, classification, and recordkeeping. These blunt the contradiction and fragmentation of social practices in order to deliver case studies exploitable by heterogeneous official actors answering, finally, a research applied to

Figure 3.2 Traces of Looting, Clandestine Digs in the Inland Niger Delta (Tou, Kouakourou). *Source*: Photo by Cristiana Panella, 2000.

the map, which is gaining more and more place also within the social sciences and humanities. It would be easy to say that the photo of a looting hole (see Figure 3.2) or the seizure of a lot of stolen objects is in this sense more spendable than the emic landscapes of the farmer-diggers. Moreover, the exponential growth of the legal approach in studies of cultural heritage and the art market seems to strengthen an assertive discourse which leaves not room for a bodily approach to the antiquities trade chains based on intersubjectivity, discontinuity, and individual ethics.

In addition, there is a presentation of the actors in place who decide between official subjects and illegal subjects without a real analysis of the interfaces between official practices and clandestine practices or mechanisms of the latter that allow the establishment and operation of the first, elements yet structural of any normative dynamics. Thus, the lack of knowledge about the first links in the market value chain (farmer-diggers, middlemen, local merchants) would seem to finally answer a lack of interest by official actors, donors, and organizations to enlighten the social ties of the trade through in-depth qualitative research, preferring short stays on the field in order to collect objective data for the reports funded by the international observatories of transnational crime.

Perhaps these reflections could contribute to a frank debate on the fundamental role of anthropology as science of the Humanness to restitute the complexity of social relations through the analysis of the hidden ties which underlie apparently averse ethical spheres.

NOTES

1. Walter E. Little kindly assisted with the translation of this chapter from the original French.

2. I truly thank Bjørn Thomassen for having drawn my attention on the work of James Leach and Gabriel Tarde.

3. International Council of Museums, International Centre for the Study of the Preservation and Restoration of Cultural Property, and International Council of Monuments and Sites, respectively.

4. In spite of the interchangeable use of the adjectives "illegal" and "illicit" in a lot of publications on "plunder" and "art crime," I consider these terms not synonym as they underlie on one side an official and pervasive normativity; on the other side a social and individual frame of values which may be not contemplated by the law.

5. See the ERC project *Global traffic in illicit cultural objects: developing knowledge for improving interventions in a transnational criminal market (GTICO)* led by the criminologist Simon Mackenzie (Mackenzie et al. 2019).

6. My last stay on the field and the period of drafting of my thesis have been funded by Leiden University, CNWS Leiden and University College London. During my research (January–April 1996, October 1996–September 1997; November 1999–February 2000), I have been working in Bamako with almost 50 actors of the African art trade (*antiquaires*, middlemen, woodcarvers) as well as 17 other actors (*antiquaries*, farmer-diggers, forgers) from the Mopti region. Three of them (one *antiquaire*, one *chef d'équipe*, and one digger) have provided the most of information on the clandestine digging in the region. Fifteen other local actors were from the Sikasso region, in the South of the country, for a total of 83 people (urban and rural traders, rural middlemen, and *navettes*) as well as civil servants.

7. As well in Europe as in Mali, I have chosen to lead open and unstructured interviews.

8. In this respect, the economist Mamadou Camara has proposed an analysis of the forces in play in the drug's supply networks by applying the game theory to reciprocity dynamics occurring between traffickers, politicians, and police, and showing that such cooperation depends from power relationships as well as by the status changes of the actors of the chain (Camara 1999).

9. I refer to the well-known strong and weak ties theory elaborated by Marc Granovetter (Granovetter 1973).

10. In his investigations of international art dealers, Simon Mackenzie relied on semistructured interviews. He reportedly used the same questionnaire in Melbourne, London, and New York, adding small variations to interviews in Thailand and Hong Kong. With few exceptions, he was able to use a recorder (Mackenzie 2005). It would have been interesting to know if Mackenzie was holding his questionnaire or asking questions without reading them; if his recorder was on the table or if he kept it on him; or what was the state of the debate around categories of sensitive objects at the time of the interview? In cultures where orality still enshrines emic ethics, like Malian ones, these "small unimportant details" make the difference, determining the success or the failure of an interview or even of a collaboration.

11. For an overview on money matters in fieldwork research, see Cajas and Pérez (2017).

12. http://anthroniche.com/darkness_documents/0375.htm, accessed on March 2, 2018.

13. http://www.aaanet.org/committees/ethics/bp2.htm, accessed on March 2, 2018.

14. https://linguistics.stanford.edu/research/linguistic-fieldwork/resources-linguistic-fieldwork/conducting-fieldwork, accessed on February 26, 2018.

15. See UNESCO (2006).

16. On the relationship between ethics and corporeality, see Panella (2014).

17. On the cultural brokerage among Senegalese art traders, see Dilley (2005).

18. This is particularly the case in war contexts, as in Syria or in Iraq (see Stone and Farchakh Bajjaly 2008; Daniels and Hanson 2015).

19. As regards, let me mention the outstanding work of Danielle de Lame in Rwanda (de Lame 2005).

20. Personal communication, Chicago, November 2008.

21. The totality of the farmer-diggers refused to be recorded. I truly thank Samou Camara for having shared with me such a difficult field research and for having carefully translated the interviews from Bamanankan to French.

22. At this time, Dolo had rehearsed his collaboration with one of the *plaque-tournantes* of the international trade in ancient terracotta. This change in the balance of our relationship put me in a sensitive position.

23. One could mention several cases of journalists who introduced themselves surreptitiously as buyers in order to get information from Malian art dealers.

24. Information on rural circuits of the antiquities trade still is rare. See, for instance, *Countering Illicit Traffic in Cultural Goods. The Global Challenge of Protecting the Worlds's Heritage*, France Desmarais, ed (ICOM 2015).

REFERENCES

Achino-Loeb, Maria-Louisa, ed. *Silence. The Currency of Power*. Oxford; New York: Berghahn Books, 2006.

Adler, Patricia A. *Wheeling and Dealing. An Ethnography of an Upper-Level Drug Dealing and Smuggling Community*. New York: Columbia University Press, 1985.

Amselle, Jean-Loup. "La corruption et le clientélisme au Mali et en Europe de l'Est: quelques points de comparaison." *Cahiers d'Études Africaines* 32, no. 128 (1992): 629–642.

Appadurai, Arjun. *Modernity at Large. Cultural Dimensions of Globalization*. Minneapolis: University of Minnesota Press, 1996.

Arnoldi, Mary Jo, Christraud M. Geary, and Kris L. Hardin, eds. *African Material Culture*. Bloomington and Indianapolis: Indiana University Press, 1996.

Atwood, Roger. *Stealing History: Tomb Raiders, Smugglers, and the Looting of the Ancient World*. New York: St Martin's Press, 2004.

Aunger, Robert. *Reflexive Ethnographic Science*. Walnut Creek: Altamira Press, 2004.

Battaglia, Debborah. "Toward an Ethics of the Open Subject: Writing Culture in Good Conscience." In *Anthropological Theory Today*, edited by Henrietta L. Moore, 114–150. Cambridge: Polity Press, 1999.

Bayart, Jean-François, Stephen Ellis, and Béatrice Hibou. *The Criminalization of the State in Africa*. London: The International African Institute, 1999.

Bedaux, R.M.A., and Michael Rowlands. "The Future of Mali's Past?" *Antiquity* 75, no. 290 (2001): 872–876.

Beeman, William. "Silence in Music." In *Silence. The Currency of Power*, edited by Maria-Louisa Achino-Loeb, 23–34. Oxford; New York: Berghahn Books, 2006.

Bernard, H. Russell. *Research Methods in Anthropology. Qualitative and Quantitative Approaches*. London; New Delhi; Thousand Oaks: Sage Publications, 1994.

Biernacky, Patrick, and Dan Waldorf. "Snowball Sampling. Problems and Techniques of Chain Referral Sampling." *Sociological Methods and Research* 10, no. 2 (1981): 141–163.

Blundo, Giorgio, and Jean-Pierre Olivier de Sardan (with N. Bako Arifari and M. Tidjani Alou). *Everyday Corruption and the State. Citizens and Public Officials in Africa*. London: Zed Books, 2006.

Boeck (de), Filip. "Garimpeiro Worlds: Digging, Dying and 'Hunting' for Diamonds in Angola." *Review of African Political Economy* 28, no. 90 (2001): 549–562.

Bouillon, Florence, Marion Fresia, and Virginie Tallio. *Terrains sensibles. Expériences actuelles de l'anthropologie*. Paris: CEA-EHESS, 2005.

Bredeloup, Sylvie. *La Diams'pora du fleuve Sénégal. Sociologie des migrations africaines*. Toulouse: IRD/Editions PUM, 2007.

Brett-Smith, Sarah C. *The Making of Bamana Sculpture: Creativity and Gender*. New York: Cambridge University Press, 1994.

Brodie, Neil, Jennifer Doole, and Peter Watson. *Stealing History: The Illicit Trade in Cultural Material*. Cambridge: McDonald Institute, 2000.

Brodie, Neil, and Colin Renfrew. "Looting and the World's Archaeological Heritage: The Inadequate Response." *Annual Review of Anthropology* 34 (2005): 343–361.

Burt, Ronald S. *Structural Holes: The Social Structure of Competition*. Cambridge: Harvard University Press, 1992.

Cajas, Juan, and Yolinliztli Pérez. "Anthropologists, Economic Retributions and Informants: Notes About Ethics in Social Research." *AGATHOS* 8, no. 1 (2017): 143–154.

Calvey, David. 2008. "The Art and Politics of Covert Research. Doing 'Situated Ethics' in the Field." *Sociology* 42, no. 5 (2008): 905–918.

Camara, Mamadou. "Économie de la drogue et théorie des jeux." *Revue Tiers Monde* 40, no. 158 (1999): 297–317.

Camara, Sory. *Gens de la parole. Essai sur la condition et le rôle des griots dans la société malinké*. Paris: Karthala, [1975] 1992.

Campbell, Peter B. "The Illicit Antiquities Trade as a Transnational Criminal Network: Characterizing and Anticipating Trafficking of Cultural Heritage." *International Journal of Cultural Property* 20, no. 2 (2013): 113–153.

Casagrande, Joseph B. ed. *In the Company of Man: Twenty Portraits by Anthropologists*. New York: Harper & Brothers, 1960.

Charney, Noah. ed. *Art and Crime: Exploring the Dark Side of the Art World*. Santa Barbara, CA; Denver, CO; Oxford; England: ABC-CLIO, 2009.

Clifford, James, and George. E. Marcus eds. *Writing Culture: The Poetics and Politics of Ethnography*. Berkeley: University of California Press, 1986.
Cissé, Youssouf Tata. "Signes graphiques, représentations, concepts et tests relatifs à la personne chez les Malinké et les Bambara du Mali." In *La notion de personne en Afrique Noire. Actes du colloque international du Centre national de la recherche scientifique*, edited by Germaine Dieterlen, 131–179. Paris: CNRS Éditions, 1973.
Comaroff, Jean, and John Comaroff eds. *Law and Disorder in the Postcolony*. Chicago: University of Chicago Press, 2006.
Conklin, John E. *Art Crime*. Westport: Praeger, 1994.
Corbey, Raymond. 2000. *Tribal Art. A chronicle of Taste. Trade and Desire in Colonial and Post-colonial Times*. Amsterdam: Royal Tropical Institute.
Crapanzano, Vincent. *Tuhami. Portrait of a Moroccan*. Chicago: The University of Chicago Press, [1980] 1985.
Daniels, Bryan, and Katryn Hanson. "Archaeological Site Looting in Syria and Iraq: A Review of the Evidence." In *Countering Illicit Traffic in Cultural Goods. The Global Challenge of Protecting the World's Heritage*, edited by France Desmarais, 83–94. Paris: ICOM.
Dembelé, Mamadi, and J. Diderick van der Waals. "Looting the Antiquities of Mali". *Antiquity* 65 (1991): 904–905.
Desmarais, France ed. *Countering Illicit Traffic in Cultural Goods. The Global Challenge of Protecting the World's Heritage*. Paris: ICOM, 2015.
De Soto, Hermine, and Nora Dudwick. *Fieldwork Dilemmas. Anthropologists in Post-socialist States*. Madison: The University of Wisconsin Press, 2000.
Diawara, Mamadou. *L'empire du verbe et l'éloquence du silence*. Studien zur Kulturkunde 120, Köln: Rüdiger Köppe Verlag, 2003.
Dieterlen, Germaine. 1981. "Réflexions sur la parole, le sacrifice et la mort dans quatre populations de l'Afrique de l'Ouest." *Systèmes de pensée en Afrique noire* 5: 61–70.
Dilley, Roy. 2004. "The Visibility and Invisibility of Production among Senegalese Craftsmen." *JRAI* 10, no. 4: 797–813.
Eilstrup-Sangiovanni, Mette, and Calvert Jones. "Assessing the Dangers of Illicit Networks. Why al-Qaida May Be Less Threatening Than Many Think." *International Security* 33, no. 2 (2008): 7–44.
Ellis, Stephen, and Janet MacGaffey 1997. "Le commerce international informel en Afrique subsaharienne. Quelques problèmes méthodologiques et conceptuels." *Cahiers d'Etudes Africaines* 145, no. XXXVII-1 (1997): 11–37.
Enwezor, Okwui, and Chika Okeke-Agulu eds. *Contemporary African Art Since 1980*. Bologna: Damiani Editore, 2009.
Errington, Shelly. *The Death of Authentic Primitive Art and Other Tales of Progress*. Berkeley: University of California Press, 1998.
Ferrel, Jeff, and Marc Hamm eds. *Ethnography at the Edge: Crime, Deviance, and Field Research*. Lebanon: Northeastern University Press, 1998.
Field, Les, Gnecco, Cristóbal, and Joe Watkins eds. *Challenging the Dichotomy. The Licit and Illicit in Archaeological and Heritage Discourses*. Tucson: The University of Arizona Press, 2017.

Finnegan, Ruth. *The Oral and Beyond. Doing Things with Words in Africa*. Chicago: The University of Chicago Press, 2007.
Fillitz, Thomas. "Art and Anthropology: Different Practices and Common Fields of Intersection." *Field. A Journal of Socially Engaged Art Criticism* 11 (2018). http://field-journal.com/issue-11/art-and-anthropology-different-practices-and-common-fields-of-intersection
Gable, Eric. "A Secret Shared: Fieldwork and the Sinister in a West African Village." *Cultural Anthropology* 12, no. 2 (1997): 213–233.
Gambetta, Diego ed. *Trust: Making and Breaking Cooperative Relations*. Cambridge: Basil Blackwell, 1988.
Geertz, Clifford. "The Bazaar Economy: Information and Search in Peasant Marketing." *The American Economic Review* 68, no. 2 (1978): 28–32.
Ghassem-Fachandi, Parvis ed. *Violence: Ethnographic Encounters*. Oxford: Berg, 2009.
Godefroit, Sophie. 2001. "La part maudite des pêcheurs de crevettes à Madagascar." *Etudes rurales* 159–160: 145–172.
Golde, Peggy. *Women in the Field. Anthropological Experiences*. Berkeley: University of California Press, 1986.
Graburn, Nelson. ed. *Ethnic and Tourist Art: Cultural Expressions from the Fourth World*. Berkeley: University of California Press, 1976.
Graeber, David. *Toward an Anthropological Theory of Value*. New York: Palgrave, 2001.
Granovetter, Marc. "The Strength of Weak Ties." *American Journal of Anthropology* 78 (1973): 1350–1380.
Grätz, Tilo. "Gold Trading Networks and the Creation of Trust: A Case Study from Northern Benin." *Africa* 74, no. 2 (2004): 146–172.
Green, Linda. *Fear as a Way of Life. Mayan Widows in Rural Guatemala*. New York: Columbia University Press, 1999.
Grégoire, Emmanuel, and Pascal Labazée. "Approche comparative des réseaux marchands ouest-africains contemporains." In *Grands commerçants d'Afrique de l'Ouest: Logiques et pratiques d'un groupe d'hommes d'affaires contemporains*, edited by Emmanuel Grégoire, and Pascal Labazée, 9–36. Paris: Karthala-Orstom, 1993.
Guyer, Jane. *Marginal Gains: Monetary Transactions in Atlantic Africa*. Chicago: University of Chicago Press, 2004.
Hart, Keith, Jean-Louis Laville, and Antonio D. Cattani. *The Human Economy*. Cambridge: Polity Press, 2010.
Herscher, Ellen. "The Antiquities Market: News and Commentary on the Illicit Traffic in Antiquities." *Journal of Field Archaeology* 10 (1983): 350–369.
Heyman, Josia McC. ed. *States and Illegal Practices*. Oxford; New York: Berg, 1999.
Hoffmann, Barbara, ed. *Art and Cultural Heritage. Law, Policy and Practice*. Cambridge University Press, 2006.
Hollowell, Julie. "Moral Arguments on Subsistence Digging." In *The Ethics of Archaeology. Philosophical Perspectives on Archaeological Practice*, edited by

Chris Scarre and Geoffrey Scarre, 69–93. New York: Cambridge University Press, 2006.

Jules-Rosette, Bennetta. *The Messages of Tourist Art: An African Semiotic System in Comparative Perspective*. New York: Plenum Publishers, 1984.

Kasfir, Sidney, and Till Förster, eds. *African Art and Agency in the Workshop*. Series: African Expressive Cultures, Indiana University Press, 2013.

Kenney, Michael. "The Architecture of Drug Trafficking: Network Forms of Organisation in the Colombian Cocaine Trade." *Global Crime* 8, no. 3 (2007): 233–259.

Kedzierska-Manzon, Agnieskza. "Words of Power: Magical Spells of Mande Hunters". In *Mande Mansa: Essays in Honor of David C. Conrad*, edited by Jan Jansen, Stephen Belcher, and Mohamed N'daou, 113–122. Zurich: Lit Verlag Gmbh & Co. KG Wien; Berlin: Lit Verlag Dr. W. Hopf, 1988.

Kemp, Wolfgang. "The Work of Art and Its Beholder. The Methodology of the Aesthetic of Reception." In *The Subjects of Art History: Historical Objects in Contemporary Perspectives*, edited by Mark A. Cheetam, 180–192. New York: Cambridge University Press, 1988.

Kloβ, Sinah T. "Sexual(ized) Harassment and Ethnographic Fieldwork: A Silenced Aspect of Social Research." *Ethnography* 18, no. 3 (2017): 396–414.

Kovats-Bernat, J. Christopher. "Negotiating Dangerous Fields. Pragmatic Strategies for Fieldwork Amid Violence and Terror." *American Anthropologist* 104, no. 1 (2002): 208–222.

Lame (de), Danielle. *A Hill among a Thousand: Transformations and Ruptures in Rural Rwanda*. Tervuren: RMCA, and Madison, WI: University of Wisconsin Press, 2005.

Lamont, Michèle. "Toward a Comparative Sociology of Valuation and Evaluation." *Annual Review of Sociology* 38 (2012): 201–221.

Leach, James 2010. "Intervening with the Social? Ethnographic Practice and Tarde's Image of Relations between Subjects." In *The Social After Gabriel Tarde. Debates and Assessments*, edited by Matei Candea, 193–209. London: Routledge, 2010.

Lee, Raymond M. *Doing Research in Sensitive Topics*. Thousand Oaks, CA: Sage Publications 1993.

Lemaire, Marianne 2009. *Les sillons de la souffrance. Représentations du travail en pays sénoufo (Côte d'Ivoire)*. Paris: CNRS Éditions-Éditions de la Maison des sciences de l'Homme.

Leyten, Harrie, ed. *Illicit Traffic in Cultural Property. Museums Against Pillage*. Amsterdam: Royal Tropical Institute, 1995.

L'Estoile (de), Benoît. *Le Goût des Autres. De l'Exposition coloniale aux Arts premiers*. Paris: Flammarion, 2007.

Luhmann, Niklas. 1973. *Trust and Power*. Hoboken: Wiley and Sons.

Mac Gaffey, Janet, and Rémy Bazenguissa-Ganga, 2000. *Congo-Paris. Transnational Traders on the Margins of the Law*. Oxford: James Currey.

Mackenzie, Simon R.M. *Going, Going, Gone: Regulating the Market in Illicit Antiquities*. Leicester: Institute of Art and Law, 2005.

Mackenzie, Simon, Neil Brodie, Donna Yates, and Christos Tsirogiannis. *Trafficking Culture: New Directions in Researching the Global Market in Illicit Antiquities.* London: Routledge, 2019.

Manacorda, Stefano, and Duncan Chappell, eds. *Crime in the Art and Antiquities World: Illegal Trafficking in Cultural Property*. New York; Dordrecht; Heidelberg; London: Springer, 2011.

Maniscalco, Fabio. "Archaeological Looting and the Protection of Cultural Property in Nigeria." *Webjournal on Cultural Patrimony* 1 (2006): 23–42. http://www.webjournal.unior.it

Martinelli, Bruno. "Entre interdit et pardon. Le pouvoir des forgerons chez les Moose et les Dogon." In *Les Dogon, le pouvoir et la chefferie*, Vol. 5, edited by Jacky Bouju. Clio en Afrique, 1998. http://sites.univ-provence.fr/~wclio af/numero/5/thematique/martinelli/index.html

Mathews, Gordon, Gustavo Lins Ribeiro, and Carlos Alba Vega eds. 2012. *Globalization from Below. The World's Other Economy*. London and New York: Routledge.

Matsuda, David. "The Ethics of Archaeology, Subsistence Digging, and Artifact Looting in Latin America: Point and Muted Counterpoint." *International Journal of Cultural Property* 7, no. 1 (1998): 87–97.

Matsuda, David. "Subsistence Diggers." In *Who Owns the Past? Cultural Policy, Cultural Property, and the Law*, edited by Kate Gibbon, 225–265. New Brunswick: Rutgers University Press, 1998.

Maurer, Bill. "The Anthropology of Money." *Annual Review of Anthropology* 35 (2006): 15–36.

Mauss, Marcel. *The Gift: Forms and Functions of Exchange in Archaic Societies.* London: Routledge, [1925] (1990).

McIntosh, R.J., Téréba Togola, and Susan Keech McIntosh. "'The Good Collector' and the Premise of Mutual Respect among Nations." *African Arts* 28, no. 4 (1995): 61–69; 110–111.

McNaughton, Patrick. *The Mande Blacksmiths: Knowledge, Power, and Art in West Africa*. Bloomington: Indiana University Press, 1993.

Médard, Jean-François. "Le "Big Man" en Afrique - esquisse d'analyse du politicien entrepreneur." *L'Année sociologique* 42 (1992): 167–192.

Médard, Jean-François. "Les paradoxes de la corruption institutionnalisée." *Revue internationale de politique comparée* 4, no. 13 (2006): 697–710.

Meskell, Lynn, and Peter Pels. *Embedding ethics*. Oxford: Berg, 2005.

Meyer, Karl. E. *The Plundered Past*. New York: Atheneum, 1973.

Möllering, Guido. "The Nature of Trust: From Georg Simmel to a Theory of Expectation, Interpretation and Suspension." *Sociology* 35, no. 2 (2001): 403–420. http://journals.sagepub.com/doi/pdf/10.1177/S0038038501000190. Accessed on March 15, 2018.

Moore, David. "Ethnography and Illicit Drug Use: Dispatches from an Anthropologist in the 'Field'." *Addiction Research* 1 (1993): 11–25.

Moreno, Eva. "Rape in the Field: Reflections from a Survivor." In *Taboo: Sex, Identity and Erotic Subjectivity*, edited by Don Kulick, and Margaret Wilson, 219–250. London; New York: Routledge, 1995.

Merryman, John H. "Text and Subtext in the International Art Trade." *International Journal of Cultural Property* 3 (1994): 61–76.

Nilan, Pamela. "'Dangerous Fieldwork' Re-Examined: The Question of Researcher Subject Position." *Qualitative Research* 2, no. 3 (2002): 363–386.

Nordstrom, Carolyn, and Antonius C. G. M. Robben, eds. *Fieldwork Under Fire. Contemporary Studies of Violence and Culture*. Berkeley: University of California Press, 1996.

Pageard, Robert. "Note sur les Diawambé ou Diokoramé." *Journal de la Société des Africanistes* 29, no. 2 (1959): 239–260.

Palmer, Nelson. *The Recovery of Stolen Art: A Collection of Essays*. London: Kluwer Law International, 1998.

Panella, Cristiana. *Les terres cuites de la discorde. Déterrement et écoulement des terres cuites anthropomorphes du Mali*. Leiden: CNWS, 2002.

Panella, Cristiana. "La vera storia delle terrecotte di Djenné. Smontaggio e ricomposizione di materiali da capolavoro." *Africa. Rivista trimestrale dell'Istituto italiano per l'Africa e l'Oriente*, LIX no. 1 (2004): 106–124.

Panella, Cristiana. "Patrons and Petits Patrons. Knowledge and Hierarchy in Illicit Networks of Trade in Archaeological Objects in the Baniko Region (Mali)." *Review of African Political Economy* 37, no. 124 (2010): 228–237.

Panella, Cristiana. "Etoiles filantes. La parabole des terres cuites anthropomorphes du Delta Intérieur du Niger (Mali): années 1940–1990." In *Ethnocentrisme et creation*, edited by Annie Dupuis, 79–102. Paris: Editions de la Maison des Sciences de l'Homme, 2014.

Panella, Cristiana. "Rhétorique du matériel, corporéité et inégalité sociale. Une réflexion biopolitique sur les représentations du « phénomène du pillage » de biens culturels." In *Mémoire africaine en péril: pillages et restitutions du patrimoine culturel et anthropologique africain*, edited by Eric Huysecom, Anne Mayor, and Vincent Negri, 39–51. Frankfurt: Monographs of the Journal of African Archaeology (Africa Magna Verlag), 2014.

Panella, Cristiana. "Lost in Translation. Unprovenanced Objects and Opacity/Transparency Agenda of Museum Policies." *ANUAC (Rivista dell'Associazione nazionale universitaria Antropologi culturali)* 4, no. 1 (2015): 66–87.

Panella, Cristiana and Kedron Thomas, eds. Special Issue: "Illegality," *Critique of Anthropology* 35, no. 1 (2015): 3-113.

Paredes Maury Sofia. "Surviving in the Rainforest: The Realities of Looting in the Rural Villages of El Petèn, Guatemala." (1999). Accessed on November 29, 2020. http://www.famsi.org/reports/95096/95096ParedesMaury01.pdf.

Pardo, Italo, ed. *Between Morality and the Law: Corruption, Anthropology and Comparative Society*. London; New York: Routledge, 2004.

Parry, Jonathan, and Maurice Bloch, eds. *Money and the Morality of Exchange*. Cambridge University Press, 1989.

Peraldi, Michel. *Cabas et containers. Activités marchandes informelles et réseaux migrants transfrontaliers*. Paris: Maisonneuve & Larose; Maison méditerranéenne des sciences de l'homme, 2001.

Punch, Maurice. *The Politics and Ethics of Fieldwork: Muddy Boots and Grubby Hands*. Thousand Oaks, CA: Sage Publications, 1986.

Rabinow, Paul, and George Marcus. *Designs for an Anthropology of the Contemporary*. Durham: Duke University Press, 2008.

Reeves, Madeleine. "Clean Fake: Authenticating Documents and Persons in Migrant Moscow." *American Ethnologist* 40, no. 3 (2013): 508–524.

Scarre, Chris, and Geoffrey Scarre, eds. *The Ethics of Archaeology. Philosophical Perspectives on Archaeological Practices*. New York: Cambridge University Press, 2006.

Schendel (van), Willem and Itty Abraham, eds. *Illicit Flows and Criminal Things: States, Borders, and the Other Side of Globalization*. Bloomington: Indiana University Press, 2005.

Schmidt, Peter, and Roderick. J. McIntosh. *Plundering Africa's Past*. Bloomington and Indianapolis: Indiana University Press, 1996.

Sender, Stefan, and Allison Truitt, eds. *Money: Ethnographic Encounters*. Oxford; New York: Berg, 2007.

Simmel, Georg. *The Philosophy of Money*. London; New York: Routledge, [1907] 1990.

Smart, Alan, and Filippo Zerilli. "Extralegality." In *A Companion to Urban Anthropology*, edited by Donald Nonini, 222–238. Malden, MA: Wiley Blackwell, 2014.

Sriram, Lekha, John King, Julie A. Mertus, Olga Martin-Ortega, and Johanna Herman eds. *Surviving Field Research: Working in Violent and Difficult Situation*. London: Routledge, 2009.

Staley, David P. "St Lawrence Island's Subsistence Diggers: A New Perspective on Human Effects on Archaeological Sites." *Journal of Field Archaeology* 20, no. 3 (1993): 347–355.

Steiner, Christopher. *African Art in Transit. The Production of Value and Mediation of Knowledge in the African Art Trade*. Cambridge: Cambridge University Press, 1994.

Stoller, Paul. "Circuits of African Art/Paths of Wood: Exploring an Anthropological Trail." *Anthropological Quarterly* 76, no. 2 (2003): 207–234.

Stone, Peter G., and Joanne Farchakh Bajjaly, eds. *The Destruction of Cultural Heritage in Iraq*. Woodbridge: Boydell Press, 2008.

Tijhuis, Antonius J.G. *Transnational Crime and the Interface between Legal and Illegal Actors: The Case of the Illicit Art and Antiquities Trade*. Nijmegen: Wolf Legal Publishers, 2006.

Titeca, Kristof. "Les OPEC boys en Ouganda, trafiquants de pétrole et acteurs politiques." *Politique Africaine* 103 (2006): 143–159.

Togola, Téréba, and Michel Raimbault. "Les pillages de sites archéologiques au Mali." *Jamana* 23 (1989): 19–21.

Trager, Lilian. “Customers and Creditors: Variations in Economic Personalism in a Nigerian Marketing System.” *Ethnology* 20, no. 2 (1981): 133–146.
Tubb, Kathryn W. ed. *Antiquities: Trade or Betrayed.* London: Archetype, 1995.
UNESCO. *Legal and Practical Measures Against Illicit Trafficking in Cultural Property.* Paris: UNESCO Handbook. International Standards Section, Division of Cultural Heritage, 2006.
Ulph, Janet, and Ian Smith. *The Illicit Trade in Art and Antiquities. International Recovery and Criminal and Civil Liability.* Oxford: Hart Publishing, 2012.
Vitelli, Karen D. *Archaeological Ethics.* New Delhi: Sage Publications Ltd, 1996.
Walsh, Andrew. “‘Hot Money’ and Daring Consumption in a Northern Malagasy Mining Town.” *American Ethnologist* 30, no. 2 (2003): 290–305.
Warms, Richard L. “Commerce and Community: Paths to Success for Malian Merchants.” *African Studies Review* 37, no. 2 (1994): 97–120.
Watson, Peter, and Cecilia Todeschini. *The Medici Conspiracy: The Illicit Journey of Looted Antiquities. From Italy’s Tomb Raiders to the World’s Greatest Museums.* New York: Public Affairs, 2007.
Zempléni, Andras. “Savoir taire. Du secret et de l’intrusion ethnologique dans la vie des autres.” *Gradhiva* 20 (1996): 23–41.
Zerubavel, Eviatar. *The Elephant in the Room. Silence and Denial in Everyday Life.* New York: Oxford University Press, 2006.

Part II

ETHNOGRAPHIES OF ILLEGALITIES AND THE REFRAMING OF NORMS AND MARGINS

Chapter 4

Street Economies, Illegality, and Rights in Antigua Guatemala

Walter E. Little

INTRODUCTION

For the last 40 odd years, Chepe has shined shoes under the portal on Antigua Guatemala's Central Plaza (see Figure 4.1).[1] Across the plaza from the cathedral, he works in a prime location in the historical heart of the city. From his initial days in the shoe shining business as boy hustling from customer to customer sitting on park benches in the plaza to his current coveted place under the portal, shaded from the sun and sheltered from the rain, where customers come to him, he has enjoyed a particular right to the city that not all workers in Antigua's street economy share. He works free from worries that the police will remove him or that city regulators, be they police or other officials, will fine him for the work he does or for being in the place he does it. He enjoys the collegiality and added safety of having others who enjoy the same privileges of earning a living on the street, such as other shoe shiners, newspaper vendors, travel guides, and photographers. While shining shoes has not made Chepe a wealthy man, it has been a secure source of income that allows him to live modestly with his wife and children and participate in Catholic religious life that is important to him. In short, he enjoys particular rights to the city that other street workers do not have. Why this is so and why other street workers, such as handicraft vendors and food sellers, do not enjoy the same rights to work in Antigua's public places is the theme of this chapter.

I will describe several different kinds of street work practiced in Antigua in order to think about David Harvey's (2008, 2012) thesis that the right to the city is a type of human right. Building on Lefebvre's (1996) work that urbanism and capitalism are intertwined processes and that cities are places of social and economic change, Harvey contends that the "freedom to make and remake our cities and ourselves is . . . one of the most precious yet most

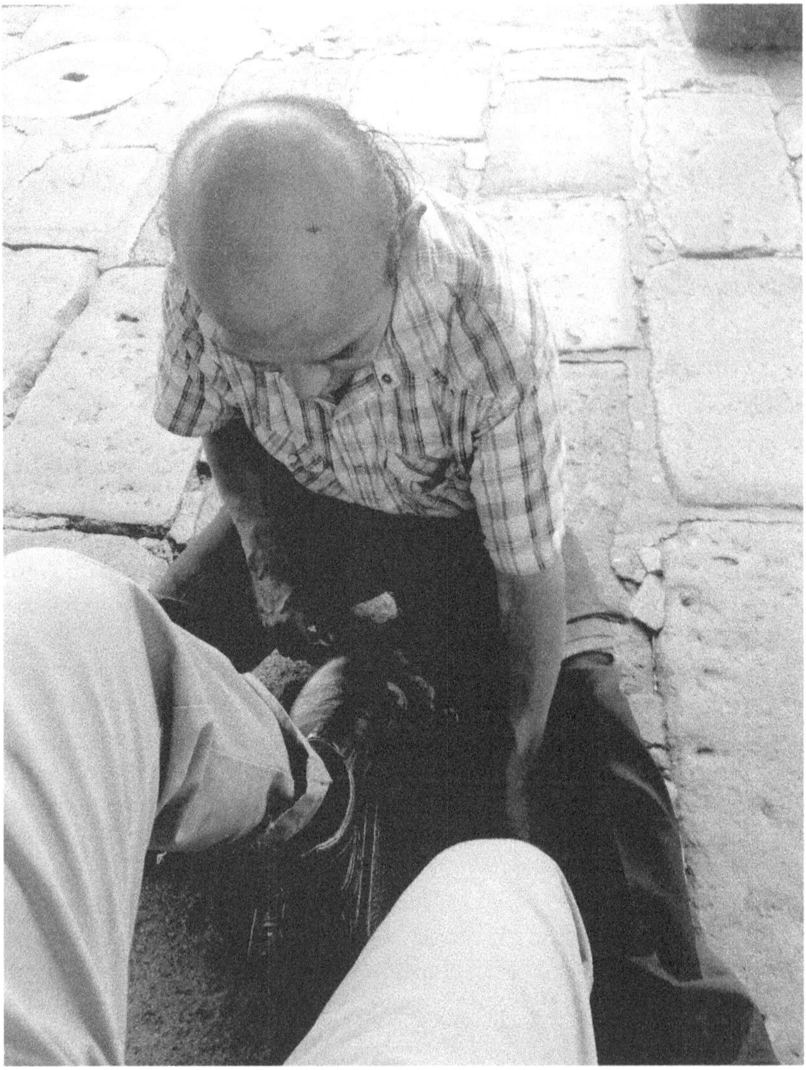

Figure 4.1 Chepe at Work Shining Shoes under the Portal. *Source*: Photo by Walter E. Little.

neglected of our human rights" (2008: 23). What I do here is bring Harvey's discussion of urbanization as a stabilization mechanism to absorb capitalism's surpluses (2008: 25) and as a process by which urban dwellers are pacified through consumerism (2008: 30) via ethnographic examples that look at one small piece of the urban experience, making a living on the street.

Harvey (2008: 33) explains that capital "surplus absorption through [urbanization is usually done] through 'creative destruction,' which nearly always has a class dimension since it is the poor, the underprivileged and those marginalized from political power that suffer first and foremost from this process." Although Harvey concerns himself with the dispossession of the poor from the places they own or rent, it is important to observe that such dispossessions can include the removal of people from places where they earn a livelihood by defining which street economic practices are legal and by redefining the acceptable or permissible uses of public space. This concept of permissibility, or urban spatial permissiveness (Little 2014) or spatial permissibility (Little 2020), as I refer to it elsewhere, is my attempt to ethnographically operationalize as the gap between regulations and how livelihoods are actually practiced on the street and in everyday public life. The lived reality of permissibility operates within a conceptual framework of -graying (Heyman and Smart 1999) and cultural intimacy (Herzfeld 2005) because unlike the either/or framework of Harvey's rights to the city position, urban places do not often operate in such ways.

This ethnographic case illustrates for Antigua that it is not as simple as Harvey argues—that it is merely "the right to the city falling into the hands of private or quasi-private interests" (2008: 38). Even though some street livelihoods are considered illegal, some others are not. And some, like the ambulatory sales of handicrafts and food, fall between legality and illegality, where municipal street vending codes and local customary practices diverge. The various street economies (see Hansen, Little, and Milgram 2013; Little 2015) I discuss here do not rest comfortably with either public or private interests but occupy the spaces between public and private. Furthermore, different street livelihoods are not equally viewed under the legal system as having the same rights and privileges. The diversity of those who work on the street and differential treatment by the municipality, local residents, and tourists tends to inhibit the formation a broad-based urban social movement, something that Harvey (2008: 39) argues needs to happen to counteract neoliberal urbanization, in general, in order to converge "on the singular aim of gaining greater control over the uses of the surplus—let alone over the conditions of its production." Lived-in UNESCO-designated World Heritage cities are sites of multiple kinds of production within and outside of tourism contexts and it is important to recognize that significant kinds of economic production take place in the public spaces of streets, plazas, and parks. Rights to be in and use these public places are complicated when they are claimed as places for making a livelihood.

By drawing on Roy's (2009) concept of civic governmentality, I look at a variety of street economy practices situated within local Antigua politics to examine what I see is Harvey's (2008, 2012) right to the city dilemma—who is it that gets to lay claim to the city? Where Harvey implies that all in the city have claims to citizenship, where the poor can be dispossessed and disenfranchised by the wealthy (capitalists) or can mobilize against them, Roy presents a different dynamic in which citizenship and governance is not envisioned from such a top-down perspective. She argues that "grassroots regimes of government both resist and comply with what may be perceived as top-down forms of rule" and, furthermore, "within the realms of civic governmentality, the urban subject is simultaneously empowered and self-disciplined, civil and mobilized, displaced and compensated" (Roy 2009: 160–61). She contends that subjects are positioned from inside citizen-making processes, which I take to be the inclusion of everyone, not just the wealthy and powerful to the exclusion and marginalization of the poor.

Looking at those who earn their livelihoods on the street, rather than through grassroots organizations as Roy does, provides an additional lens from which to view the relationships of the production of space, governance, and citizenship. One of the reasons I began this chapter with the shoe shiner Chepe is that his street economic subjectivity places him in an ambiguous nexus: his work is a permissible practice according to the municipality but it is out of sync with the conventions of heritage regulations and predominant touristic interests, in that he is not a typical subject for the tourism gaze (Urry 1990) and only rarely provides his service to tourists. Technically, his work is contrary to the official regulations in which all work on the streets is prohibited. On the other hand, handicraft and food vendors intersect with this nexus of public street vending codes, heritage regulations, and tourism interests in, yet, other ways. The municipality deems both kinds of street sales illegal, but these economic actors and their street work articulate with local residents, workers, and tourists in distinct and varied ways that shape the production of space in Antigua's streets and plazas. So, while Roy is concerned with organizations, my interest is in individuals' economic practices as situated in public space. Like her, however, I believe this case is a way to explore "the relationship between . . . regimes of inclusion and the production of space" (Roy 2009: 161). This space of human and social and economic activity "characterizes the human body according to its relational strategies within a production framework" (Panella 2015). To grasp the production framework and regimes of inclusion is to understand the experience of those who work on the streets and the complex matrix of forces and contexts that make that work permissible.

ANTIGUA AS A UNESCO WORLD HERITAGE SITE AND TOURISM ATTRACTION

Antigua Guatemala is a well-known tourism destination and has been for now over one hundred years (Little 2004). Beginning in the 1900s as a place for urban dwellers from Guatemala City and random foreigners to relax away from the bustle of the capital, Antigua has changed over time with global tourism trends. By the late 1920s and through the 1930s, it emerged as an ethnic tourism route that served the same kinds of elite American and European tourists who were also traveling to Oaxaca and Bali, all of which were given increasing ethnographic attention. Guidebooks of the period placed an emphasis on the Mayas who came from smaller villages in the countryside to sell handicrafts and agricultural goods in the municipal marketplace, which was a recommended stop for tourists.

The Guatemalan historian, Jorge Luján Muñoz (1966), noted that by 1941 the city's dominant Spanish Baroque architectural style began gaining recognition by locals, national leaders, and the international community, providing an additional rational for tourism development. At the same time, this change contributed to defining Antigua as a non-Maya place, despite many of the manual laborers, gardeners, and vendors working there were Mayas coming into the city from their homes in the highlands. Beginning on March 30, 1944, the city's architectural characteristics began to garner accolades, first from the Guatemalan national government declared it a National Monument. Then the Pan American Institute of Geography and History declared it a Monumental City of the Americas on July 7, 1965. Its most significant designation was in October 1979 when UNESCO named it Cultural Heritage of Humanity site (now called a World Heritage property). What is consistent through these various designations is the emphasis on architecture, rather than people or intangible forms of culture—be it Maya, Ladino, and foreign people or their cultural practices.

However, since the beginning of modern international tourism in the 1920s (Fussell 1980), not just the last 40 years, political violence has been the biggest impediment to tourism development in Guatemala (Carmack 1988; Little and Smith 2013). Although Antigua has largely been spared from it, making the city safe for Guatemalans and foreigners, the specter of violence haunts tourists' decisions to visit the country. Estimates by INGUAT and the Banco de Guatemala, the Guatemala Chamber of Tourism, and the Instituto Guatemalteco de Turismo place the numbers of tourists—national and foreign—at nearly 2.5 million visitors with the greatest concentration during Holy Week.[2] Notwithstanding, Guatemala's legacies of violence, national and international tourists and locals, too, enjoy the city's mix of Spanish Baroque-style architecture, indigenous Maya vendors and workers dressed in colorful hand-woven clothing, and a diverse cosmopolitan culinary and music scene. Hence, tourists may be drawn to Antigua because of architecture heritage, but they do not limit their experiences to the architecture and tourism businesses only articulate with it. To experience Antigua on the streets, the most publicly accessible places of the city, means interacting with the city' vibrant street economies: handicrafts vendors, watercolor artists, food sellers, and shoe shiners, Polaroid photographers, freelance tour guides, and others.

This dynamic between architecture and people is constantly shifting tourism landscape. Tourists' interests in Maya handicrafts seem to come in cycles, as does their interest in Spanish language studies, volunteering for medical NGOs or animal welfare organizations, and Catholic religious pageantry, especially, Holy Week. From street vendor entrepreneurs and fixed place businesses, most members of the business community are trying to develop intangible cultural practices, even expanding to culinary experiences in recent years (Little 2020, 2021), because what keeps tourists in Antigua and spending their money are the intersubjective cultural experiences, not the architecture. This intersubjective and liminal (Thomassen 2009) space is constantly in a state of becoming and unbecoming through the interactions between people, buildings, and public places. Because these are often spaces that exist between what is officially sanctioned (laws and regulations) and norms on the ground where it is possible to experience the kinds of cultural intimacies (Herzfeld 2005) that reveal urban spatial permissibility in practice.

Antigua Street Economies

Like other Latin American urban heritage sites, Havana (Hill 2012, 2007), Salvador da Bahia (Collins 2015), Quito (Middleton 2009), and Cuzco (Seligmann 2013), street livelihoods in Antigua articulate with the conditions of heritage regulations and touristic structures and tourism trends. Such heritage and tourism conditions encourage economic and political strategies that can distinguish these street workers from those vendors and workers in other parts of the Global South (Brown 2006; Cross and Morales 2007; Clifton and Seale 2013; Hansen, Little, and Milgram 2013).

Although street vendors and others practicing their livelihoods on the street may end up there precisely because of the dispossession and creative destruction that Harvey (2008, 2012) describes, street worker economies and political actions in urban heritage sites are shaped by more than these factors. Unlike vendors who claim public city spaces through traditional forms of political action and resistance (Cross and Morales 2007; Goldstein 2016; Mendiola García 2017), those working in heritage and tourism site, rely on strategies that play on their ambivalent and tenuous relations to tourists and the tourism industry, in order to foster a pro-vendor image as rightfully in the public touristic spaces in which they work (Castañeda 1996; Little 2005, 2008). These tourism and heritage contexts constrain their political strategies, offering additional reasons to understand why urban social movements struggle to be "converged on the singular aim of gaining greater control over the uses of the surplus—let alone over the conditions of its production" (Harvey 2008: 39). Nor do these vendors embrace grassroots institutions to advocate for themselves and to democratize public places, as Roy (2009) discusses, even when they are ubiquitous jobs like shining shoes that can be found in just about every city in the world.

In this section, I sketch brief ethnographic profiles of shoe shiners, Polaroid photographers, ambulatory Maya handicraft vendors, and mobile food vendors to highlight the ways they make a living on public streets. Many other ambulatory or mobile vendors and street workers work in Antigua, such as prostitutes and drug dealers (though they are few), who are not desired by locals, other street workers, city officials, and tourists. There are, also, watercolor artists who are universally liked by locals, other street workers, city officials, and tourists. The vendors I discuss, here, fall into in-between economic and political spaces: not quite legal, not quite illegal; respected by some political sectors yet reviled by others; and sometimes considered to be public nuisances, health and traffic hazards, or just plain bothersome to locals and tourists. Yet, they are persistent presences in the street economies of the city, despite their ambivalent legal status. What these street workers are permitted to sell is discussed in the following section.

Shoe Shiners

All shoe shiners are identifiable by the tools of their trade: a small wooden stool for them to sit on, a wooden box with a flat beveled surface for their customer to rest their shoe while the shiner does his work. The box contains the cleaning solutions, polishes, pastes, rags, and brushes needed. This street work is exclusively done by men and boys who have enjoyed a privileged place in the Central Plaza (see Figure 4.2).

In the 30 years I have conducted ethnographic research in Antigua, there have been no women shoe shiners or photographers. Some shoe shiners like Chepe, a Ladino, are able to do their work under the portal protected from the weather, but most, like Juan, a K'ichee' Maya man, ply their trade in the Central Plaza, approaching locals and tourists who sit on the park benches or linger in conversation with friends. Fewer, still are the shoe shiners who maintain ambulatory routes throughout the city where they serve regular local customers in their homes and businesses.

For their services, there is a sliding price scale, depending on the polish used, how dirty the shoes are, the type of shoe, and the quality of the work. This sliding scale has contributed to many misunderstandings when national and international tourists have their shoes shined. Their local clientele understands these price differences, but they are not transparent to outsiders and conflict over prices can make some shiners leery of business with those who are not known customers.

Polaroid Photographers

The photographers, who also are all men, work exclusively in the plaza, where they take photos of young local couples on the park benches, national

Figure 4.2 Antigua's Central Plaza. *Source*: Photo by Walter E. Little.

tourists in front of the fountain, and occasionally Maya families on business in the city. The Polaroid photographers carry the tools of their trade, cameras, including now digital cameras, the images of which they will email to their clients or print at a photo-processing shop a block from the plaza. They also carry shoulder bags with their supplies and sample photo albums of their work. Unlike the shoe shiners, they have opted to professionalize themselves by wearing identification badges and adopting a uniform: tan baseball caps and vest identifying work, Instantaneous Digital Technology, their organization, on the back, Association of Photographers of the Central Park of Antigua Guatemala. They also carry a document, that they say gives them permission to work in the plaza. In fact, the dog-eared copies of the original document, signed in 1998 by the, then, mayor of Antigua Victor Hugo del Pozo, were written by a self-formed collective of street car washers who solicited permission from the mayor to allow them to continue their work without being arrested. I will discuss this document shortly, as it gets at the ways in which street workers conceptualize their rights to work in Antigua.

Maya Handicraft Vendors

Maya handicraft vendors are ubiquitous on the streets with their numbers fluctuating between a few dozen during the slower midweek days to hundreds during peak tourism periods like Christmas, Easter week, and weekends

Figure 4.3 A Photographer and Shoe Shiner Converse in the Plaza. *Source*: Photo by Walter E. Little.

from June to August. The majority of the vendors are women from nearby Kaqchikel Maya towns, but others come from some quite distant other Maya towns. The women, especially, but also some men are easily identifiable by the clothes they wear and the different Maya languages they speak.

They sell a wide range of handmade products that generally correspond with the interests of tourists. Although I have consistently listened to tourists say that they want "authentic experiences with Mayas" and "will only buy real hand-made Maya clothes, traditional clothes," few in reality do. Besides, the shock they experience when they hear the prices—a new complete woman's outfit from San Antonio Aguas Calientes can be more $1,000—few want to carry these heavy, bulky clothes in their luggage. Vendors respond to the market by making cheaper goods: change purses, various bags, bracelets and other inexpensive jewelry, and lightweight scarfs, all of which can be purchased for $1–$40.

Because Maya handicraft vendors look distinctive, they are the subjects of many tourists' photos. Unlike similar vendors in Spanish colonial-style cities in Mexico and Peru, who ask to be paid for photos (Seligmann 2013; Steele 2008), the vendors in Antigua do not, believing that they can use the photo opportunity to convince the tourist into purchasing handicrafts from them. In order to maximize their sales, they capitalize on the typical touristic representations that juxtapose them with colonial architecture. They follow routes that take them by hotels, restaurants, museums, and historical buildings. Until 1998, many Maya handicraft vendors were able to claim a place on the street to sell and stay there. Some families controlled places in the plaza and on city street corners for generations. As I have explained elsewhere (Little 2004), this came to an end with the major, forced restructuring and regulation of all street vendors in 1998. Those who had enough capital and merchandise went to the newly opened handicraft marketplace and those who did not have the money or small inventories, either went out of business or sold on the streets as ambulatory vendors. They devised various strategies to entice tourists to buy their goods and avoid being arrested and fined, but their main one is to keep on the move and to be with tourists, since police are reluctant to enforce street vending regulations when foreigners are present.

Food Vendors

Like the handicraft vendors, most food vendors are highly mobile, but they interact with tourists only in rare instances. Often, the food they sell is not known by the tourists and, if it is, tourists are fearful of eating it. Unlike Maya handicraft vendors, whose primary customers are foreign tourists, food vendors almost exclusively sell to local workers. They provide a service, an alternative to the city's expensive restaurants and more convenient than the cheaper restaurants in the municipal marketplace on the edge of the city. Food vendors have enjoyed periods in which they, too, were able to set up their stands or place their baskets of food for sale and wait for their customers. Now, this is not as easily done (Little 2020), but like shoe shiners and Polaroid photographers, some of them have working arrangements with city officials and local workers that help them maintain visible regular places to sell.

Food vendors tend to have two different kinds of selling strategies, both of which articulate with local consumers, rather than tourists, or even out-of-town Guatemalans visiting the city. There are vendors who prepare complete

Figure 4.4 Handicraft Vendors Buy a Snack from a Food Vendor. *Source*: Photo by Walter E. Little.

meals and serve regular local clientele of city workers, including other street workers. These vendors prepare meals in their homes and set-up pop-up serving stations throughout the city. With meals typically ranging from US$1.50 to $2.50, they provide an affordable meal option for the cities workforce who do not make enough to afford restaurant food that can cost US$10 and up per meal. Tourists do not eat from these vendors for a couple of reasons. Vendors tend to prepare only enough meals for their regular clients and tourists tend to be cautious about eating prepared street food.

By contrast, the ambulatory food vendors have routes that take them by as many businesses as possible, including a circuit that follows the same routes as the Maya handicraft vendors, who are some of their biggest customers. They tend to sell snacks and rely on their mobility to insulate them from the police instructed to remove them for selling. The more stable and successful ambulatory vendors establish reliable customers through regular sales to a set number of fixed-place businesses and grade schools where employees and students purchase food for their morning and afternoon snacks. Those who do not maintain such regular clientele and known places to sell on their routes are much more subject to having their food seized and being fined.

URBAN HERITAGE REGULATION OF STREET LIVELIHOODS

All street workers described above are working in violation to the municipal laws and codes. Yet, shoe shiners and Polaroid photographers are permitted to work in public places without fear of being arrested and fined. By contrast, Maya handicraft vendors and food vendors work under more precarious and shifting political and social conditions that make them vulnerable to harsh legal repercussions. In order to understand this gray space (Yiftachel 2009), in which urban spatial permissibility plays out in variable ways, it is important to look beyond official codes[3] that regulate street use and national heritage regulations. How these and other kinds of street economies articulate between legal and illegal spaces, the street codes, and heritage regulations need to be taken into consideration alongside locals' and foreigners' conceptualizations of who the vendors are and the kinds of cultural intimacies that take place in the economic and social transactions between the street workers and their customers. How these workers' identities are conceptualized by others, be they locals or tourists, contributes to how they conceive of their rights to the city and how others conceive of these street workers' right to be in the city.

Briefly, the 1969 law, "Ley protectora de la cuidad de La Antigua Guatemala" (Decreto número 60–60) and the subsequent UNESCO World Heritage inscription in 1979 are only concerned with the architectural aesthetic of the city. Much local debate about the city—who gets to use it and how it is used—is tied to the regulation of architecture. For instance, police officers and city officials have confessed to me that food vendors and Maya handicraft vendors should be removed, because they are out of sync with the city's heritage aesthetic. Some residents, knowledgeable of the 1969 law and UNESCO inscription, have pointedly told me that there are no provisions for these kinds of street workers, vendors, or services. Simply put, they are all illegal occupations.

Why, then, are some permitted and others not? How is it that those street economies that supposedly are not allowed persist anyway? One simple answer is that it is because of customary practices (see Thompson 1991), but it is difficult to relegate handicraft sales to the noncustomary, given that Maya street vendors have sold to foreign tourists since at least the 1920s. Instead, I would argue that the kinds of street economies I describe in the previous section persist with, and without, being pursued and fined by the police, because of the ways that Antigua has developed economically and socially. Certainly, the social construction of space in Antigua illustrates the "accumulation by dispossession" that Harvey (2008) theorizes for urbanization, but affluent forms of urbanization in Antigua come from both the wealthy deciding to make it their home and from foreign tourism. The street vendors and other street service providers who make their livelihoods on the street provide goods and services that are not being provided through legally recognized, tax-paying businesses. For instance, food vendors are permissible because they feed Antigua's workforce. A lunch with a mobile street vendor can cost as little as 1 US dollar, but a meal in a modestly priced restaurant can be between $5 and $10, with many much more expensive meal options. Many workers do not have the time during their breaks to walk to the inexpensive marketplace restaurants. So mobile food vendors serve an important niche, despite the municipal and national discourse being that street food is dangerous, a discourse that matches that from tourism and helps explain why few tourists eat food from these vendors.

For Maya handicraft vendors, the presence of tourists is crucial to explaining why they are permitted to sell, yet also subject to municipal laws and regulations. Local sentiment in Antigua has been to remove these vendors and since the early 1990s, I have watched successive municipal officials and police employ strategies to expel them from the city. Even with the threat of jailtime, usually over night or a couple of days, fines for selling, and the loss of merchandise through police seizer, Maya vendors rationalize the benefits of selling in Antigua outweigh the costs. As one vendor cynically commented to me, "I have to worry more about thieves taking my stuff and my money than the police. Usually, the police are too afraid to stop us if there are tourists, but thieves don't care. They'll take our goods, our money, the tourists' money and the tourists' things." Another added, "That were we're the same, tourists and us, the police won't help either of us. That's why we *ambulantes* have to take care of each other and of the tourists."

One of the things that also distinguishes official and customary positions on who belongs in the city, especially belongs in relation to livelihood choices, is ethnicity. One thing that I have witnessed with regularity is the persistent police pressure on Mayas, including those who do not have the street economy-based livelihoods and are in Antigua for school or other business. They are asked to vacate the park benches, upon which they rest and to not loiter in front of businesses. Police even break up conversations between these Mayas, some of who are actually tourists from other parts of Guatemala, and foreign tourists. Mayas (not vendors) who were talking to me have been interrupted by police on multiple occasions for speaking a Maya language and, then, were told to leave the park. Although police profile Mayas according to cultural features—the languages they speak and the clothes they were—Maya handicraft vendors know that these same characteristics are what attract tourists and, hopefully, sales. Savvy restaurateurs, hotel managers, and Spanish-language school directors, too, recognize that Maya vendors attract tourists, and provide havens for these vendors when the police threaten fines and arrests.

This urban spatial permissibility plays out in a social, economic, and political context of gray spaces (Yiftachel 2009) that are, in turn, related to a double sense of cultural intimacy. One is as Herzfeld describes, that is "a source of external embarrassment but nevertheless provide insiders with their assurance of common sociality" (2005: 3). Shoe shiners, photographers, handicraft vendors, and food vendors are potential sources of embarrassment, especially, when viewed alongside idealized heritage relations and touristic representations. When everyone plays along—locals and visitors—these street workers are permitted to work and their customers get the services and goods they want. The question of the illegal nature of the work only comes to the fore when there is a greater transgression—cheating a customer or a customer claiming to be cheated, physically intimidating locals and visitors, obstructing businesses or causing traffic problems. The shared intimacy between the street workers and their customers is in knowing that what is normal and permitted is not limited to formal laws and regulations but for practiced in the everyday workings of the city.

The second sense of cultural intimacy comes from that of shared experience, not between those described above who know the rules and live by other social and economic norms, but those who do not know them and do not comprehend what is out-of-sync and embarrassing. This is the cultural intimacy that exists between Maya handicraft vendors and tourists. It operates when the vendors share their struggles with tourists. Vendors play on their cultural differences to provide tourists with a glimpse into their lives and with that can come even more intimate knowledge of how they are poorly treated in Antigua by the police and many residents. It can be a successful ploy to make a sale, but it can also serve as a way to mobilize tourists to advocate on behalf of the vendors in small ways that keep police at bay on the streets and in bigger ways when they speak up for them in public municipal forums (Little 2008). Cultural intimacy in this sense still results in "embarrassment, rueful self-recognition" that "describe the collective representation of intimacy" (Herzfeld 2005: 6) itself. Tourists siding with and supporting vendors in material ways by purchasing their handicrafts and in political ways by signing their petitions to sell legally are, frankly, embarrassing for city leaders.

Cultural intimacy comes through sharing and conspiring and supporting each other in a liminal space for both the handicraft vendors and tourists who do not know each other and the other street workers and locals who know each other. All are in the know—that this economic activity is illegal but nonetheless practiced in plain view, sometimes serving a pragmatic function, shoes shined and people fed, and sometimes serving symbolic roles, capturing a moment in a photo or representing touristic distinctiveness through a hand-woven textile.

Here, I want to return to the letter the photographers carry with them, the letter mentioned earlier in this chapter. It serves as an important symbolic capital for some street workers. Originally, it was, in fact, written by a loose collective of car washers that no longer exists, and explain what it means. First, it does not grant the car washers (or the photographers who now carry the letter) permission to work in the plaza, nor are the occupations of car washing, street photography or shoe shining, or food sales permitted in the municipal codes. The city stamp from the secretary merely acknowledges the letter was received.

Car washers petitioned the city to be allowed to work, because they were being threatened by violent street criminals and pressured by the police to quit working or pay fines. Car washers during that time also claimed that police tried to extract bribes from them too. Their proposition was that they and the police work together to improve the overall safety for residents and visitors, as well as do minor things to help keep the city clean. Maya handicraft vendors have made similar, unsuccessful overtures to the municipal government, including offering to pay a municipal fee and pay taxes in order to be assured a legal place in the public street economy (Little 2008).

In Antigua, today, street car washers largely do not exist, due to extortion from organized gangs and police and increased hostility from local home and business owners, as well as drivers. I got to personally know two car washers. One was the son of food vendor who sold drinks and snacks to marketplace handicraft vendors. He was a grade schooler when I met him and his father but, by the time he was a teen, he struggled in school and did not want to work alongside his father. With some other youths, they used tactics of intimidation to "sale their car-washing and protection services" to drivers visiting Antigua. Their activities were soon noticed by both the police and a violent street gang that forcibly recruited them. Antigua's civic leaders are quick to respond to such threats as drug dealing, criminal gangs, and prostitution. While certainly these elements exist, they certainly do not enjoy the public urban spatial permissiveness that the vendors discussed in this chapter do and, ultimately, the car washers were not successful in cultivating a secure economic space between the regulations and norms. They found themselves outside of the norms of everyday economic and social practice, regarded as criminals by drivers, property owners, police, tourists, and bonafide criminals. The food vendor's son was later murdered by the gang that conscripted him. The other youth who followed a similar path was from Santa Cruz del Quiche, a distant K'ichee' Maya town. He, too, saw washing cars and extorting money from drivers as a way to quick, easy cash in comparison to selling handicrafts or staying home and working as an agricultural laborer. He, however, while managing to dodge the gangs and police, decided the risk was too great. He is now a part-time vendor, sometimes selling handicrafts and sometimes selling dried nuts, and part-time farmhand, living between his hometown and Antigua.

That the car washer letter has been copied by other street workers beyond the original petitioners, the car washers, to the photographers and to some of the younger shoe shiners from Santa Cruz del Quiche, and various mobile food vendors is significant. Older shoe shiners have ignored it, as have Maya handicraft vendors who for distinct reasons have judged it useless. Why the letter is, at least, symbolically powerful for some, the photographers, for instance, and not for others, Maya handicraft vendors, has to do with particular economic and political relationship that each has with the city. The Maya handicraft vendors considered it useless because they knew it was not going to stop the police from hassling them, nor did they think it would help legitimize them to their main customers, tourists, or help them live more peacefully with local residents. Besides, said one woman, "If I carry this letter, it will confirm to the Ladinos [non-Maya Guatemalan], that I am just a dumb Indian."

For the photographers, the letter symbolizes their economic insecurity. Making a living in this profession is incredibly difficult, since most residents and national and international tourists have their own cameras, most often on their cell phones. With a shrinking clientele, their ability to make a living and stay in the city becomes more precarious. In conversations with the photographers, they explained that when they ask people in the plaza if they would like their photo taken it is "not the same as the Indian (Maya) vendors who pester tourists and try to cheat them." One photographer said, "No, we have a legitimate business. We provide a service." He, then, tapped his identification badge—a badge that they invented and one not issued by the city. They are also quick to present the letter to their clients, who are not given the time to actually read it. Police officers do not pay any attention to it. In short, the letter is for the photographers themselves, a symbolic security blanket, and for tourists, used to help distinguish themselves as non-Maya and, hence, more suited to be in Antigua, a place that is officially defined by local, national, and international heritage conventions in ways that exclude Mayas and Mayanness.

Given that shoe shiners enjoy the most privileged place in Antigua's street economy, accepted by locals and local officials, it may seem odd that some carry the car washers' letter. This, in part, has to do with the younger shoe shiners' insecurities about their ethnicity and the common experiences of being discriminated in Antigua. Being poor and Maya, with minimal literacy skills is not easy. The letter symbolizes a form of power, a mimesis of when police officers hold up legal pamphlets to Maya handicraft vendors when threatening arrests or fines. Where the photographers show the letter to their potential customers, the young Maya shoe shiners show it to police and other officials they worry will make them leave the plaza. Like their older counterparts, Chepe and Juan, the police do not pay any attention to them. Since they only guardedly speak K'ichee', the language of their home communities, and do not wear ethnically identifiable clothing, the police do not interrupt their work or expel them from the plaza, as happens with Maya handicraft vendors. In this case, the letter is still a form of security, but one that references the insecurity of being in a place in which these young Maya men do not yet feel comfortable.

CONCLUSIONS

I want to return to the issue of workers' rights to the city. In his discussion of rights to the city, Harvey (2008: 39) advocates the mobilization against the most well-offs' accumulation by dispossession and "the developmental drive that seeks to colonize space for the affluent." In advocating such resistance, even revolution, according to his terms (Harvey 2008: 40), to alter the urban production of space, he leaves aside the question of governance, which Roy (2009) takes up. The point I want to make, here, is that the right to the city can be achieved through persistent economic practices and relation to the particular kinds of relationships the street workers have with other members of the city, be they permanent residents or transient international tourists. These practices may be officially illegal—contrary to municipal codes and regulations—but are, nevertheless, permitted out of a combination of customary practices, local and tourist consumer expectations, and pragmatic functions, even, that help the city work and people work in the city.

Although sectors of the street economies have mobilized, there has been no mobilization of social movement or revolution that Harvey (2008, 2012) references as appropriate responses to affluent forms of urbanization. Nor has there been the development of grassroots organizations that serve to advocate for the poor, as described by Roy (2009). However, these street vendors and street service providers occupy similar in-between legal–illegal places, like those discussed by Roy. They are concerned with participating in their own governance. The social, political, and economic conditions, of which I have only been able to briefly touch upon, allow for the street livelihoods described here. They are the result of the processes of "accumulation by disposition" where K'ichee' boys and young men seek new opportunities to landlessness and poor wages in the countryside and Kaqchikel Maya women weavers seek to economically colonize the spaces of affluent tourism by selling handmade crafts linked to their ethnicity.

For those whose ethnicity may not be on display—the food vendors, the shoe shiners, the photographers—their places in the city depend on the social construction of space too. Unlike the Maya handicraft vendors who play a major part in the touristic representation of the city and are expected by foreigners, these other street workers are largely absent from those representations. Instead, they provide services that locals need or desire. Despite these occupations' official illegality in public places, their permissibility indicates socially constructed spaces based on recognizable customary practices. By working in the city, they just do not reconfigure public places, they change the conditions by which they have rights to the city. Indeed, the plaza is a more interesting and dynamic place for locals and tourists alike because of the diversity of street workers. These kinds of livelihoods are not as dramatic as Harvey's revolution or Roy's grassroots organizations political mobilizations, but I would argue they are more common and that they indicate far subtler ways for the less affluent to have their rights to and in the city recognized.

NOTES

1. An early version of this chapter was presented at the conference—"Urban Property, Governance and Citizenship in the Global South"—Copenhagen, June 23–26, 2015.
2. *Boletín Estadístico, Banco de Guatemala*, see http://www.banguat.gob.gt/ (last accessed August 17, 2018); Cámara de Turismo de Guatemala, see http://www.camtur.org/ (last accessed August 17, 2018); Instituto Guatemalteco de Turismo, see http://www.inguat.gob.gt/estadisticas/boletines-estadisticos.php (last accessed September 5, 2018).
3. Reglamento Municipal que prohíbe el uso de La Vía Pública para la Exhibición, Alquiler, Venta y Comercialización de Bienes y Servicios en el Municipio de La

Antigua Guatemala. Reglamento Municipal que prohíbe el uso de La Vía Pública para la Exhibición, Alquiler, Venta y Comercialización de Bienes y Servicios en el Municipio de La Antigua Guatemala.

REFERENCES

Brown, Alison, ed. *Contested Space: Street Trading, Public Space, and Livelihoods in Developing Cities*. Warwickshire: ITDG Publishing, 2006.

Carmack, Robert M. *Harvest of Violence: The Maya and the Guatemalan Crisis*. Norman: University of Oklahoma Press, 1988.

Castañeda, Quetzil. "On the Correct Training of *Indios* in the Handicraft Market at Chichén Itzá: Tactics, Tactility of Gender, Class, Race, and State." *Journal of Latin American Anthropology* 2, no. 2 (1996): 106–143.

Collins, John F. *Revolt of the Saints: Memory and Redemption in the Twilight of Brazilian "Racial Democracy."* Durham: Duke University Press, 2015.

Cross, John, and Alfonso Morales, eds. *Street Entrepreneurs: People, Place and Politics in Local and Global Perspective*. London: Routledge, 2007.

Evers, Clifton, and Kirsten Seale, eds. *Informal Urban Street Markets. International Perspectives*. London: Routledge, 2014.

Goldstein, Daniel M. *Owners of the Sidewalk: Security and Survival in the Informal City*. Durham: Duke University Press, 2016.

Hansen, Karen Tranberg, Walter E. Little, and B. Lynne Milgram, eds. *Street Economies in the Urban Global South*. Santa Fe: SAR Press, 2013.

Harvey, David. *Rebel Cities: From Right to City to the Urban Revolution*. London: Verso, 2012.

Harvey, David. "The Right to City." *New Left Review* 53 (2008): 23–40.

Herzfeld, Michael. *Cultural Intimacy: Social Poetics in the Nation-State*. New York: Routledge, 2005.

Heyman, Josiah McC, and Alan Smart. "States and Illegal Practices: An Overview." In *States and Illegal Practices: An Overview*, edited by Josiah McC Heyman, 1–14. Oxford: Berg, 1999.

Hill, Matthew J. "'The Return to the 'Historic Center': Heritage Landscapes and the Reterritorialization of Urban Space in Late Socialist Cuba." In *Global Downtowns*, edited by Gary McDonough and Marina Peterson, 186–205. Philadelphia: University of Pennsylvania Press, 2012.

Hill, Matthew J. "Reimagining Old Havana: World Heritage and the Production of Scale in Late Socialist Cuba." In *Deciphering the Global: Its Scales, Spaces and Subjects*, edited by Saskia Sassen, 59–78. New York; London: Routledge, 2007.

Lefebvre, Henri. *Writings on Cities*. Oxford: Blackwell Publishers, 1996.

Little, Walter E. "Chapter 9: Street Food to Restaurant: Politics of Eating and Cultural Heritage in Antigua Guatemala." In *The Cultural Politics of Food, Taste, and Identity: A Global Perspective*, edited by Steffan Igor Ayor Díaz, 147-160 (. New York: Bloomsbury Books, 2021.

Little, Walter E. "Antigua Street Food Vendors." *Revista del CESLA: International Latin American Studies Review* 25 (2020): 209–232.
Little, Walter E. "Urban Economies and Spatial Governmentalities in the World Heritage City of Antigua." *Economic Anthropology* 2, no. 1 (2015): 42–62.
Little, Walter E. "Façade to Street to Façade: Negotiating Public Spatial Legality in a World Heritage City." *City & Society* 26, no. 2 (2014): 196–216.
Little, Walter E. "Crime, Maya Handicraft Vendors, and the Social Re/Construction of Market Spaces in a Tourism Town." In *Economies and the Transformation of Landscape*, edited by Lisa Cliggett and Christopher A. Poole, 267–290. Walnut Creek: Altamira Press, 2008.
Little, Walter E. "Outside Social Movements: Dilemmas of Indigenous Handicrafts Vendors in Guatemala." *American Ethnologist* 31, no. 1 (2005): 43–59.
Little, Walter E. *Mayas in the Marketplace: Tourism, Globalization, and Cultural Identity*. Austin: University of Texas Press, 2004.
Little, Walter E., and Timothy Smith. *Mayas in Postwar Guatemala: Harvest of Violence Revisited*. Tuscaloosa: University of Alabama Press, 2009.
Luján Muñoz, Jorge. *Permanencia de Antigua*. Guatemala City: Universidad de San Carlos Guatemala, 1966.
Middleton, Alan. "Trivializing Culture, Social Conflict and Heritage Tourism in Quito." In *Cultural Tourism in Latin America: The Politics of Space and Imagery*, edited by Michiel Baud and Annelou Ypeij, 199–216. Leiden: Brill Publishers, 2009.
Panella, Cristiana 2015. "Rhétorique du matériel, corporéité et inégalité sociale. Une réflexion biopolitique sur les représentations du 'phénomène du pillage' au Mali." In *African Memory in Danger—Mémoire africaine en peril*, edited by Anne Mayor, A., Vincent Negri, and Eric Huysecom, 39–51. Frankfort: Africa Magna Verlag, 2015.
Roy, Ananya. "Civic Governmentality: The Politics of Inclusion in Beirut and Mumbai." *Antipode* 41, no. 1 (2009): 159–179.
Seligmann, Linda. "The Politics of Urban Space among Street Vendors of Cusco, Peru." In *Street Economies, Politics, and Social Movements in the Urban Global South*, edited by Karen Tranberg Hansen, Walter E. Little, and B. Lynne Milgram, 115–136. Santa Fe, NM: School for Advanced Research, 2013.
Steel, Griet. *Vulnerable Careers: Tourism and Livelihood Dynamics Among Street Vendors in Cusco, Peru*. Amsterdam, Netherlands: Rozenberg Publishers, 2008.
Smart, Alan, and Filippo Zerilli. "Extralegality." In *A Companion to Urban Anthropology*, edited by Donald M. Nonini, 222–238. New York: John Wiley, 2014.
Thompson, E. P. *Customs in Common*. London: Penguin Press, 1991.
Thomsassen, Bjørn. "The Uses and Meanings of Liminality." *International Political Anthropology* 2, no. 1 (2008): 5–27.
Urry, John. *The Tourist Gaze: Leisure and Travel in Contemporary Societies*. London: Sage, 1990.
Yiftachel, Oren. "Critical Theory and 'Gray Space': Mobilization of the Colonized." *City* 13, no. 2–3 (2009): 240–256.

Chapter 5

Informal Economies, Illegal Subjects

Roma and Senegalese Traders in Rome

Isabella Clough Marinaro and Cristiana Panella

Rome is currently undergoing dramatic changes in its urbanity, linked to immigration and to the rapid development of new economic sectors. Italy's capital offers a crucial vantage point for close analysis of informal migrant economies by virtue of its Mediterranean position which continues to make it a crossroads of East-West and South-North migrations and related economic exchanges. Indeed, urban change in the city is in many ways a result of global patterns which emerge out of smaller linkages and less visible networks than those represented by high finance and transnational corporations, but that constitute, in our view, an equally important part of global capitalism.[1] It is striking that within Italy's national context of sluggish economic growth (ISTAT 2018), formal businesses run by immigrants have expanded massively in recent years (CESPI 2017). In 2017, migrant workers' contribution to economic activity accounted for 8.9% of Italian GDP; in the province of Rome, businesses owned by non-EU migrants made up nearly 20% of companies—almost twice the national average (MdL 2017).[2] Yet, this economic integration is occurring within a national political setting of increasingly visible racism, expressed through violent attacks against foreigners and in often openly xenophobic statements by some members of Italy's political elite (Lunaria 2018).

Although there is still a dearth of ethnographic investigation into many aspects of contemporary Roman society, recent urban anthropological and migration studies are developing a body of literature increasingly reflective of the kaleidoscopic normative landscapes in the country and more specifically in Rome. The city is in fact a locus of multiple daily arrangements where law, practical norms, and temporalities are negotiated, made up of heterogeneous spheres of value and interdependent legal, informal, and illegal political and economic networks (Carter 1997; Knights and King 1998; Lombardi-Diop

2009; Broccolini 2009; DeMaria Harney 2012; Tuckett 2018; Piazzoni 2020). The literature on African migrants has tended to stress individual employment trajectories and their networks in host countries (Carter 1997; Riccio 1999; Riccio and degli Uberti 2013), while that on Roma in Italy has only recently moved beyond a focus on social exclusion to explore communities' participation in urban economic life (Solimene 2016; Santilli 2017; Clough Marinaro 2018) and forms of inclusion through informality.[3]

In order to enrich in-depth ethnographic approaches to the emergence of immigrant transnational economies (Thomassen and Vereni 2014), we propose a grounded analysis of informal and illegal commodity flows and value production in a local/global setting from the perspective of Senegalese and Roma migrants mostly residing and operating in the city of Rome.[4] In particular, we focus on the social dynamics of market exchange occurring in the marginal spaces of capitalist globality by comparing the production, supply, and circulation networks of both groups in relation to social organization, trust/risk relationships, and market trajectories. The fieldwork evidence shows that these informal commercial strategies constantly negotiate and adapt to official representations of illegality while at the same time enhancing several dynamics of social integration generated through the informal/illegal practices themselves. Despite widespread public and political discourses constructing both groups as outsiders and marginal economic actors, Senegalese and Roma traders emerge as profoundly integrated in urban and regional commercial relations and flows. Nevertheless, their divergent migration trajectories and social and financial organization, as well as the different representations of their alterity within Italian society, produce highly differentiated investment, accumulation, and sales strategies. Rather than sectors of relegation and exclusion, the informal markets within which our ethnographies are located provide an ever-shifting landscape of daily negotiations. Movable arrangements are made with the law and its representatives, while bodily, social, and financial resources are activated within a balance of visible and invisible temporalities. It is through the variable (in)visibilities of informal and clandestine trades that new light can be shone on how value chains operate. For example, in the symbolic transition of a handbag that is created through the opaque production practices of a *fake* but acquires the connotations of *real/authentic* once it is exposed in a licensed shop. It is also within these in-between spaces and contested arenas that value most clearly emerges in its essence as a process of meaning-making that engages both individual and official ethics.

In his analysis of liminality, understood as "the experience of finding oneself at a boundary or in an in-between position, either spatially or temporally," Bjørn Thomassen (2015: 40) underlines the social connotations of individual and collective experiences of such threshold states. Borrowing from Van Gennep (2004) and Turner (1967), he highlights the centrality of processes of transitioning from one social status or condition to another. He thus correctly identifies similarities between apparently heterogeneous phenomena such as mourning, puberty, political minorities, carnival, and revolutions, which he considers states where the social norm is suspended, that is, liminal ones (Thomassen 2015: 48–49). In the specific cases of Roma and Senegalese traders, liminal conditions manifest themselves in so far as these actors base their trades on relationships and interdependencies within multiple sociopolitical contexts in-between which, and on whose borders, they operate. These interrelations concern the practical organization of their sourcing and resale networks and the commercial choices they make, such as their debt/credit relations and their management of risk. However, they also reveal differing scales of value through the discrepancies between how they depict their activities and how these are instead portrayed in public rhetorics on illegality. Roma see themselves as providing a social service through recycling secondhand goods in neighborhood flea markets, while Senegalese traders are involved in political claims-making through regional and national labor union activities, for example, mobilizing against exploitation of migrant agricultural workers. They participate in national political debates as active subjects, while nevertheless remaining illegal subjects and a minority. We consequently borrow the concept of "moral economy" (Carrier 2018; Fassin 2009), understood as a dynamic network of interactions and adjustments occurring within value scales that are imbricated in everyday life, rather than as a set of homogeneous norms emanating from a given community (Keane 2019). Our ethnographic lens reveals the disconnect between self-perceptions and public representations in the context of claiming rights. We thus analyze the junctures between how these groups are made visible and invisible in public representations and the variety of strategies that make up their daily lives, comparing the materiality of processes through which they are objectified as illegal subjects with the emic dimensions of their trades.

THE SOCIAL ORGANIZATION OF SOURCING MERCHANDISE

The Senegalese community in Italy is mostly made up of men (73%) and constitutes the largest sub-Saharan African population in the country, ranking thirteenth among foreign nationals (MdL 2017b).[5] Employment levels are higher than the average rate among immigrants, with 68% formally employed;[6] it is the fifth most active in terms of entrepreneurship and the third highest (after Filipinos and Bangladeshis) in volume of remittances.[7] Between January 2016 and September 2018 the Senegalese community alone sent 853,766 million euro from Italy in remittances.[8] In 2016, there were 2,167 Senegalese formally resident in Rome, over 80% of them men.[9] They tend to live in small or medium-sized groups (ranging from 3 to 20 people under one roof), often originating from the same towns in Senegal. These traders are highly mobile both nationally and internationally, generally traveling for 4–6 months a year. In Rome, they are spread throughout numerous and often distant neighborhoods, most notably Pigneto, Torpignattara, Boccea, and Salario. In the over 200 interviews from which we draw, it was possible to trace complete individual biographies of 156 traders between 2012 and 2018.[10] Of these, 115 currently have legal residency permits while 18 lost theirs between 2013 and 2015 due to legal proceedings connected to their sale of counterfeit goods. Two also spent time in prison. The individualized paths of Senegalese migration profoundly shape traders' commercial dynamics, which are characterized by intense mobility and adaptability.

Since most Senegalese migrants work for themselves and are not inserted in close-knit kinship or other trade alliances, they build much looser intergenerational relationships than those developed among Roma. All the interviewees were exempted from paying board and lodging during their first two or three months in Italy in order to invest in stock. As one Senegalese seller of African art in Rome put it, "when Senegalese people arrive in a new country, if they don't have anything, they will sell their watch to start up a business" (Interview 04/07/2011, Esquilino). Those who lack their own funds are given credit in the form of objects to sell by relatives or small traders already integrated in distribution circuits for craftwork and counterfeits. These objects are loaned at a fixed price; whatever profit the vendor makes on top of that is his to keep. This reflects initial accumulation strategies widespread in many market sectors in Francophone West Africa. Senegalese traders differ from Roma ones also because of highly diversified accumulation patterns: one young Senegalese trader who sells various categories of goods (tourist art, commissioned copies of bronze statues, but also illegal wares such as fake Rolex watches) is able to make a greater profit than an artisan with more years of experience whose atelier is in Dakar and who therefore limits his economic risks to a single commercial channel. A number of Senegalese migrants who arrived in Italy in 1980s first began by selling socks, underwear, and lighters before they went on to integrate informal and illegal goods.[11] The trajectory of Moustapha[12] provides some interesting insights into the dynamics of what can be considered the first phase of Senegalese migration to Italy (1980–1989). Moustapha comes from a family of pharmacists in Dakar; he left Senegal in 1989 with a little over one million FCFA: 700,000 provided by his father and 350,000 accumulated as savings.[13] At that time, 125,000 FCFA (equivalent to approximately 190 euro today) were enough to apply for a residency permit.[14] According to him, at the end of the 1980s there were still few Senegalese in Rome and they only sold craftwork in the streets.[15] After two weeks in Rome, Moustapha moved to a town in Central Italy, where he started selling cigarette lighters while taking Italian language courses offered by the CISL trade union.[16] Since only tobacconist shops were licensed to sell lighters, any alternative sales circuits were illegal. During his first weeks Moustapha was exempted from contributing to his household's grocery shopping. He began with an initial inventory of 25 boxes of lighters, worth 125,000 lire (about 60 euro), bought from a Senegalese wholesaler. Each box bought at 5,000 lire was resold for 10,000; on good days he could sell almost a whole box in 24 hours. He subsequently turned to wholesalers in San Marino, whose prices were much lower (75,000 lire per box). In less than two months, Moustapha transitioned to becoming a wholesaler himself, selling boxes of lighters for 120,000 lire each. While in San Marino, he saw the first Zippo lighters stocked by his suppliers; these were not yet available on the streets of his town of residence. Local tobacconist shops sold them for 50,000 lire while his wholesaler provided them for 3,000 each. Moustapha thus began selling them in the streets for 25,000 lire, supported by his San Marino supplier who, out of friendship, ensured that he had a monopoly of Zippos in his town which he alternated with the "normal" [*sic*] Bic lighters. Moustapha invested part of the ensuing income in a Renault 18 car for 2,500,000 lire, allowing him to avoid taking the train and thus lowering his risk of being stopped by the Financial police (*Guardia di Finanza*).

In the subsequent decade, new Senegalese traders in Italy instead tended to launch businesses directly through selling counterfeits; primarily DVDs and CDs, before transitioning, after a few years of experience, into bags and other fashion accessories. At the end of the 1990s, however, sale of counterfeit bags was still quite rare and the market was predominantly for "sunglasses, watches, lighters and, more recently, pirated CDs" (Riccio 2000: 22). Partly due to the changes in media technologies by the early 2000s, the new arrivals generally entered the market by selling belts, scarves, and wallets which required a less onerous initial investment than bags and shoes. At the time of the fieldwork, Senegalese vendors generally bought 4,000–6,000 euros of goods weekly or biweekly from wholesalers, although these quantities could increase to 8,000–9,000 euros with intensified tourism in the summer months. A wallet bought from a wholesaler cost a street vendor 8–10 euros, compared to 20–25 euros on average for the cheapest bags. Many of those involved in selling counterfeits soon came into contact with wholesalers in the region of Campania, especially in Naples and its environs, and Florence. The wares go through numerous transnational movements, originating in China and, more recently, in Senegal, and flowing into Italian ports, especially Genoa, Livorno, Naples, and Salerno. Those vendors who are able to make large-scale profits or obtain significant loans often become wholesalers themselves.

In this case, many sources came straight from Chinese producers in Italy or stock ordered from Greece and Turkey, thus bypassing Italian middlemen.[17] The physical mobility of these goods is matched by entrepreneurial fluidity between typologies of commercial activity.

The trade chain requires diversification of merchandise and the maintenance of fluid distribution channels, accommodating a variety of objects of disparate origin and levels of legality. Those who move from street vending to wholesale tend to keep the same categories of goods (bags and accessories) but may shift to different elements within the same production chain; for example, a counterfeit bag vendor may choose to convert to selling fake fashion brand tags and labels. Some do, however, move into other counterfeit sectors, such as watches. A second category of business mobility emerges with those who switch from craftwork to counterfeits or vice versa. In this latter case, they transition from a trade that is entirely illegal in Italy (unlicensed sale of "fakes") to a hybrid one (unlicensed sale of artisanal goods that are not banned). A third option is to manage businesses in Italy and Senegal in parallel. When counterfeit trades allow capital accumulation dynamics, income sources multiply, for example, by setting up a shop, farm, taxi firm, or import/export of spare parts for cars and household appliances. This requires traders' intense mobility along the distribution chain; for example, wholesalers travel back to Africa various times a year to source new artisanal goods, in some cases commissioning family members to produce sculptures for sale on the Italian market.[18] In some rare cases, objects are crafted directly in Italy by sculptors who have been resident there for many years.

From their neighborhoods in Rome, these migrants operate within a vast local and national-level social context populated by a range of Italian actors: customers, shopkeepers, wholesalers, civil society organizations, public institutions, small entrepreneurs, labor unions, state authorities. Relations of trust are developed early on with locals who rent them garages and other places to store stock and with Italian wholesalers who often allow vendors to prolong repayment deadlines. Those who have been sourcing from Neapolitan wholesalers for about 20 years can now obtain as much as 40,000 euros worth of goods on credit, with repayment times that range from a week to a month.[19] In some cases where a vendor has not been able to honor a debt due to unforeseen events, such as health problems, Italian merchants have even cancelled thousands of euros of debt. Apart from the friendships underlying such behavior, the fact of wiping a debt fosters gratitude that reinforces the relations of dependency between buyer and supplier which, in turn, strengthens their collaboration and limits the risk of the buyer turning to another distributor. It is notable that most of the interviewees underlined the friendly welcome they received from Neapolitan wholesalers from their very first encounters and the gestures of courtesy that usually characterize their transactions, such as sharing a coffee, an invitation to lunch or during the festivities, a lift in the car to Rome. When relations are consolidated, the merchant may even help the Senegalese client economically when faced with various family expenses (gifts, funeral costs), sometimes going as far as to invest in parallel businesses such as buying a taxi, a restaurant, or land in Senegal and occasionally becoming a partner in the firm. In addition to facilitating access to credit, trust relations also affect the price of merchandise, especially at the high end of the market, such as Louis Vuitton or Liu-Jo bags which can cost as much as 120–130 euro each wholesale.[20] For example, Alioune, who has been trading in counterfeit bags for almost 30 years, is well known among Italian and Chinese suppliers, allowing him to obtain lower prices than other middlemen. A further, albeit indirect, feature of integration is the fact that some Neapolitans who supply Senegalese informal traders with counterfeit shoes and bags also provide stock to regularly licensed Italian shopkeepers. According to one Senegalese watch dealer, this also goes for "fake" Rolexes sold in Italian stores for 100–200 euro each.[21]

The patterns of social organization, mobility, and financial accumulation of Roma in Rome are profoundly different from those discussed above. Clear demographic data does not exist because of the diversity of nationalities involved (Italy does not systematically collect ethnic-specific data: ISTAT 2017) and the fact that a significant part of the population is undocumented or de facto stateless. Nevertheless, the Italian government estimates that there are between 120,000 and 180,000 Roma, Sinti, and Caminanti living in Italy, half of whom are Italian citizens (PCM 2012). These groups are highly differentiated and generally do not consider themselves a single ethnic grouping. Indeed, the shorthand umbrella term "Roma," with which a broad variety of sub- and related groups are designated, conceals great heterogeneity among people who define themselves as such or are labeled thus by outsiders. Nevertheless, they share a history of social, spatial, and economic marginalization in Italy which has resulted in them experiencing similar challenges to inclusion and often developing similar responses. Around 40,000 people are originally from former Yugoslavia, having mostly migrated to Italy between the 1960s and 1990s. Consequently, many members of this group—including the community discussed here—have been resident in the country for decades, with second, third and, in some cases, fourth generations born there. Despite this long-term presence, only a small proportion have been able to naturalize as Italian citizens due to ambiguities in their documents determined by the breakup of Yugoslavia as well as Italy's increasingly restrictive residency and naturalization legislation for non-EU migrants, especially those lacking long-term employment contracts.

As has been widely documented (Sigona 2005; PCM 2012; Clough Marinaro 2014; ECRI 2016), deep-rooted prejudice against Roma in Italy intertwines with the fact that a high proportion (approximately 26,000, of which 9,600 from former Yugoslavia) live in conditions of "housing emergency" in camps of various types (Associazione 21 luglio 2017).[22] The largest number of such camps, both those provided by the municipality and unauthorized self-built ones, is located in Rome, housing around 6,900 people (ibid). These are generally positioned in isolated locations on the urban fringes, adding spatial exclusion to the legal complexities of their residents. These factors, combined with widespread hostility, mean that many Roma are—circularly—unable to access registered employment that would allow them to more easily resolve problems of documentation and obtain mainstream housing. Consequently, numerous reports underline that camp-dwelling Roma are extremely underrepresented in the legal labor force (Fondazione Casa della Carità 2012;[23] PCM 2012; ISTAT 2017[24]). The lack of formal data hides a reality of widespread informal entrepreneurship present within Roma communities in Rome. Generally, this is organized through the participation of various members of extended family groups who tend to live close together for reasons of sociality and mutual support, but also because their physical proximity facilitates the logistical and spatial management of their work. While camp conditions are highly problematic and their isolation exacerbates difficulties in accessing services and business networks, they do present a number of social and economic advantages. The case-study camp is emblematic of this intertwining of liminal housing situations and the organization of informal economic activities. It has long been *tolerated* by the municipal authorities but is now officially slated for demolition. Positioned on isolated wasteland beyond the city ring-road, with countryside behind and the nearest residential area 2 kilometers away, it does not immediately appear connected to Rome's economic and social fabric. Yet, the numerous vans parked within, the overflowing dumpsters across the road, and the frequent coming-and-going of visitors, belie this impression.

A further paradoxical benefit of the camp's marginalized and unofficial housing status is the municipality's refusal to connect it to the electricity and water grid. This means that residents have very few overhead costs beyond food, mobile phone expenses, car insurance, and petrol. This factor contributes to an overall economic model which is fast, highly precarious and fluid, low in investment, and equally low in accumulation. The approximately 100 people who live there divide themselves into two large extended family groupings, with clear spatial boundaries between them that demark deep social and economic tensions. Each area is laid out to ensure that families who work together are geographically close, creating spaces between the shacks and camper vans in which to strip, clean, reassemble, and stockpile materials. Unlike the Senegalese vendors who specialize in limited typologies of products, these traders work with a vast range of goods, mostly sourced without any financial outlay.[25] These include metals, construction tools and materials, electronic equipment, clothing, toys, home furnishings, often gleaned from their expansive network of personal contacts. Indeed, despite endemic anti-Roma prejudice, the individual community members have woven extensive relationships with residents throughout the city, thanks to outreach from NGOs and religious organizations and friendships forged at school and in the neighborhood. Their long-term residence in the area has facilitated this: they settled in the camp in the early 1990s, although some families were already living in tents and camper vans scattered nearby a decade earlier. In contrast to the stereotype of Roma's alleged nomadism, it has been this geographical rootedness that has enabled them to build the local social capital necessary for their entrepreneurial operations. Indeed, while various studies highlight the centrality of circular migration for many Roma entrepreneurs who trade between Italy and their countries of origin (Cingolani 2011; Solimene 2014; Agoni 2016; Tosi Cambini 2016), this particular group has lost most ties with their hometowns.

Although international travel is rare, these traders are regionally very mobile, traveling to other areas of the Lazio region whenever work opportunities present themselves. They also traverse vast distances within the city to source goods or negotiate deals. The activities carried out by Mirko over the last 25 years exemplify the fluidity of goods and trade channels and the entrepreneurial intertwinement of family members. Having successfully completed middle school, he began working as a teenager in the early 1990s, buying roses in bulk from wholesalers and selling them to tourists in the city center.[26] As competition from other migrants intensified and sales dwindled by mid-decade, he used his same contacts in the plant distribution system to instead buy bonsai trees that he resold in the commercial streets of residential neighborhoods near his camp.[27] Once demand for these plants waned, he began to buy wholesale materials to make sand pictures in glass bottles, and involved his siblings, nephews, and nieces in assembling them. These, again, he sold to acquaintances in nearby areas, as did his younger relatives whenever they could get a lift from the camp. Meanwhile, he obtained a stable cleaning job in a local parish church which enabled him to build up further relations of trust. Although he eventually gave up the job to pursue other opportunities—a choice he has since regretted—the five years spent there proved a great asset in enhancing his relational networks in ways that continue to pay off. From the late 1990s to 2014 he traveled widely with his brother-in-law through Rome and nearby towns, responding to phone calls from contacts asking them to pick up their bulky waste or scouting for abandoned metals in illegal waste dumps or outside construction sites.

While multiple goods were gleaned, to be traded within their long-established network of shopkeepers and friends, the core income came from metals sold to scrap dealers. Before being sold on, metals and other bulky items involve significant physical labor to strip off plastic, break them down, and harvest still functioning motors or electronic parts. This activity requires both open spaces to store and work the materials safely, and the availability of a flexible number of helpers. The income made by Mirko and his brother-in-law not only covers the immediate expenses of their respective nuclear families but also integrates that made by Mirko's mother and two sisters through begging. The past half decade has, however, forced further change in strategies for sourcing and reselling goods. Since around 2012, the prices offered by scrap metal dealers have fallen from 25 cents per kilogram to the current 8–10 cents per kilogram, while at the same time, Italy's struggling economy since 2008 had generated competition from a growing number of other gleaners. Tightening regulations in the scrap metal sector and crackdowns on informal sales have further reduced the viability of this trade (Clough Marinaro 2018). Instead, Mirko and his partner now exploit the full range of networks, regional and local, developed over the decades, to collect whatever secondhand goods are available: unused paints, tools and wood from building sites, unsold stock from wholesalers. Other odd jobs that they are commissioned to do, such as clearing cellars, reap the double benefit of cash payment and objects to sell. The stock collected through these multiple streams is covered in plastic and stored briefly in the open areas of the camp, before being taken to a flea market for resale. Disused construction materials and other bulky waste are illegally dumped across the street by outsiders, providing further free goods to be mined. As with every other good that they source, the families first evaluate whether they are of immediate domestic utility; better quality window frames for their shacks, containers to plant flowers in, and so on (see Figure 5.1). They simultaneously assess each item's potential value for resale, effecting a cost-benefit analysis of the relative labor, time and petrol expenditure, and their probable profit. Whatever is deemed unlikely to appeal to the tastes of their habitual buyers is returned to the dumpster. Two typologies of goods emerge from this filtering process: a mass of small household objects (stickers, picture frames, toys) to be sold at the market; and a range of products that they collect systematically, knowing that they can resell them in bulk directly to middlemen. These include collectors' items for the Italian market, such as vintage comics, old sewing machines, cameras and TVs, and goods sourced by migrants for export. The latter often collect the goods—tools, spare parts for domestic appliances, sports shoes—directly from the camp. Some of these traders are Senegalese; it is here that the two otherwise separate local/global trade flows discussed in this chapter intersect.

Figure 5.1 Objects Dumped or Stored Near the Camp, Awaiting Evaluation for Domestic Use or Sale. *Source*: Photo by Isabella Clough Marinaro.

RESALE: TEMPORALITIES AND SPACE

The above section demonstrates how an ethnographic approach to informal and illegal trades reveals extensive forms of social integration despite the political role attributed to counterfeit sellers as illegal and marginal actors.[28] Nevertheless, the lack of authorization for the goods they sell does profoundly condition the resale practices of both groups. The illegality of counterfeits makes Senegalese vendors particularly vulnerable to police intervention when they display their merchandise, and Roma's frequent lack of legal documentation, both for themselves and their goods, also forces them to develop commercial strategies that reduce exposure to police fines and confiscations. In this section, therefore, we explore the different ways in which the temporal and spatial organization and material practices of resale are determined by the liminal status of the wares and the dominant representations of illegality of both groups.[29]

Senegalese vendors who trade in counterfeits must do so by positioning themselves fleetingly on the street, timed according to the reduced likelihood of municipal police patrols. They therefore mostly display their goods at lunchtime (between 1 and 3 p.m.) or after 6 p.m. Rather than set up stalls, they use a white sheet which is easy to fold, along with *rambo* bags (often large Ikea ones) to move the goods, should they need to hurriedly "*plier bagage*" (pack up) to avoid the police. At times they simply hold the goods in their hands to accelerate their escape. Street sales, but also interactions with wholesalers, can be carried out in just a few minutes, often by appointment, thereby enabling them to keep their goods out of sight in the back of a car. Due to the fragmented temporal nature of these transactions, the relational spaces of Senegalese vendors are much more mobile and transitory than those of Roma. This is also linked to the transnational scope of their trade chains and diversification of income sources. Indeed, their multiple business activities are not only the result of individual and family entrepreneurial plans (e.g., opening a shop for relatives in Senegal), but simultaneously respond to a need to cushion the inevitable losses made when the authorities seize their merchandise. The risk of confiscation and forfeiture of their invested capital is the reason why some Senegalese migrants in the 1990s preferred the physical effort of selling along the beaches of Rimini to using fixed sales locations, thereby limiting their potential losses to the goods they could carry on their backs (Riccio 1999).

Risk is managed through very different strategies by Roma traders. The danger of their work arises—paradoxically, given their stereotypical labeling as nomads—from their territorial stability in the city. The presence of entire family groupings in Rome and the absence of a transnational escape route mean that exposure to the police must be reduced as much as possible. It is for this reason that members of the camp avoid illegal activities where they can. While a few individuals sporadically deal drugs and fence stolen goods, limiting their clients to trusted personal contacts and transacting in the seclusion of their homes, this is frowned upon by others who view it as unnecessarily exposing the whole community to vulnerability. Indeed, past cases of high-profile arrests triggered threats from the municipality to evict the entire camp: a possibility which persists given its liminal legal status. Maintaining a low profile is therefore essential to family stability and cohesion. Roma's centuries-old essentialization as criminal actors is materialized in camps as the perceived fulcrum of illegal activities, in public opinion and policy approaches.[30] The high urban visibility of their housing gives Roma a traceability that dispersed and mobile Senegalese vendors can avoid,[31] while the inherent precarity of living in such liminal environments conditions the declared desire of many of their residents to achieve financial and operational stability. Part of the reason for preferring the collection and resale of household goods rather than bulky metals, for example, is its transportability by car rather than the far more obtrusive vans that are more likely to be stopped by the police and their contents scrutinized for documentary evidence of their origin. While the objects themselves are not illegal, they rarely conform to the complex bureaucratic requirements for collection, transportation, and sale of "waste" materials and secondhand goods and are thus vulnerable to confiscation (Santilli 2017; Clough Marinaro 2018).

In contrast to Senegalese vendors' fleeting commercial encounters with their clients, many of them tourists passing through, it is the relative predictability and possibility of controlling their sales environment that appeals to many Roma sellers. Their preferred flea market is a semiformal one located in a nearby peripheral residential area which offers temporal regularity—it opens twice a week, from dawn to noon—and attracts loyal clients who live or work in the western quadrant of the city: migrants and impoverished Romans who source toys, household necessities, and work materials there, as well as wealthier vintage collectors and antiques dealers scouting for any valuable new arrivals. While Roma vendors are able to avoid capital investment in stock required of Senegalese traders, their investment is in time. The rhythms of the market are slow: an hour can be spent on hard bargaining over an antique lamp, a client commissions a set of goods over a drawn-out coffee, friendly conversations extract detailed knowledge of buyers' tastes and interests. Goods are displayed with this information in mind; the same objects will only appear a few times before being relegated to the dumpster, their temporariness dictated both by their low exchange value and the fact that storage space at the camp must be cleared for the next delivery of goods. What at first glance may appear a collection of random objects on a stall—art books, dolls, electronic components, ornaments, shoes, and jackets; a mass of homogeneously valued junk—is in fact calculated to appeal to clients' potential preferences and needs. Thus, a carved wooden (and slightly battered) swordfish is prominently displayed in the hopes of appealing as potential décor for a fish shop or restaurant, while donated clothes and accessories are often discarded unless they carry fashionable brands. In this, Roma claim that they indirectly compete with counterfeit vendors, stating that customers prefer secondhand *authentic* fashion-label goods to new *fakes*. They also assert that there is a significant demand for stolen high-brand goods (cameras, jewelry, perfumes, and accessories) which is in part catered to by mobile and furtive vendors operating outside the market's gates. Roma who instead work within the market very rarely sell any stolen goods, well aware that plain clothes police monitor the space.[32]

Just as apparently undifferentiated junk in fact reveals complex evaluations of objects' symbolic and financial value, so the discursive homogenization of Roma poverty and social exclusion advanced in media and political portrayals is contradicted in the market's sociospatial organization. Internal hierarchies of wealth and urban rootedness among Roma groups are reflected in its layout: those with long-established relations in the city were able to register early for market stalls and to negotiate higher-visibility sales spots than more recent arrivals, especially Romanians.[33] Indeed, the social and cultural capital of historically settled actors is closely tied to the circulation and the value of goods: their extensive social networks enable them to source more profitable items, while others are less able to offer a diversity of merchandise and to display it profitably.

Thus, Senegalese traders produce trajectories of progressive investment; the temporal and spatial frames of their economic activities are extensive, with goods bought on protracted credit, transported across great geographical distances involving high shipping costs, and potentially stockpiled for long periods. It is the transnational nature of these high-investment, high-profit strategies which ensure that businesses in Senegal and Rome support each other: risks in one location are sustained by profits generated in the other. Roma operations are the opposite. Financial investment is minimal; these actors are gleaners, receivers, and sorters of goods, not investors. Theirs is a hand-to-mouth economy, with the cash earned spent almost immediately on food and short-term needs of all family members. Their risks concern time wasted if goods are confiscated and, more importantly, the danger of upheaval of their very precarious family budget if they are arrested, or their vehicles impounded, and the even greater physical precarity if evicted.

OBJECTIFYING ILLEGAL BODIES

Corporeality is a core dimension of the trade activities, simultaneously involving the criminal connotation attributed to the vendors, and the ways in which they represent their work and the ethics of risk associated with it. The *resistant* body is exposed together with the goods: where there is merchandise, the body is equally present in its gestures, words, attention to the customer, and to everything occurring nearby. In the case of Senegalese vendors, it is with the body that one carries wares along streets and beaches, runs when the police arrive, exposes oneself not only to the authorities but also, in places like Naples, to criminal groups who control local sales turfs.[34] All of this plays out in a state of continuous day-to-day precarity which becomes, in the eyes of its actors, the measure of their tenacity, sense of responsibility, acceptance of risk, and thus of their ethical value. This bodily dimension of ethics, which is shared by other marginal actors such as Malian gold-diggers and antiquities farmer-diggers (Panella 2007, 2014), is in sharp contrast with their official construction as "illegal subjects" with which not only their merchandise but also their bodies are marked, given their frequent lack of legal documents. These constitute moral economies in that the illegal/

informal nature of the commercial activities requires assuming risks (which can extend to deportation or imprisonment) and the consequent management of relations of trust.

Since in-depth ethnographic studies on the circulation of informal and illegal goods are still rare (Panella 2002; Aguiar 2013; Hansen et al. 2014; Crăciun 2014; Galemba 2017), there is a tendency both in academia and popular narratives to portray sale of stolen goods, fakes, and discarded objects as a single and largely undifferentiated gray market (Mackenzie and Yates 2016). Our ethnographic data demonstrates that traders' commercial strategies are based on evaluations of the relative costs and benefits of operating within sectors of differential (il)legality. An intrinsic component of these migrant vendors' calculations is the varied ways in which they are reified as illegal subjects. Recent scholarship demonstrates that Roma are perceived more negatively in Italy than migrants generally: prejudice toward Roma is chronic and "open, direct, racist, full of negative emotions like reject[ion] and fear" (Fontanella et al. 2016: 487). In terms of group-specific stereotypes, both Roma and Senegalese are subjected to criminalization, but in different ways: Roma are widely associated with theft, burglaries, their mere presence assumed to "cause criminality" (Villano et al. 2017: 35). Sub-Saharan Africans are subjected to frequent racial profiling by police, although the presence of Senegalese in Italian jails is around 0.48% (Gonnella 2018), and they appear to be targeted by less extreme generalized prejudice than Roma.

This symbolic emphasis on the absolute illegality of counterfeit goods is complicated by the ambiguous status of Senegalese actors in Italy. Some interviewees report that various Senegalese conationals operate in criminal environments. Our ethnographic data, however, does not point to specific subordinate relations of the traders to Italian organized crime. Various Senegalese actors have achieved visibility in civil society organizations that campaign against exploitative work or housing conditions. The case of the evictions of Senegalese migrants who had been renting at exploitatively high prices in two buildings in the Pigneto neighborhood is particularly cogent. A first eviction was annulled in June 2011 by the Lazio administrative court (TAR), declaring the street a Social Protection Zone (*Zona a Tutela Sociale*). Nevertheless, on February 19, 2019, the Financial Police (*Guardia di Finanza*) definitively evicted 15 Senegalese citizens who still lived there, after various individuals were found with counterfeit goods. The repeated evictions, ostensibly due to precarious structural conditions, appear more plausibly connected to the gentrification interests of local real estate owners as well as authorities' conviction that one of the buildings was a base for storage and sale of counterfeit bags and accessories (see Figure 5.2). In both cases, neighborhood residents and associations protested actively in support of migrants' housing and work rights.[35] These demands for legality, asserted by *illegal* subjects (some of them directly targeted by police in the Via Campobasso evictions), underline how integration in informal markets is often accompanied by claims of belonging and citizenship on the part of migrants as ways of coping with liminal situations of semilegality (Kubal 2013).

The ways in which Roma navigate the variable opportunities for inclusion through informal circuits are marked by their much more defined and crystallized *aura of illegality* than that of Senegalese migrants. For example, Roma are the only ethnic group in Rome for which a targeted police unit exists (*Gruppo Sicurezza Pubblica ed Emergenziale*, *Polizia Locale di Roma Capitale*). While their dominant portrayal as criminals in Italy is partly juxtaposed by romanticized views of their alleged freedom, the latter characteristics are naturalizing ones that do not mitigate perceptions of their deviance in relations with outsiders (Villano et al., 2017). Despite some civil society demonstrations to counter their criminalization in Rome, sometimes in alliance with NGOs (e.g., Lisi 2018), on the whole Roma make less use of rights-based claims for inclusion than Senegalese actors. Instead, the group studied here organizes its work in direct response to criminal labels, honing strategies to become "less illegal" by seeking to demonstrate their "deservingness" through "traces of long-term presence and good conduct" (Chauvin and Garcés-Mascareñas 2014: 422). By anchoring themselves socially in the neighborhood, by developing less informal ways of trading through

Figure 5.2 Pigneto, Neighborhood with a mural by Mr. Klevra. *Source*: Photo by Cristiana Panella, 2015.

registering with a semiauthorized flea market, and by avoiding explicitly criminal trades, they thus seek to become less evictable or deportable (see Van Baar 2017). The discrepancy that emerges between the images of illegality of the two groups and the concrete legal status of their daily transactions is not coincidental, therefore, but reflects the ties between real economic trajectories and political representations of (non)citizenship.

The tendency to conflate undocumented migration with unauthorized trade continues to this day, expressed in many initiatives by national and regional government as well as by consumer and producer associations. The same message is also conveyed in some sociological literature, such as Izzi's (2010) claim that counterfeiting is one of a series of interconnected trades, along with drugs and migrant smuggling, managed by Italian organized criminals, without, however, providing data from the field. Even in situations where the link between immigration and illegal trades is demonstrated, ethnographic evidence points to a reality that is nuanced and in constant flux. For example, while illegal immigration was a dominant source of income in the 1990s for organized crime, since 2000 the counterfeits market has overtaken it, in part due to the growing importance of the port of Naples for Chinese imports and exports (Becucci 2011). In the case of Senegalese traders working in Naples, while it is true that the supply of counterfeit goods is managed by the Camorra at all stages of the production and distribution chain (ibid), our findings show that in Rome street traders and small wholesalers work individually and autonomously.

CONCLUSIONS

Through an ethnographic approach to Roma and Senegalese communities in Rome, we have illustrated the role played by informal and illegal trades in their social integration, due to the liminal status of the actors and their sales channels. Senegalese vendors are strategic entrepreneurs, operating within a relational network set up for economic autonomy and, where possible, accumulation. Roma adopt an opposite approach, working collectively and seeking to redefine the terms of their intense visibility. On the one hand, their transportation practices strive for invisibility from the authorities because of the legal ambiguity of their goods; on the other, gleaning merchandise depends on visibility, as do sales. Their visibility actively contests the ways in which Roma tend to be cast through popular representations (evictions, arrests, criminality frames) by performing "deservingness" (Chauvin and Darcés-Mascareñas 2014). Theirs is not merely a reaction or adaptation to how they are overarchingly represented politically and culturally. However, they act on their own terms, as a means of maintaining autonomy by organizing their own work rhythms and relationships. The liminal conditions within which these actors operate should therefore not be read as merely passive ones, forged by dynamics of political and social discrimination—although these are of course present. They are active in that the people involved develop modes of adaptation that oscillate between visibility (the exposure of illegal bodies and goods) to carry out their commerce, and invisibility. This is epitomized in the traceless trust-based bonds upon which relations of debt and credit are founded, the means through which value is measured, and the strategies honed for managing risk.

Heterogeneous trajectories of migration determine spaces of absence and emergence, where absence, according to the conceptualization advanced by Bonaventura de Sousa Santos (de Sousa Santos 2002, 2007), is viewed as a state of social and/or political underrepresentation that creates 'emergent' dynamics of creation and social change (Panella 2012). This perspective stands as an alternative to a linear approach to time and infers the existence of *in fieri* temporalities, nonetheless constituting full-fledged epistemological states in their own right. There is an urgent need to develop and to articulate anthropologically informed approaches to the nature of markets and to the degree to which they can come to rely upon culture-dependent types of political representation. The absence of links between the legal discourse and the daily life of the migrants perpetuates the cleavage between real economic trajectories and political representations of citizenship. In this sense, Senegalese traders could be considered as "shadow groups" because they display no economic visibility and identify themselves collectively as resisting infringements by the State. Within this context, ethnographic evidence suggests that a component of moral economies lies in the discrepancy between how actors perceive their business, based on strategic planning that involves managing trust relations and risk, and the essentialist representations of "illegal subjects" by the authorities and the media that do not recognize the ethical nature of corporeality within the individual migratory trajectories. Because of their marginal status, therefore, these actors participate in socially and juridically heterogeneous contexts through various gradations of formal, informal, and illegal economies. This confirms, as Chauvin and Garcés-Mascareñas (2014: 426) have also noted, that the "gradational character of (il)legality" does not simply produce exclusion, and that migrants do not only integrate in informal networks but also formal ones. The multiple strategies and experiences involved in the informal and illegal trades discussed above highlight how inclusion and exclusion overlap in the vast terrain of informality and reveal how the construction and management of official norms implies structural links with informal and illegal spheres.

NOTES

1. We are very grateful to Bjørn Thomassen for his contribution to this discussion (see Clough Marinaro and Thomassen 2014). Isabella Clough Marinaro assisted with translations in the chapter.

2. Estimated at 130 billion euro, the gross value added of migrant workers in Italy alone outweighs the entire GDP of countries such as Hungary, Croatia, and Slovenia (FLM 2017, based on Eurostat data).

3. See the Special Section of *Cities* (95, 2019 and 96, 2020) dedicated to this issue. A crucial discussion of Roma economies across Europe is provided in Brazzabeni et al. (2016).

4. The study brings together data collected through long-term fieldwork by the two authors: on the one hand, over 200 interviews mostly held between 2011 and 2015 (a few in 2018) with Senegalese wholesalers and street vendors of craftwork and counterfeit goods navigating informal and illegal trade networks that span from the neighborhood to the intercontinental level. On the other hand, 20 years of ethnographic research within a community of around 100 Roma individals originally from former Yugoslavia residing in a "nomad camp" in Rome. The capillary reach of the interviews in the Senegalese community in Rome was achieved thanks to the constant support of local assistants. Cristiana Pelliccetti (Progetto Diritti, Pigneto), Alessandra Conte, and the late Dario Simonetti (Comitato di quartiere Pigneto Prenestino e CSOA-Snia) also provided invaluable help and insights.

The term "resident" is used here broadly to refer to migrants living in Rome with a residency permit, those waiting for a permit, and those who lack documents and are consequently invisible in administrative records.

5. MdL (Ministero del Lavoro e delle Politiche Sociali) 2017b. "La comunità senegalese in Italia", http://www.lavoro.gov.it/documenti-e-norme/studi-e-statistiche/Documents/Rapporti%20annuali%20sulle%20comunit%C3%A0%20migranti%20in%20Italia%20-%20anno%202017/Senegal-Report-2017.pdf, accessed January 14, 2019.

6. As opposed to 50% average employment among officially resident foreigners MdL (Ministero del Lavoro e delle Politiche Sociali) 2017b.

7. The MdL 2017b study only considers documented residents. On remittances by the Bangladeshi community, see Rahaman and Kabir (2012).

8. Bank of Italy, http://www.bancaditalia.it/statistiche/tematiche/rapporti-estero/rimesse-immigrati/, accessed January 29, 2019.

9. Comuni-Italiani, http://www.comuni-italiani.it/statistiche/stranieri/sn.html, accessed November 29, 2020. Among the fieldwork informants, very few live in Rome with their wife or partner; the majority cohabit with relatives or friends they already knew in Senegal. Only two traders interviewed are women.

10. Twenty-five of the people interviewed have since returned to Senegal and seven others have died. Considering the instability of counterfeit street trade, the extreme mobility of Senegalese migrants, and the different types of residency documents, these statistics simply indicate contingent patterns and do not aim to be generalizable.

11. Among the interviewees, the first group arrived in Rome between 1987 and 1989 (except two people who came in 1981 and 1982).

12. All names have been changed to protect anonymity.

13. *Franc de la Communauté Financière Africaine.*

14. Law 39, passed in February 1990 and known as the "Legge Martelli," was the first legislative attempt to regulate migratory flows into Italy by regularizing those who were already present in the country on December 31, 1989, and introducing entry visas. The number of documented Africans thus more than doubled, from 99,878 in 1989 to 238,130 in 1990, http://www.adir.unifi.it/rivista/2000/dibello/cap1.htm, accessed October 29, 2018.

15. Two traders sold African art on the Porta Portese flea market: the first one died in the early 2000s; the second one was around 75 years old in 2012; the others were itinerant street vendors.

16. It is interesting to note that Moustapha was viewed with suspicion by the first Senegalese he met in this town, who advised him to swap his elegant clothing for more modest attire to avoid being mistaken for a drug dealer by Italians. Comments made by Italians about migrants wearing designer items appear incognizant of the fact that these are often counterfeits of low economic value, often bought by the traders from their own wholesalers. In other cases, they are received as change by wholesalers short of cash.

17. Relations with Greek suppliers waned after 2012 when—concomitantly with the economic crisis—law enforcement controls on counterfeits that had previously been tolerated were intensified.

18. An interesting case is that of a Senegalese vendor who in 2011 ran a stall on a weekly Roman street market while his wife traveled multiple times a year to Cameroon and Nigeria to source artworks, especially copies of the famous Ife bronze statues.

19. Comparing interviews in 2012 and 2015, it is evident that there was a tightening of deadlines for repaying credit, from 30 to 15 days. This is partly due to official clampdowns on counterfeits not only in Italy but also in countries that were once more lenient, such as Greece.

20. The interview data indicates that Vuitton and Liu-Jo labeled bags are more expensive at source, and consequently on the street, than Gucci and Prada, probably due to higher demand.

21. Conversation in a working-class neighborhood of Rome, April 2012.

22. *Associazione 21 luglio*. 2017. "Rapporto annuale 2017", http://www.21luglio.org/21luglio/wp-content/uploads/2018/04/Rapporto_Annuale-2017_web.pdf, accessed January 14, 2019.

23. Fondazione Casa della Carità. 2012. "*Rapporto nazionale sull'inclusione lavorativa e sociale dei rom in Italia*", http://www.casadellacarita.org/eu-inclusive/rapporto.html, accessed 14 January 2019.

24. ISTAT. 2017. "Fonti di dati sulla popolazione Rom, Sinti e Caminanti", https://www.istat.it/it/files/2017/02/Fonti_di_dati_sulla_popolazione_RSC.pdf, accessed January 14, 2019. ISTAT. 2018. "Le prospettive per l'economia italiana nel 2018", 22 May, https://www.istat.it/it/files/2018/05/Previsioni_mag22_fin22mag18a.pdf, accessed January 14, 2019.

25. We focus here only on the work of small-scale trades most typical of camp-dwelling Roma in the city. We recognize, however, that some Roma participate in highly lucrative trades—both legal and illegal—as is the case with other groups of Italians and foreigners.

26. He bought these for the lire equivalent of 2.50 euro for 20 roses and resold them for 1.50–2.00 euro each.

27. These were bought for 1.50 euro each and resold for 10–15 euro.

28. Campaigns against street vendors were first initiated in Rimini by shopkeepers in 1988–1989 (Riccio 1999) and intensified nationally following the introduction of more restrictive immigration legislation in 1992 ("Bossi Fini" Law 189).

29. The liminal nature of "fakes" lies in the fact that the same object may be sold in the street or in shops, depending on the traders' circuits, and acquired by various categories of buyers (tourists, private individuals who resell to friends, shopkeepers, etc.).

30. See, for example, the following newspaper articles: Galli (2018), Mancinelli and Di Corrado (2018), Rame (2018).

31. All formal and 'tolerated' camps are mapped by the authorities and these maps are publicly accessible.

32. Tensions in fact simmer between the stall holders who pay both an annual and weekly fee to trade within the legal confines of the market, and unauthorized ones outside who are perceived as attracting the hostility of residents and attention from the authorities, thereby jeopardizing the future of the market itself.

33. See Solimene (2014) on the construction of hierarchies between Roma from former Yugoslavia and Romania.

34. https://www.cronachedellacampania.it/2017/01/camorra-ecco-come-funziona-pizzo-per-gli-ambulanti-i-pentiti-cosi-si-arricchiscono-i-clan-sulle-griffe-false/.

35. The synergy between migrants and social justice activists in Pigneto has also extended to national issues, such as a demonstration in Rome on January 13, 2012, organized by the CIGL trade union against *caporalato* (exploitative recruitment of undocumented farm labourers), which included migrant workers displaced from the Calabrian town of Rosarno where in January 2010 African seasonal agricultural workers revolted against extreme conditions of exploitation by local mafias.

REFERENCES

Agoni, Marianna. "Etnografia delle migrazioni e degli spostamenti di alcune famiglie di rom romeni tra Gradina e Milano." In *Italia Romani vol. 6*, edited by Stefania Pontrandolfo, and Leonardo Piasere, 141–158. Roma: CISU, 2016.

Aguiar, José Carlos G. "Smugglers, *Fayuqueros, Piratas*: Transitory Commodities and Illegality in the Trade of Pirated CDs in Mexico." *PoLAR: Political and Legal Anthropology Review* 36, no. 3 (2013): 249–265.

Becucci, Stefano. "La criminalità organizzata cinese in Italia. Caratteristiche e linee evolutive." Rapporto di ricerca. CNEL, Osservatorio socio-economico sulla criminalità. 2011. https://www.tgcom24.mediaset.it/documento/13.$plit/C_4_documento_12_upfDocumento.pdf, accessed February 19, 2019.

Brazzabeni, Manuela Cunha, and Martin Fotta, eds. *Gypsy Economy: Romani Livelihoods and Notions of Worth in the 21st Century*. New York: Berghahn, 2016.

Carrier, James G. "Moral Economies: What's in a Name." *Anthropological Theory* 18, no 1 (2018): 18–35.

Carter, Donald M. *States of Grace. Senegalese in Italy and the New European Immigration*. Minneapolis and London: University of Minnesota Press, 1997.

CESPI. "Osservatorio nazionale sull'inclusione finanziaria dei migranti in Italia, VI Rapporto." 2017. http://www.integrazionemigranti.gov.it/rapportiricercaimmigrazione/Rapporti%20Nazionali/VI-Rapporto-sullaInclusione-Finanziaria-dei-Migranti-in-Italia-2017.pdf, accessed January 14, 2019.

Chauvin, Sébastien, and Blanca Darcés-Mascareñas. "Becoming Less Illegal: Deservingness Frames and Undocumented Migrant Incorporation." *Sociology Compass*, 8, no. 4 (2014): 422–432.

Cingolani, Pietro ed. "(Rom)eni tra Italia e territori di partenza." 2011. https://www.fieri.it/wp-content/uploads/2011/12/Romeni-tra-italia-e-territori-di-partenza.pdf, accessed January 14, 2019.

Clough Marinaro, Isabella. "'Sporco zingaro'. I rom e l'integrità del corpo della nazione." In *L'Italia postcoloniale*, edited by Cristina Lombardi Diop, and Caterina Romeo, 93–108. Florence: Le Monnier-Mondadori Accademia, 2014.

Clough Marinaro, Isabella. "Salvaging Rome: Roma Waste Traders and the City's 'Garbage Crisis'." *Etnografia e ricerca qualitativa* 9, no. 1 (2018): 11–31.

Clough Marinaro, Isabella, and Marco Solimene. "Navigating Urban (In)formalities: Roma, Urban Life and Governance in Rome." *Cities* 96 (2019): 102402.

Clough Marinaro, Isabella, and Bjørn Thomassen. "Introduction. Into the City. The Changing Faces of Rome." In *Global Rome: Changing Faces of the Eternal City*, edited by Isabella Clough Marinaro, and Bjørn Thomassen, 1–18. Bloomington: Indiana University Press, 2014.

Crăciun, Magdalena. *Material Culture and Authenticity. Fake Branded Fashion in Europe*. London: Bloomsbury, 2013.

DeMaria Harney, Nicholas. "Migrant Strategies, Informal Economies and Ontological Security: Ukrainians in Naples, Italy." *International Journal of Sociology and Social Policy* 32, no. 1–2 (2012): 4–16.

ECRI. "ECRI Report on Italy." 2016. https://rm.coe.int/fifth-report-on-italy/16808b5837, accessed January 14, 2019.

Fassin, Didier. "Les économies morales revisitées." *Annales, Histoire, Sciences Sociales* 64, no. 6 (2009): 1237–1266.

Fontanella, Lara, Paola Villano, and Marika Di Donato. "Attitudes Towards Roma People and Migrants: A Comparison through a Bayesian Multidimensional IRT model." *Quality & Quantity: International Journal of Methodology* 50, no. 2 (2016): 471–490.

FLM (Fondazione Leone Moressa). *Rapporto annuale sull'economia dell'immigrazione. La dimensione internazionale delle immigrazioni*. Bologna: Il Mulino, 2017.

Galemba, Rebecca B. *Contraband Corridor. Making a Living of the Mexico-Guatemala Border*. Redwood City: Stanford University Press, 2017.

Galli, Andrea. "Auto, droga, furti: le isole criminali del campo rom di via Bonfadini." *Corriere della Sera*, September 18, 2018. https://milano.corriere.it/notizie/cronaca/18_settembre_27/auto-droga-furti-isole-criminali-campo-rom-via-bonfadini-8c297490-c216-11e8-85a4-d6c3d427f951.shtml?refresh_ce-cp, accessed January 14, 2019.

Gonnella, Patrizio. "Stranieri in carcere: Il grande bluff populista." In *Dossier Statistico Immigrazione*, edited by IDOS, 191–195. Roma: Centro Studi e Ricerche IDOS, 2018.

Hansen Tranberg, Karen, Little, Walter, and Lynne Milgram, eds. *Street Economies in the Urban Global South*. Santa Fe: School for Advanced Research Press, 2014.

Izzi, Stefano (with Antonello Colosimo). *Lotta alla contraffazione. Analisi del fenomeno, sintesi e strumenti di contrasto*. Milano: Franco Angeli, 2010.

Keane, Webb. "How Everyday Ethics Becomes a Moral Economy, and Vice Versa." Economics Discussion Papers, No 2019-9, Kiel Institute for the World Economy. 2019. http://www.economics-ejournal.org/economics/discussionpapers/2019-9, accessed February 18, 2019).

Kubal, Agnieszka. "Conceptualizing Semi-Legality in Migration Research." *Law & Society Review* 47, no. 3 (2013): 555–587.

Lisi, Nino. "Oggi rom e sinti in piazza contro i rischi di deriva xenofoba." *Articolo 21*. 2018. https://www.articolo21.org/2018/08/oggi-rom-e-sinti-in-piazza-contro-i-rischi-di-deriva-xenofoba/, accessed January 14, 2019.

Lombardi-Diop, Cristina. "ROMA RESIDENCE: Senegal, Italy and Transnational Hybrid Spaces." *Interventions: International Journal of Postcolonial Studies* 11, no. 3 (2009): 400–419.

Lunaria. "Il ritorno della 'razza.'" June 2018. https://www.lunaria.org/wp-content/uploads/2018/06/Focus-N4_ilritornodellarazza.pdf, accessed November 29, 2020.

Mackenzie, Simon, and Donna Yates. "What is Grey about the 'Grey Market' in Antiquities." In *The Architecture of Illegal Markets: Towards an Economic Sociology of Illegality in the Economy*, edited by Jens Beckert, and Matias Dewey, 70–86. Oxford: Oxford University Press, 2016.

Mancinelli, Silvia, and Valentina Di Corrado. "Armi, soldi e gioielli: la bella vita nel campo rom." *Il Tempo*, May 17, 2018. https://www.iltempo.it/roma-capitale/2018/05/17/news/roma-magliana-campo-rom-via-candoni-armi-soldi-gioielli-1066993/, accessed November 29, 2020.

MdL (Ministero del Lavoro e delle Politiche Sociali). "La presenza dei migranti nella Città Metropolitana di Roma Capitale." 2017. http://www.lavoro.gov.it/documenti-e-norme/studi-e-statistiche/Documents/La%20presenza%20dei%20migranti%20nelle%20aree%20metropolitane,%20anno%202017/RAM-2017-RomaCapitale.pdf, accessed January 14, 2019.

Panella, Cristiana. *Les terres cuites de la discorde. Déterrement et écoulement des terres cuites anthropomorphes du Mali. Les réseaux locaux*. Leiden: CNWS Publications, 2002.

Panella, Cristiana. "L'éthique sociale du *damansen*. Éducation familiale et orpaillage artisanal dans le Basidibé (Wasolon, Mali)." *Cahiers d'Etudes Africaines* 186, no. 2 (2007): 345–370.

Panella, Cristiana. "Looters or Heroes? Production of Illegality and Memories of 'Looting' in Mali." *European Journal on Criminal Policy and Research* 20, no. 4 (2014): 487–502.

PCM (Presidenza del Consiglio dei Ministri). "Strategia nazionale d'inclusione dei rom, dei sinti e dei caminanti." 2012. https://www.comune.roma.it/resources/cms/documents/Strategia_italiana_rom.pdf, accessed January 14, 2019.

Piazzoni, Francesca. "Visibility as Justice: Immigrant Street Vendors and the Right to Difference in Rome." *Journal of Planning Education and Research* (2020): 1–16. https://doi.org/10.1177%2F0739456X20956387.

Rahaman, Md Mizanut, and Mohammed Alamgir Kabir. "Moving to Europe: Bangladeshi Migration in Italy." ISAS Working Paper 142, 2012. https://www.files.ethz.ch/isn/137192/ISAS_Working_Paper_142_-_email_-_Moving_to_Europe_-_Bangladesh_Migration_to_Italy_07022012143721.pdf, accessed January 28, 2019.

Rame, Sergio. "Dopo i clandestini, tocca ai campi rom. Salvini: 'Li chiudo tutti entro 5 anni'." *Il Giornale*, September 25, 2018. http://www.ilgiornale.it/news/politica/i-clandestini-i-campi-rom-salvini-li-chiudo-tutti-entro-5-1580226.html, accessed November 29, 2020.

Riccio, Bruno. "Senegalese Street-Sellers, Racism and the Discourse on 'Irregular Trade' in Rimini." *Modern Italy* 4, no. 2 (1999): 225–239.

Riccio, Bruno. "Spazi transnazionali. Esperienze senegalesi." *Africa e Orienti* 3, no. 4 (2000): 17–25.

Riccio, Bruno, and Stefano degli Uberti. "Senegalese Migrants in Italy: Beyond the Assimilation/Transnationalism Divide." *Urban Anthropology and Studies of Cultural Systems and World Economies Development* 42, no. 3 (2013): 207–254.

Santilli, Cristina. "I rom che raccolgono il ferro a Roma. Vuoti normativi, economia informale, antiziganismo." *ANUAC* 6, no. 1 (2017): 141–163.

Sigona, Nando. "Locating 'The Gypsy Problem'. The Roma in Italy: Stereotyping, Labelling and 'Nomad Camps.'" *Journal of Ethnic and Migration Studies* 31 no. 4 (2005): 741–756.

Solimene, Marco. "The Rootedness of a Community of Xoraxané Romá in Rome." In *Global Rome: Changing Faces of the Eternal City*, edited by Isabella Clough Marinaro, and Bjørn Thomassen, 129–142. Bloomington: Indiana University Press, 2014.

Solimene, Marco. "'I Go for Iron': Xoraxane Roma Collecting Scrap Metal in Rome." In *Gypsy Economy: Romani Livelihoods and Notions of Worth in the 21st Century*, edited by Micol Brazzabeni, Manuela Cunha, and Martin Fotta, 107–126. New York: Berghahn, 2016.

Thomassen, Bjørn. "Thinking with Liminality. To the Boundaries of an Anthropological Concept." In *Breaking Boundaries. Varieties of Liminality*, edited by Agnes Horvath, Bjørn Thomassen, and Harald Wydra, 39–58. New York: Berghahn, 2015.

Thomassen, Bjørn, and Piero Vereni. "Diversely Global Rome." In *Global Rome: Changing Faces of the Eternal City*, edited by Isabella Clough Marinaro, and Bjørn Thomassen, 21–34. Bloomington: Indiana University Press, 2014.

Tosi Cambini, Sabrina. "Da un villaggio del Sud delle Romania a una città del centro Italia. Alcuni elementi di riflessione intorno al tempo, allo spazio e al senso nella migrazione di una rete di famiglie di rudari." In *Italia Romani vol.* 6, edited by Stefania Pontrandolfo, and Leonardo Piasere, 159–184. Roma: CISU, 2016.

Tuckett, Anna. *Rules, Paper, Status: Migrants and Precarious Bureaucracy in Contemporary Italy*. Stanford: Stanford University Press, 2018.

Turner, Victor. *The Forest of Symbols: Aspects of Ndembu Ritual*. Ithaca, NY: Cornell University Press, 1967.

Van Baar, Huub. "Evictability and the Biopolitical Bordering of Europe." *Antipode* 49, no. 1, (2017): 212–230.

van Gennep, Arnold. *The Rites of Passage*. London: Routledge, [1909] 2004.

Villano, Paola, Lara Fontanella, Sara Fontanella, and Marika Di Donato. "Stereotyping Roma People in Italy: IRT Models for Ambivalent Prejudice Measurement." *International Journal of Intercultural Relations* 57, no. 1 (2017): 30–41.

Chapter 6

Repositioning the Edge

The Resilience of a Wholesale Vegetable Market in Benguet Northern Philippines

B. Lynne Milgram and Lorelei C. Mendoza

INTRODUCTION

In the northern upland Philippines, Benguet provincial newspapers repeatedly report on the wellbeing of the region's extensive trade in highland vegetables (e.g., cauliflower, broccoli, potatoes, carrots, cabbage, beans) as this industry, comprising "80 percent of vegetable market inputs nationwide" (Alimondo 2020; Catajan, M.E. 2018), substantially contributes to the provincial economy. Central to this trade is the LTVTP, the region's major wholesale vegetable market located in La Trinidad, Benguet's provincial capital (see Figure 6.1). Local media reports continue, for example, that "The La Trinidad Vegetable Trading Post on a normal day is as busy as a beehive" (Sun Star Baguio 2015:4). "The local trading post is a jump off point for the transport of highland vegetables to the lowlands, home to traders, disposers and buyers" (Catajan, M. E. 2012) and represents the "biggest income generating endeavor of the municipal government of La Trinidad" (Catajan, B. 2016a:3–4).[1]

Thus, in preparation for the revised Association of Southeast Asian Nations (ASEAN) Free Trade Area agreement that, by 2015 would open Philippine borders to vegetable imports from ASEAN countries, in late 2010, the Benguet government began construction on the Benguet Agri Pinoy Trading Center (BAPTC) (BAPTC 2015). BAPTC, a vegetable wholesale facility three times the size of the current LTVTP, promised to give provincial administrators more control over the province's lucrative wholesale vegetable trade (BAPTC 2015; Catajan, M.E. 2014:1,4). Although the BAPTC facility officially opened in late 2015, "experimental trading" did not take place

Figure 6.1 La Trinidad Vegetable Trading Post, La Trinidad, Benguet, Philippines, 2018.
Source: Photo by B. Lynne Milgram.

until late 2016 (Membrere 2016) as heated negotiations about the ultimate fate of LTVTP businesses and, in particular, of the essential jobs it offers continued between government officials and LTVTP traders. Anticipating that the BAPTC one-size-fits-all marketing plan would threaten the Trading Post's viability, LTVTP traders refused to move to BAPTC. When the then La Trinidad mayor ordered the closure of the LTVTP effective the end of February 2016, traders compiled a 1,000-signature petition to protest their eviction. Association leaders subsequently obtained a 20-day Temporary Restraining Order to forestall their move (Catajan, M.E. 2016:1,4; Sun Star Baguio 2016a:1,3) and eventually won assurances from the municipal government that, "La Trinidad Vegetable Trading Post has been created through a legislative enactment and thus it can only be closed through legislation" (Catajan, B. 2016b:1,4; see also Empian 2016:1,37). When the mayor failed to be reelected in May 2016, city officials took no further action to close the LTVTP that to date continues to conduct business as usual (Alimondo 2020; Sun Star Baguio 2016b).

As evidenced in the redevelopment plan for the LTVTP, a range of political-economic processes exert increasing pressures on people working in what Global South governments consider the urban margins (e.g., public markets, street vending) (Hansen et al. 2013). Migrating neoliberal models of governance and "appropriate" development often promote policies that marginalize other-than-mainstream work (Filipi 2013; Milgram 2015). Ideals of world-class cities, which are usually unaccommodating of the urban poor and even of the lower-to-middle classes, have made their way into cities in the Global South with considerable effects. Many cities are thus being modernized and sanitized through evictions, face-lifting, and other forceful measures intended to eliminate undesirable remnants of traditional trade—forms of work that often encompass informally negotiated and often "extralegal" modes of organization (Smart and Zerilli 2014; see Hansen et al. 2013). At the same time, controlling such marginal sites currently constitutes a last frontier for capital expansion. Governments thus devise new strategies to penetrate these persistent informal or alternative economic activities in order to extract value from them often resulting in struggles over land, livelihood rights, and access to urban resources.

This chapter engages these issues by analyzing the mainstream channels and the edgy side roads through which LTVTP wholesale traders sustain their provisioning livelihoods, given the municipal and provincial government policies that have threatened their businesses' viability. We argue that within a contested context privileging large-scale municipal developments, LTVTP traders have used "everyday politics" (e.g., occupying public spaces for business) (Kerkvliet 2009) to innovatively leverage informal and "not-yet-legal" practices within a mainstream commodity flow (Smart and Zerilli 2014:226). In order to ensure reliable deliveries from farmers and ample avenues of distribution to buyers, LTVTP marketers continually create new personalized trade nodes grounded in trust and in elastic business arrangements (Milgram 2019). What emerges is a complex, multichannel flow of goods among farmers, a range of middle traders and buyers that enable wholesalers to quickly respond to shifting consumer tastes and business opportunities—improvised practices that have, in effect, become the norm. That market wholesalers have regularized their individual and informally arranged economic agreements through repeated practice and that the municipal government has, in effect, enabled these ad hoc actions by looking-the-other-way or by collecting additional administrative fees for minor infractions, evidence that both the city and LTVTP traders are complicit in using informality and extralegality as urban organizing logics when it is to their mutual advantage—increased income for the city and optional trade channels for marketers (AlSayyad and Roy 2004; Roy 2014).

Since launching the 2015 initiative to replace the LTVTP with the larger BAPTC facility, municipal and provincial Benguet government policies have tried to regularize, subordinate, tolerate, and finally eradicate the former wholesale market. Traders' advocacy, however, has meant that LTVTP continues to provide much-needed employment for a host of market players as well as consumption options for residents both of which materialize a rich urban texture of "cityness" (Robinson 2006:10) that can respond to different peoples' needs across sectors. The resultant mix of work and consumption opportunities LTVTP's trade offers we suggest emerges as the driving force that fashions this marketplace's constant reshaping, perseverance, and vitality.

To situate the shifting trajectories of trade within the LTVTP, we explore the scholarship advocating for inclusive cities, and that charting public market transformation and alternative or gray spaces of trade. We then investigate the extent to which the LTVTP marketers can secure their long-standing food provisioning channels despite the modernizing development challenges they face.

ADVOCATING FOR AN INCLUSIVE "CITYNESS"

With rapid urbanization, municipal governments worldwide tend to adopt development priorities specifically designed to enhance their city's global cultural and economic positioning (Douglass et al. 2008; Marcuse 2012; Parnell and Robinson 2012; Perera and Tang 2013). By seeking to modernize urban centers—to attain a so-called world-class status—governments may limit the ability of many urban residents to establish viable and diverse livelihoods when formal sector work options are not widely available. Such a development agenda, clearly evident in the La Trinidad government's BAPTC initiative, could have had devastating consequences for many urban residents in terms of equality of service access, and provision and redistribution of goods (Douglass 1998:111; Milgram 2013, 2015; Roy 2011). Rather than governments imposing a universal image of "cityness" that privileges more well-off urbanites and large-scale businesses, Jennifer Robinson (2006:108, 170) argues for policies to adopt an "ordinary city" perspective—an approach that "considers the city as a whole in all its diversity and complexity." Such a "reterritorialisation" would have governments more relevantly address the on-the-ground needs of urbanites across sectors rather than direct efforts outward to achieve some symbolic global position for their cities (Robinson 2006:10; Parnell and Robinson 2012).

By considering all cities as "coeval," as existing in the same time (rather than along a developing-developed) continuum, we can more relevantly operationalize the potential of a city's alternative economies (Go and Bunnell 2013; Schappo and van Melik 2017). Work such as public market trade, rather than indicating activities of underdevelopment, evidence how traders operationalize proximity in economic interactions to foster relations of trust between individuals and organizations and thus materialize what Alan Scott and Michael Storper (2015:3) term a "reflexive city." As Mike Douglass et al. (2008:3) remind us, in situations of limited infrastructural development such as that in the northern upland Philippines (e.g., poor housing and social service provision, insecure employment), the street, public markets, and other public spaces become crucial settings for inventing ways of being sociable, earning a living, and gaining recognition. Finding ways of being modern in cities worldwide then is realized, not only in the built environment, but also in flexible private and public spaces and enacted in personal performances, cultural practices, and innovative actions such as those of the LTVTP wholesale traders.

MARKETPLACES AND GRAY SPACES OF TRADE

Scholars analyzing public marketplace transformation support the spirit of Robinson's (2006) inclusive "cityness" by demonstrating how these sites generate interdependent social, cultural, economic, and historical processes to foster a pulsating "urban bustle" (Garcés and Bedon 2017:169; see also Black 2012; Polese and Prigarin 2013; Ünlü-Yücesoy 2013).[2] As "cosmopolitan canopies" (Anderson 2011) marketplaces bring together people from across socioeconomic sectors within often loosely managed operations that, in effect, enable alternative business strategies and personalized patterns of consumption (Bonnin 2018; Endres 2014).

While the majority of research on market transformation has focused on informal or extralegal markets in the Global South, especially regarding street vending (e.g., Hansen et al. 2013), increasingly fixed and regulated markets worldwide are undergoing similar redevelopment pressures, albeit through more subtle and often less violent processes of change. To analyze such regularized market redevelopment, Sara González (2017:2) suggests a three-part framework that considers markets as "frontiers for gentrification . . . as spaces for resistance and political mobilization . . . [and as] spaces for development of alternative practices of production and consumption."

In this light, given that many regularized city markets occupy prime central urban locations, it is not surprising that municipal governments seek to develop these sites to maximize income. Once the mega-wholesale site BAPTC was operational, for example, the La Trinidad municipal government had planned to redevelop the LTVTP into a retail boutique center (Catajan 2013:1) offering specialized and costly "one-town-one-product" goods targeted to more well-off residents and tourists. As Sharon Zukin et al. (2009:48) argue, such gentrification identifies an area as safe for commercial investors who then upgrade services and raise rents, both of which inevitably displace many of the original stores who cannot afford the new higher rates (see also Seale 2016; Seligmann and Guevara 2013).

Such market gentrification, however, as evidenced at LTVTP, is often challenged by market traders and indeed by other urban actors (e.g., neighbors, consumers) as different government and private stakeholders may hold conflicting visions of viable and sustainable development. As Robinson (2006:84) argues, establishing a diverse "cityness" is often only achieved through contestation as subaltern actors are regularly perceived as being "out-of-step" with, or in defiance of, the position of official policy makers (see also Milgram 2015; Perera and Tang 2013; Polese and Prigarin 2013). Such "contestation" around market transformation, Gonzalez (2017:10) notes, "often extends to broader debates about the 'right to the city'" for the more disenfranchised sector of the population such as those working in various niche-trade capacities at the LTVTP (see also Bayat 2012; Marcuse 2012).

As studies of retail and wholesale markets have widely documented, moreover, these sites not only facilitate finite economic sales, but also provide inclusive social spaces in which traders and consumers can develop relations of trust and alternative circuits of exchange which diverge from the homogenized urbanism of cities that privilege mega-developments and privatization. Such receptive sites are essential in cities with high unemployment as they provide a first stop for unskilled residents and new arrivals to access entry-level work options (e.g., porters, packers, cleaners) (Morales 2009; Ünlü-Yücesoy 2013; Watson 2009).

To maintain and secure the vibrancy of their enterprises, market traders thus continue to exploit both mainstream and under-the-radar informally negotiated gray spaces of practice.[2] "Gray spaces," Oren Yiftachel (2012:153) argues "have become a dominant feature of contemporary urbanism" created both "'from above' by powerful groups linked to the centers of power," but more commonly from below by city residents whose rights have been marginalized. The latter, rather than "being powerless recipients of [unfavorable] urban policies [however], . . . generate new mobilizations and insurgent identities" by using gray spacing to create "bases for self-organization, negotiation, and empowerment" (Yiftachel 2012:153; see also Smart this book). La Trinidad's public market traders use "everyday politics" (Kerkvliet 2009) to create such ambiguous gray spaces by, for example, contravening market guidelines when they expand their product displays into public market aisles or by conducting retail sales in a wholesale-only market.

Although such gray spaces are rarely fully integrated into or eliminated from contemporary urban organization, they persist partially outside of or tolerated by the knowledge of state authorities when the latter can benefit from looking the other way or from encapsulating informal gray-space practices into regulated frameworks (Smart and Zerilli 2014:229; Smart and

Smart 2017). Understanding that gray spacing is a quiet ongoing process of refashioning socioeconomic spatial relations (Yiftachel 2012:15; Bayat 2012) dissolves any formal/informal or legal/illegal dichotomy to yield a more inclusive sphere Smart and Zerilli (2014:222) term “extralegality.”

The steamroller model of urban redevelopment then cannot be assumed, as marketplace actors across the Global North and South activate grassroots initiatives to mitigate the “hypercommodification” (Robinson 2006:2) of urban centers. Responding to Susan Parnell and Jennifer Robinson’s (2012) call for inclusive cities, Yves Cabannes and Cecilia Marocchino (2019) urge policy makers to integrate public food markets into urban planning agendas arguing like Susan Parnham (2012:61) that by foregrounding such “food quarters” urban planners can create not only “convivial” and much-needed food spaces but also realize the potential of marketplaces as “engines for urban growth” (Janssens and Sezer 2013:169).

Through these cross-sector approaches we can understand the avenues through which wholesale traders, such as those in LTVTP, have decentered the municipal and provincial governments’ urban development strategy to materialize a diverse and self-styled cityness that can better meet their and consumers’ livelihood needs.

ESTABLISHING THE LTVTP

La Trinidad, the capital city of Benguet province with a population of 150,000, is the regional center for agricultural development and education, and as noted, functions as the northern Philippine hub for the wholesale collection, sale, and distribution of highland vegetables. As the altitude of much of Benguet province is above 1,500 meters, the cool temperatures enable farmers to grow temperate climate vegetables that those in the hotter lowlands cannot produce such as broccoli, cauliflower, beans, potatoes, carrots, cabbage, and lettuce. Benguet farmers, along with other highland Cordillera producers, supply the LTVTP wholesale marketers who distribute these vegetables throughout the country. At the retail level, such upland vegetables are available to consumers generally, in public retail markets, in neighborhood stores, and in supermarket venues.

Until the late 1980s, Benguet’s wholesale upland vegetable trade was channeled through the Hanger Wholesale Vegetable Market of the Baguio City Public Market (BCPM), the province’s largest retail and wholesale public market at that time (Reyes-Boquiren 1989). Baguio, with a population of 300,000, is one of the region’s industrial, cultural, and education centers. Throughout the 1970s, ongoing rural to urban migration and increasing consumer demand saw the rapid expansion of the province’s wholesale vegetable trade resulting in more traffic congestion in and around Baguio's public market. To circumvent the long delays farmers, traders, and buyers experienced in order to deliver, purchase, and pack their vegetables, some Manila buyers started to intercept farmers en route to the BCPM offering to purchase the latter's produce on the roadside, a process commonly termed, *harang*.

By the early 1980s, it became evident that the physical limitations of the BCPM site could not adequately accommodate the expanding wholesale trade, in particular. Some farmers whose land is located closer to La Trinidad thus began to sell their produce to wholesale buyers directly from their trucks that they parked along La Trinidad's downtown streets, in public parking lots, and in private parking facilities. As many farmers did not have information about current market prices, traders often purchased the latter's vegetables in the aforementioned informal market sites, at prices lower than farmers would have received at Baguio's wholesale market, a transaction termed *alok* (to offer). The advantage of the latter system for farmers, however, was that they could quickly sell their produce eliminating travel time to the BCPM, waiting time to enter the market, and the risk of having their produce spoil due to delays in market access.

In order to claim the tax revenue that governments realized they were losing from these gray zone transactions, in 1982 the La Trinidad government, with additional provincial and USAID financial support, designated 2 acres of municipal land on which to construct a new downtown wholesale vegetable market—the LTVTP which opened for business in 1989 (Municipality of La Trinidad 2009). The LTVTP subsequently saw its wholesale vegetable trade expand dramatically following the 1990 earthquake in Baguio that destroyed part of the city's Hanger Wholesale Vegetable Market further constraining the building's facilities and resulting in some Baguio wholesalers moving to the LTVTP. Southern Luzon (Manila) buyers welcomed this move as the larger LTVTP parking lots could accommodate their enormous 20- to 24-wheel trucks eliminating the time and expense of having to transport their extensive purchases from the BCPM to off-site parking lots.

From the early 1990s, Benguet's wholesale highland vegetable trade has continued to take place across these two markets but with the BCPM relegated to a secondary role handling smaller wholesale deliveries and purchases. To secure their enterprises, some Baguio market wholesalers developed a niche-trade by stocking vegetables cultivated in smaller volumes and different from the standard LTVTP produce (e.g., sweet peas, bell peppers, turmeric, herbs). Wholesalers in both markets, however, maintain an active personalized dialogue of cross-sourcing. When wholesalers in either the LTVTP or BCPM need specific produce to complete an order or to fill their truck when extra room is available and they cannot purchase the required produce from their farmer deliveries or from fellow wholesalers, they source the goods they need at the neighboring city's wholesale market. At the same time, some farmers explain that they prefer to continue to work with their longtime traders at the BCPM rather than forge new personalized relations with LTVTP wholesalers. Such cross-sourced or horizontal commodity flows between markets highlight how multiple arteries feed into a larger vertical commodity chain (Fine 2002).

ORGANIZATION OF LTVTP AND ITS PARAMETERS OF TRADE

The 2-acre site on which LTVTP is situated is organized into five major trading sectors. These include the main central trading or *bagsakan* area occupied by individual self-employed wholesale traders or "disposers," two lanes on either side of the *bagsakan* area reserved for farmers to deliver their produce, the parking area reserved for buyers to load vehicles with their purchased goods, and enclosed stalls located along the outer perimeter of the grounds—most of which are rented by farmer cooperatives and in which farmers sort their produce.

The *bagsakan* area, a covered 15-X-75 meter concrete platform with open sides, is the major area for the collection and distribution of Benguet's wholesale vegetables (see Figure 6.1). This area, in turn, is divided into three parallel trade zones or lanes located on either side of a central aisle. Within these lanes white painted floor lines indicate the specific space or cubicle that traders or disposers rent for their businesses. While the cubicles do not have walls, they are specifically designated physical locations for which traders pay a 50-peso ($1.00) daily rent whether or not they are on site. As formalized as these cubicles were originally intended to be, traders create "gray spaces" of operation by expanding or contracting the physical space they occupy depending upon the volume of that day's deliveries and orders (Smart this book; Yiftachel 2012). In addition, if fixed-site traders are absent one day, other traders simply expand their businesses into these vacant spaces for the whole or part of the day rooted in an understanding of mutual exchange, but one that contravenes the LTVTP Market Code in which only the market administration can allocate alternative selling sites (Municipality of La Trinidad 2009).

The LTVTP Market Code outlines that market business is reserved solely for the wholesale trade of highland vegetables (Municipality of La Trinidad 2009). What has emerged, however, is a situation in which traders conducting business from rented cubicles in the center market aisle sell *sari-sari* produce or mixed vegetables, including some lowland produce (e.g., eggplant, baby corn, assorted greens), and primarily work with smaller-volume retail sales. Center-aisle retail traders have the flexibility to purchase small quantities of the aforementioned vegetables directly from farmers while simultaneously purchasing, for retail sales, small amounts of highland vegetables stocked by their *suki* (trusted) wholesale disposers operating in the lane directly behind them. Such retail sales, besides contravening the LTVTP Market Code, jeopardize the livelihoods of the La Trinidad Public Market vegetable retailers operating businesses just down the street. That both LTVTP administrators and city officials enable such retail sales in their hallmark wholesale facility materializes how the government is complicit in formalizing such informally organized and extralegal transactions to augment administrative coffers (Smart and Zerilli 2014; Smart and Smart 2017).

The continuing growth of the industry, moreover, has meant that the outer of the three trade lanes—the Farmers' Lane formerly reserved for farmers' short-term use at no cost—has been converted into cubical spaces that can be rented for the standard daily 50-peso rate. The Market Manager justifies formalizing the previously ad hoc and free Farmers' Lane sites as he explained that, "Farmers are not delivering produce each day but only when they have harvested their crop and need to deliver produce to their disposer. Farmers can manage the inconvenience of working from the narrow space between the Farmers' Lane and the parking areas on a first-come-first-serve basis" (see Figure 6.2). Objecting to this municipal policy, one farmer states,

> Although the same farmer does not deliver produce each day, there are enough of us to consistently use the Farmers' Lane slots. City officials just want to collect more fees. We continue to occupy these restricted sites when we see they are vacant; indeed, some market officials welcome our personal payments to them to do so.

Farmers' everyday political actions thus render the variably regulated Farmers' Lane sites as gray spaces of trade that move in and out of legal to not-so-legal status depending upon how the occupant has secured access.

During busier harvest seasons, farmers may experience delays in readily accessing the market. Fixed site and periodic disposers thus risk not being able to fill their buyers' orders on time while farmers risk losing produce to spoilage if their goods are exposed to the sun for extended periods. To address this periodic challenge both parties have developed an additional artery of trade to effectively accumulate the produce they need. While waiting in market entry lines, farmers use their cell phones to text their positions to their disposers who then inspect the produce on-site and negotiate an agreed-upon price for the goods. Upon completing their on-the-spot

Figure 6.2 La Trinidad Vegetable Trading Post, La Trinidad, Benguet, Philippines, 2018. Wholesale vegetable traders conducting business in a narrow lane between the main trading area and the parking lot. *Source*: Photo by B. Lynne Milgram.

agreements, disposers hire their own porters to unload the farmers' trucks by the side of the road and transport the produce back to the Trading Post via hand-pulled wooden carts that are free to enter the wholesale grounds at any time.

Similar spontaneous public roadside transactions also take place when LTVTP disposers cannot fill an order from that day's prearranged farmer deliveries. To compensate for the produce shortfall, disposers either purchase the produce they need from other market wholesalers, including those at the BCPM or, to save the middle-person markup, they canvas the farmers in the cooperative stalls as well as those waiting in line to enter the market to identify the available produce they seek. If the vegetables that disposers seek are in high demand, to ensure they can fill their orders, disposers may purchase a farmer's entire truckload in a process termed, *buhos* (to capture). Such personally orchestrated trade negotiations thus emerge as an integral alternative channel of Benguet's large-scale, wholesale vegetable trade, as we demonstrate further in the following case studies.

OPERATIONALIZING THE POTENTIAL OF PRODUCE SPECIALIZATION

Patricia Tacio,[3] in her mid-50s with six adult children, moved her wholesale vegetable business from the BCPM's Hanger Wholesale Vegetable Market to the LTVTP in 1995 given the latter market's potential for increased business growth (see Figure 6.3). Patricia's husband works in contract wage labor. Focusing on wholesale sales of cauliflower and green onions, Patricia's trade strategies are similar to those of other LTVTP disposers who rent permanent cubicle spaces in the market's primary *bagsakan* area and specialize in one or two highland vegetables. Patricia begins work at 5:00–6:00 a.m. and will work until 8:00 or 9:00 p.m. to meet late-arriving buyers. Patricia has three employees who work full time to transport, clean, and pack her produce, and as needed, she hires additional part-time workers.

In a typical LTVTP trade pattern, Patricia purchases the majority of her produce directly from farmers and to ensure she obtains the quality and quantity of goods she needs she advances inputs (seed, fertilizer, pesticides) rather than cash to her approximately 20 *suki* (trusted) farmer suppliers. Given her

Figure 6.3 La Trinidad Vegetable Trading Post, La Trinidad, Benguet, Philippines, 2018. Cauliflower is stacked and wrapped in newspaper in preparation for shipping. *Source*: Photo by B. Lynne Milgram.

limited space for produce storage and processing, Patricia explains, "I give the farmers a schedule for their deliveries to avoid receiving all my produce at one time. I receive, sort, and pack cauliflower in the morning for my buyers' mid-day pick up and later in the day I go the bus station to collect farmers' shipments of green onions." To reduce the cost and time required to personally transport produce to the LTVTP, farmers with smaller-volume crops, such as green onions, peppers, and sweet peas, may ship their produce to La Trinidad via bus.

Following farmers' cauliflower deliveries, Patricia weighs and sorts the produce by quality paying farmers accordingly. This entails also paying for the weight of the outer green leaves which is a bonus for farmers as the leaves are usually trimmed and discarded before final sale. Patricia adheres to a relationship of trust with her suppliers as she pays for deliveries shortly after receipt of her produce. If she finds a marked discrepancy in product quality after her rough sorting, Patricia discusses this issue with the farmer in the next delivery. As Patricia explains, "We need to maintain a mutual understanding to benefit both of our businesses."

Although the common practice in which disposers advance inputs to farmers potentially increases farmers' vulnerability, such advances simultaneously function as a social safety net to assist farmers with unexpected expenses such as for education or health care. The lack of adequate government support to farmers in the form of health and crop insurance and of easily accessible bank loans (Hutchcroft and Rocamora 2012:98) means, as William Davis (1973:211) notes in his early work on Philippine public markets, that only by forming personal networks of trusted relationships can those in business overcome the barriers posed by weaknesses in formal institutional credit and legal facilities (see also Turgo 2016). The complexity of such social capital relations emerges, however, when one considers the accompanying "dark sides" of social capital such as the potential for "downward levelling norms" on product prices and unreasonable "claims [of allegiance] on group members" if producers remain in debt to disposers (Portes and Landolt 2000:532). Farmers, like traders, thus employ "everyday politics" (Kerkvliet 2009:235)—whatever resources are at their disposal—to negotiate the most advantageous agreements.

To gauge how they can best leverage the fluctuating supply and demand for wholesale vegetables, for example, farmers increasingly use cell phones to access up-to-date information about product prices. Farmers also canvas market disposers to ask about the daily "running price" for their particular product and to monitor the demand. If farmers determine that their products are in short supply or *singit*, or when they see that their deliveries sell quickly, they may ask disposers for a higher price. At the same time however, farmers can gain higher produce prices only if disposers agree to decrease their markup or convince their buyers to pay more. Such variable parameters of trade at the LTVTP encourage ongoing negotiations between farmers and traders as Patricia explains,

> I consistently monitor my business relations with both farmers and buyers. If I want to keep the trust of my supplier, I need to offer farmers a fair price often with a bonus. My morning routine now is to make the rounds of other disposers to see the prices they offer as well as check prices with those I trust at Baguio's Wholesale Hanger Market. Losing any of my suppliers can mean loosing my buyers.

Most disposers, like Patricia, have regular weekly orders from two to five large-scale buyers whose purchases anchor their businesses. Patricia's two largest Manila buyers pick up their cauliflower orders on Wednesdays and Fridays. On average, Patricia sells twenty 50-kilogram sacks of cauliflower per day or 1,000 kilograms most of which is preordered and reserved for these regular clients. Within this large-scale national trade, however, Patricia's fine-grain processing includes sorting the cauliflower according to size and condition or class and trimming the produce in one of four styles according to her buyers' specifications. As Patricia explains,

> Buyers with retail outlets and some buyers from Bicol province retain the cauliflower's outer green leaves for more attractive displays while others request a "half green trim"; some buyers from the southern Luzon provinces of Bulacan, Angeles, and Manila's large Divisoria market request a "bald cut" in which the green leaves are removed to the lower edge of the white cauliflower florets while buyers from Palawan want an "ice cream cut" where the green leaves are trimmed to below the florets to reduce product weight for longer shipments.

What emerges in Patricia's trade, as we found with other LTVTP disposers, is an elastic, multistranded sourcing chain that expands or contracts as needed. As Patricia continues,

> Sometimes I purchase a farmer's extra stock just to maintain that farmer's allegiance. In such cases, I inform other disposers I have surplus cauliflower to sell. If I have extra vegetables at the end of the day, I wait for the late afternoon buyers to arrive. When I do not have enough produce to fill a buyer's order, I contact my network of free-lance "pickers" who locate produce from their personal sources or I purchase goods from other LTVTP or Baguio Wholesale Hanger Market disposers. The additional middle people involved in these transactions raises my expenses. Thus, to keep my buyer's allegiance, I reduce my mark-up to maintain my original quoted price. By late afternoon, if I have no produce to

> display and no cauliflower is available, I purchase any available vegetable from farmers to give me some end-of-the-day business. To survive in business you have to be willing to give and take.

DISPOSERS WITH NO FIXED SITE

While the permanent fixed-site disposers like Patricia form the core of regular trading activity, a range of part-time disposers holding daily LTVTP business permits can operate from any available site along a narrow edge-lane bordering the Farmers' Lane and the parking lots (see Figure 6.2). The Trading Post's periodic disposers work on variable schedules trading only when their farmer-contacts deliver their produce or when their *suki* buyers have orders for which disposers sleuth out the applicable goods. Disposers use cell phones to communicate with farmers and buyers about where they are located on any specific day. When spaces permitted for trade are not available, periodic disposers operationalize gray and extralegal sites of trade by conducting business in the streets around the LTVTP or in the Trading Post parking lots. Irene Nunag, 38 years old and formerly a farmer, for example, has been working as a freelance disposer since 2012 conducting business at the LTVTP two to four days a week. Like many mobile traders, Irene does not specialize in a specific type of vegetable but rather she sells different highland vegetables her *suki* farmers produce as well as purchasing produce from farmers as needed. That some of Irene's family members are farmers means she is fairly certain of receiving regular vegetable deliveries. In discussions about the challenges of her trade, Irene outlines that,

> When I decided to sell rather than farm, first I had to meet buyers. I regularly introduced myself to buyers in the LTVTP parking lots as they loaded their trucks. Because I am not at the Trading Post each day, farmers who come to sell their products on speculation do not know me and this limits my business opportunities. In my in-between position, my challenge is to secure the produce I need in sufficient quantities for the orders I anticipate receiving. The most satisfying part of my work is when I am able to successfully make a match.

Conversely, John Tayad, 42 years old, and a part-time LTVTP disposer who does not have relatives in farming, outlines that he needs to use tactics different from those of Irene to secure his business. As John states,

> I try to give inputs to farmers thereby forming a partnership with them. In this situation, a disposer owns part of the harvest and earns income accordingly. I am working on commission such that the higher the price I can secure for a farmer's

> harvest, the more we both earn. Farmers often choose you as their disposer so they know they have a representative at the market fighting for them. Thus, we both have an investment to protect. If the crop fails, we both lose. When vegetable prices drop disposers are responsible for finding a remedy so farmers still make a gain and we keep their allegiance.

In this light, Irene explains that the small scale of her business precludes her ability to advance inputs to farmers. She continues,

> Importantly, I have to foster good relations with permanent disposers to keep informed about shifting prices and to encourage them to refer their buyers to me if they do not have a specific type of produce on hand. The competitive nature of this trade means I need to balance risk, trust, and confidence. Only by fostering interlocking supply chains can I ensure receiving the goods I need when I need them for my orders.

John and Irene maintain, moreover, that their particular work niche in the region's wholesale vegetable trade has enabled their self-employment albeit on a sliding scale of success. As Irene explains, "As a mobile disposer, your feet get tired canvassing the market for good buyers to purchase your produce at the best price." John and Irene both agree that the viability of their enterprises depends upon the number and strength of their *suki* relations with both farmers and buyers as John summarizes, "How well you do in disposing farmers' produce spreads by word of mouth to other farmers and by selling high-quality goods to buyers we ensure their repeated business."

PORTERS AND CONSUMERS

The movement of Cordillera wholesale vegetables into, out of, and within the LTVTP goes nowhere without the essential service of market porters—a popular forum of work for unskilled laborers and new immigrant residents. LTVTP porters belong to their own member association that has established standard rates of pay depending upon the weight of each delivery and the distance porters carry it (e.g., 0.50 pesos per kilogram or 50 pesos per 100 kilograms) (Municipality of La Trinidad 2009). Informal or unlicensed porters may also obtain work by relying on personalized village connections to learn the "tricks of the trade." Although the Market Manager can evict these extralegal workers at any time, we never heard of this occurring. Porters receive one rate of pay, for example, when they manually carry produce in 20-kilogram bags within the *bagsakan* area between disposers as well as between the *bagsakan* area and buyers' and farmers' trucks located in any of the on-site parking lots. Porters earn additional payments when they transport produce outside the market usually to buyers' trucks waiting in private or public off-site lots. Whether using hand-pulled wooden carts or by packing and unpacking goods in a jeepney (open-back truck) required for longer trips, porters' rate of pay depends on the distance traveled and on the number of bags of produce they carry as noted. The role of porters thus emerges as a key node in the multistranded flow of LTVTP's wholesale vegetables (Fine 2002; Gerber et al. 2014).

While the majority of LTVTP's wholesale vegetables are sold to buyers supplying retail outlets such as supermarkets, smaller grocery stores, and public marketplaces, we were able to talk with shoppers who regularly make retail purchases in the LTVTP market's central *sari-sari* vegetable aisle. Consumers explained that they often purchase vegetables at their neighborhood stores while shopping for general dry goods due to the convenience, but added that they also try to shop in public markets when possible (see also Green 2015). One consumer outlined, for example, "I like to personally choose my vegetables to ensure I obtain the freshest and safest items. And who is there at the supermarket to ask about these concerns? The staff just stock the shelves." Another shopper continued that, "Since we now divide our trash into solid waste and compostable materials, the plastic and Styrofoam in which most vegetables in supermarkets are packaged contributes to our household trash accumulation; the added material may mean we exceed our collection limit."

Food safety is another important issue that most consumers acknowledge. Although private sector and government agricultural reports, which to date have not been effectively acted upon, acknowledge the extensive use of pesticides in Benguet's intensive vegetable cultivation (Lu 2009; Reyes and Laurean 2007), the fear of food safety has not precipitated a total move away from public markets toward supermarkets. As the head provincial agriculturalist in Benguet explained, "Most Benguet consumers believe that produce procured from any source contains chemicals and is therefore potentially unsafe. With no conclusive way to know the origin of produce unless one purchases it directly from the farmer, consumers' best recourse is to purchase from market vendors who they trust are procuring the safest possible produce" (see also Sun Star Baguio 2018). Trust, as noted then, emerges as the closest thing to a guarantee that people have regarding the safety of the goods they consume (Gerber et al. 2014:57–58). Once traders, generally, have earned the confidence of their customers through ongoing purchases, the latter tend to regularly secure their produce from the same retailer or wholesaler, as evidenced in LTVTP's business patterns.

CONCLUSIONS

Despite the Benguet provincial government's establishment of the Benguet Agri-Pinoy Trading Center, the mega-wholesale site that foreshadowed certain demise for LTVTP enterprises, the latter's viability and popularity as an essential source of provisioning for farmers, disposers, buyers, and consumers, endures. As popular media sources continue to document, "Even with the pressure of BAPTC, the La Trinidad Trading Post remains one of the busiest vegetable trading hubs in Northern Luzon" (Catajan 2018; see also Alimondo 2020). LTVTP traders formally advocated for the right to continue their enterprises when BAPTC opened in 2015 and through a "subaltern mode of spreading-out" to secure "opaque urban spaces" (Bayat 2012:123, 121) they expanded and diversified the commodity flows that could further anchor their businesses. That municipal and provincial officials legalized LTVTP wholesalers' tenancy and continue to tolerate their informal-and-not-so-legal initiatives demonstrates how traders' cumulative actions have, in effect, normalized their previously marginalized trade to significantly "upset the prevailing urban order" (Yiftachel 2012:152). In so doing, LTVTP wholesale traders have thus mitigated, to date, the threat of being displaced by BAPTC which, despite its sprawling grounds, continues to operate substantially under full capacity (Membrere 2017:1; Palangchao 2020).

The resultant dynamics and ongoing need for the LTVTP's provisioning systems highlight the futility of crafting urban development after a model that potentially jeopardizes livelihoods and consumption options across sectors. Understanding cities as "multiplex" and "internally differentiated" spaces encompassing relations that span "interaction and disconnection, sociability and alienation" materializes the diversity of ordinary cities and how urbanites such as LTVTP wholesale traders can use their voice to more advantageously craft the character of their work and the consumption options they offer (Robinson 2006:10, 171–72). That LTVTP market players have effectively sustained and diversified patterns of fresh food provisioning in the face of government constraints evidences how conflict and reconciliation, civic engagement, and everyday politics can be negotiated when competing ideologies clash over rights to livelihood, marketplace modernization, and the best way to facilitate a city's quality of life for and by its residents.

ACKNOWLEDGMENTS

The fieldwork for this chapter has been conducted from 2013 to 2020. Financial support has been provided by the Social Sciences and Humanities Research Council of Canada (2012–2016) and by the University of the

Philippines Baguio. In the Philippines, Lynne Milgram is affiliated with the Cordillera Studies Center, University of the Philippines Baguio working with Lorelei Mendoza in the College of Social Sciences. We thank our research assistant, Corinna Villanueva, who assisted us in the Philippines and informed Lynne of events during the year. To all those working and shopping at the LTVTP and who answered our numerous questions, we owe a debt of gratitude.

NOTES

1. Following the LTVTP closure in late March 2020 due to the pandemic of COVID-19, the LTVTP reopened for business on April 14, 2020, with appropriate health precautions in place (Alimondo 2020).
2. Parts of this section build on and expand previously published material in Milgram (2019:54–55).
3. All personal names of people are pseudonyms.

REFERENCES

Alimondo, Lauren. "Private Vegetable Trading Operations Resume." *Sun Star Baguio*, April 14, 2020. https://www.sunstar.com.ph/.../Private-vegetable-trading-operations-resume, accessed September 28, 2020.

AlSayyad, Nezar, and Ananya Roy. "Prologue/Dialogue—Urban Informality: Crossing Borders." In *Urban Informality: Transnational Perspectives from the Middle East, Latin America, and South Asia*, edited by Ananya Roy, and Nezar AlSayyad, 7–30. Lanham, MD: Lexington Books, 2004.

Anderson, Elijah. *The Cosmopolitan Canopy: Race and Civility in Everyday Life*. New York: W.W. Norton, 2011.

Baguio Midland Courier (Staff). "Court Stops Trading Post Closure with 20-Day TRO." *Baguio Midland Courier*, March 6, 2016: 1, 23.

BAPTC (Benguet AgriPinoy Trading Center). *Benguet AgriPinoy Trading Center: Farmers Representatives*. Benguet, Philippines: BAPTC Institutional Development & Extension Services, 2015.

Bayat, Asef. "Politics in the City-Inside-Out." *City & Society* 24, no. 2 (2012): 110–128.

Black, Rachel E. *Porta Palazzo: The Anthropology of an Italian Market*. Philadelphia, PA: University of Pennsylvania Press, 2012.

Bonnin, Christine. "Grand Designs? State Agendas and the Lived Realities of Market Redevelopment in Upland Northern Vietnam." In *Traders in Motion: Identities and Contestations in the Vietnamese Marketplace*, edited by Kirsten W. Endres, and Ann Marie Leshkowich, 55–68. Ithaca, NY: Cornell University Press, 2018.

Cabannes, Yves, and Cecilia Marocchino, eds. *Integrating Food into Urban Planning*. London, UK: UCL Press, 2018.

Catajan, Maria Elena. "Trading Post Closure Upcoming." *Sun Star Baguio*, September 7, 2013: 1, 13.

Catajan, Benjamin. "Alcala Assures Guv on Agri-Pinoy." *Sun Star Baguio*, October 3, 2014: 1, 4.

Catajan, Benjamin "Benguet Dads Okay Trading Post Budget." *Sun Star Baguio*, March 2, 2016a: 3–4.

Catajan, Benjamin. "Trading Post Can Only be Closed by LT Council." *Sun Star Baguio*, March 23, 2016b: 1, 4.

Catajan, Benjamin. "Tabanda Issues Eviction Notice." *Sun Star Baguio*, February 5, 2016: 1, 4.

Catajan, Benjamin. "La Trinidad as an Economic Hub." *Sun Star Baguio*, March 16, 2018. https://www.sunstar.com.ph/article/1501863/Baguio/Feature/La-Trinidad-as-an-economic-hub, accessed September 29, 2020.

Davis, William G. *Social Relations in a Philippine Market: Self-Interest and Subjectivity*. Berkeley, CA: University of California Press, 1973.

Douglass, Mike. "World City Formation in the Asia Pacific Rim: Poverty, 'Everyday' Forms of Civil Society and Environmental Management." In *Cities for Citizens*, edited by Mike Douglass, and Jonathan Friedman, 107–137. Chichester, UK: John Wiley, 1988.

Douglass, Mike, K.C. Ho, and Giok Ling Ooi "Globalization, the City and Civil Society in Pacific Asia." In *Globalization, The City and Civil Society in Pacific Asia*, edited by Mike Douglass, K.C. Ho, and Giok Ling Ooi, 1–26. London; New York: Routledge, 2008.

Empian, Ofelia C. "Only Legislation Can Close LT Trading Post." *Baguio Midland Courier*, March 27, 2016: 1, 37.

Endres, Kirsten W. "Downgraded by Upgrading: Small-Scale Traders, Urban Transformation and Spatial Reconfiguration in Post-Reform Vietnam." *The Cambridge Journal of Anthropology* 32, no. 2, 2014: 97–111.

Filipi, James. "Privatized Transformation of Public Space: Construction of a Marketplace through the Cooptation of Public Space by Private Enterprise and the Aesthetic of Exclusion/Inclusion." *Built Environment* 39, no. 2 (2013): 236–244.

Fine, Ben. *The World of Consumption: The Material and Cultural Revisited*. 2nd edition. London; New York: Routledge, 2002.

Garcés, Eduardo K., and Erika Bedón. "Popular Culture and Heritage in San Roque Market, Quito." In *Contested Markets/Contested Cities: Gentrification and Urban Justice in Retail Spaces*, edited by Sara González, 166–178. London; New York: Routledge, 2017.

Gerber, Jonathan, Sarah Turner, and B. Lynne Milgram. "Food Provisioning and Wholesale Agricultural Commodity Chains in Northern Vietnam." *Human Organization* 73, no. 1 (2014): 50–61.

Goh, Daniel P. S., and Tim Bunnell. "Recentering Southeast Asian Cities." *International Journal of Urban and Regional Research* 37, no. 3 (2013): 825–833.

González, Sara. "Introduction: Studying Markets as Spaces of Contestation." In *Contested Markets/Contested Cities: Gentrification and Urban Justice in Retail Spaces*, edited by Sara González, 1–18. London; New York: Routledge, 2017.

Green, Maia. "Making Africa Middle Class: From Poverty Reduction to the Production of Inequality in Tanzania." *Economic Anthropology* 2, no. 2 (2015): 295–309.

Hansen, Karen Tranberg, Walter E. Little, and B. Lynne Milgram, eds. *Street Economies of the Urban Global South*. Santa Fe, NM: SAR Press, 2013.

Hutchcroft, Paul D., and Joel Rocamora "Patronage Based Parties and the Democratic Deficit in the Philippines: Origins, Evolution and the Imperatives of Reform." In *Routledge Handbook of Southeast Asian Politics*, edited by Richard Robinson, 97–119. London; New York: Routledge, 2012.

Janssens, Freek, and Ceren Sezer. "Marketplaces as an Urban Development Strategy." *Built Environment* 39, no. 2 (2013): 168–171.

Kerkvliet, Benjamin J.T. "Everyday Politics in Peasant Societies (and Ours)." *Journal of Peasant Studies* 36, no. 1 (2009): 227–243.

Lu, Jinky L. "Total Pesticide Exposure Calculation among Vegetable Farmers in Benguet, Philippines." *Journal of Environmental and Public Health* (2009): 1–5. doi: 10 1155/2009/412054.

Marcuse, Peter. "Whose Right(s) to What City?" In *Cities for People Not for Profit: Critical Urban Theory and the Right to the City*, edited by Neil Brenner, Peter Marcuse and Margit Mayer, 24–41. London; New York: Routledge, 2012.

Membrere, Elamae. "BAPTC Trading Starts." *Sun Star Baguio*, December 15, 2016. https://www.sunstar.com.ph/article/115770/Business/-BAPTC-trading-starts-, accessed October 2, 2020.

Membrere, Elamae. "Smooth Operation Assured in BAPTC: Empty Stalls?" *Sun Star Baguio*, January 16, 2017: 1.

Milgram, B. Lynne. "Taking the Street into the Market: The Politics of Space and Work in Baguio City, Philippines." In *Street Economies in the Urban Global South*, edited by Karen Tranberg Hansen, Walter E. Little, and B. Lynne Milgram, 71–92. Santa Fe, NM: SAR Press, 2013.

Milgram, B. Lynne. "Unsettling Urban Marketplace Redevelopment in Baguio City, Philippines." *Economic Anthropology* 1, no. 2 (2015): 77–89.

Milgram, B. Lynne. "Gift-Commodity Entanglements: Repositioning (In)formality in a Transnational Philippine Market Trade." *Anthropologica* 61 (2019): 51–63.

Morales, Alfonso. "Public Markets as Community Development Tools." *Journal of Planning Education and Research* 28, no. 4 (2009): 426–440.

Municipality of La Trinidad. *Municipal Ordinance No. 5-2009*. La Trinidad Vegetable Trading Post Code. Municipality of La Trinidad, Province of Benguet, Republic of the Philippines: Office of the Sangguniang Bayan, 2009.

Palangchao, Harley. "'Salad Bowl' Farmers Face ASEAN Market Challenges." *Baguio Midland Courier*, September 30, 2020. http://www.baguiomidlandcourier.com.ph/anniv17_article.asp?mode=anniv_2017/supplements/harley.txt, accessed September 30, 2020.

Parham, Susan. *Market Place: Food Quarters, Design and Urban Renewal in London*. Cambridge, UK: Cambridge Scholars Publishing, 2012.

Parnell, Susan, and Jennifer Robinson. "(Re)theorizing Cities from the Global South: Looking Beyond Neoliberalism." *Urban Geography* 33, no. 4 (2012): 593–617.

Perera, Nihal, and Wing-Shing Tang, eds. *Transforming Asian Cities: Intellectual Impasse, Asianizing Space and Emerging Translocalities*. London; New York: Routledge, 2013.

Polese, Abel, and Aleksandr Prigarim. "On the Persistence of Bazaars in the Newly Capitalist World: Reflections from Odessa." *Anthropology of East Europe Review* 31, no. 1 (2013): 110–136.

Portes, Alejandro, and Patricia Landolt. "Social Capital: Promise and Pitfalls of Its Role in Development." *Journal of Latin American Studies* 32 (2000): 529–547.

Reyes-Boquiren, Rowena. "The History and Political Economy of the Vegetable Industry in Benguet." *CSC Working Paper Series*. Baguio City, Philippines: Cordillera Studies Center, University of the Philippines Baguio, 1989.

Reyes, Gaudelia, and Carlito Laurean. "A Comprehensive Assessment of Pesticide Residues in Two Vegetable-Farming Municipalities in Benguet." *Northern Luzon Research Journal* 1 (2007): 39–54.

Robinson, Jennifer. *Ordinary Cities: Between modernity and development*. London; New York: Routledge, 2006.

Roy, Anaya. "Slumdog Cities: Rethinking Subaltern Urbanism." *International Journal of Urban and Regional Research* 35, no. 2 (2011): 223–238.

Roy, Anaya. "Worlding the South: Towards a Post-Colonial Urban Theory." In *The Routledge Handbook on Cities of the Global South*, edited by Susan Parnell, and Sophie Oldfield, 9–20. Abingdon, OX: Routledge, 2014.

Schappo, Patricia, and Rianne van Melik. "Meeting on the Marketplace: On the Integrative Potential of the Hague Market." *Journal of Urbanism* 10, no. 3 (2017): 318–322.

Scott, Alan, and Michael Storper. "The Nature of Cities: The Scope and Limits of Urban Theory." *International Journal of Urban and Regional Research* 39, no. 1 (2015): 1–15.

Seale, Kirsten. *Markets, Places, Cities*. London: Routledge, 2016.

Seligmann, Linda J., and Daniel Guevara. "Occupying the Center: Handcraft Vendors, Cultural Vitality, Commodification, and Tourism in Cusco, Peru." *Built Environment* 39, no. 2 (2013): 203–223.

Smart, Alan, and Josephine Smart. "Formalization as Confinement in Colonial Hong Kong." *International Sociology* 32, no. 4 (2017): 437–453.

Smart, Alan, and Filippo Zerilli. "Extralegality." In *A Companion to Urban Anthropology*, edited by Donald M. Nonini, 222–238. New York: John Wiley, 2014.

Sun Star Baguio (staff). "Cordillera to Depend on Agri-Industry in AFTA 2015." *Sun Star Baguio* October 5 (2014): 1, 4.

Sun Star Baguio (staff). "20-day TRO for Trading Post." *Sun Star Baguio*, March 2, 2016a: 1, 3.

Sun Star Baguio (staff). "Trading Post to Remain Open." *Sun Star Baguio*, April 5, 2016b: 1, 4.

Sun Star Baguio (staff). "Local Veggies Still Best for Consumers." *Sun Star Baguio*, February 16, 2018: 3–4.

Turgo, Nelson. "'Laway lang ang kapital' (Saliva as Capital): Social Embeddedness of Market Practices in Brokerage Houses in the Philippines." *Journal of Rural Studies* 43 (2016): 83–93.

Ünlü-Yücesoy, Eda. "Constructing the Marketplace: A Socio-Spatial Analysis of Past Marketplaces of Istanbul." *Built Environment* 39, no. 2 (2013): 190–202.

Watson, Sophie. "The Magic of the Marketplace: Sociality in a Neglected Public Space." *Urban Studies* 46, no. 8 (2009): 1577–1591.

Yiftachel, Oren. "Critical Theory and 'Gray Space': Mobilization of the Colonized." In *Cities for People Not for Profit: Critical Urban Theory and the Right to the City*, edited by Neil Brenner, Peter Marcuse, and Margit Mayer, 24–41. London; New York: Routledge, 2012.

Zukin, Sharon V. Trujillo, P. Frase, D. Jackson, T. Recuber, and A. Walker. "New Retail Capital and Neighborhood Change: Boutiques and Gentrification in New York City." *City & Community* 8, no. 1 (2009): 47–64.

Chapter 7

Normal Uncertainties in a Malagasy Mining Town

Andrew Walsh

Ambondromifehy is an artisanal (small-scale) mining town that, like many communities elsewhere in Madagascar and around the world, is perhaps best understood in terms of its perfectly normal uncertainties. In 1996, this formerly small roadside village of rice farmers and cattle herders was enveloped by a thriving sapphire trade, with prospecting miners, petty traders, entrepreneurs, and other usual suspects of a mining boom packing themselves in alongside the community's few longtime residents. Over a matter of months, a communal landscape once dotted with family compounds, sacred trees, and shady gathering spots was transformed into a maze of tightly packed huts, trading stands, and shops. From the very start of the boom, Ambondromifehy was reckoned by outside observers and residents alike as chaotic, disorderly, and abnormal—a place of drifters and criminals, of shady deals and illegal mining, of shallow social connections easily broken. In postboom years, however, the town has continued along its own distinctive developmental path toward a new normalcy—still fundamentally unlike the small community it had once been, but normal nonetheless in the sense of being familiar, and even comfortable, to those who continue to abide its unquestionable uncertainties.

In this chapter I tell just a small part of the story of Ambondromifehy's development, drawing especially from the accounts of two men who, although postrush arrivals, considered themselves responsible residents of the town. In situating and discussing their reflections on the role that the Malagasy state and its representatives have (and have not) played in fostering and addressing the uncertainties of life in this place, I hope to illustrate how an outwardly marginal-seeming community like this one has maintained its own kind of order—an order founded not in the familiar centers of state and/or traditional governance but in the distinctive uncertainties presented by lives and livelihoods enabled by the local sapphire trade.

ENCOUNTERING THE ABNORMAL IN AMBONDROMIFEHY

I first heard about Ambondromifehy on a plane, in 1997, on my way back to the Ankarana region of northern Madagascar where I had lived and conducted ethnographic research for almost two years from 1992 to 1994. My seatmate had recently traveled the highway I would shortly be taking into Ankarana and told me to look out for Ambondromifehy, assuring me that I wouldn't miss it. He was right. I had traveled that highway dozens of times in previous years without ever taking notice of the place, but when I encountered it later that day, the apparent chaos of it was overwhelming. Thousands of young men and women crowded the road, forcing the bush taxi I was riding in to a crawl.

Over the years since that first encounter, I have returned to Ambondromifehy often, applying ethnographic methods to the task of making sense of what this rush and its aftermath have brought to the region. As others working in artisanal mining communities have noted, I have found that the apparent chaos that accompanies a mining rush often belies patterns of social and economic organization and exchange that, while unfamiliar at first, are unquestionably linked to the traditional, mainstream, or otherwise normal systems and ideologies in contrast to which the chaotic is defined. In the early years of the rush, for example, both outside observers and longtime residents of Ambondromifehy often highlighted the outrageous, conspicuous spending habits of the boomtown's young men as indicators of the community's abnormality, telling me stories of how sums of money that might elsewhere have supported families for years were being spent by miners in single nights of hedonistic consumption. This wasn't all hyperbole. I too was shocked by the apparent shortsightedness of so many of the young men I met while doing research in Ambondromifehy in those early years. But there was also something familiar about these young men, not least in how they invited accusations of irresponsibility from elders and other critical observers. Although the stakes had changed considerably, the conspicuous consumption and other apparently abnormal and transgressive habits they were engaging in weren't really so far from other sorts of "daring" behavior (fighting, drinking alcohol, wrangling cattle, driving fast, and the like) for which young Malagasy men in other, apparently normal, communities are so well known and so commonly admonished (Walsh 2003). Another genre of story offered by observers of Ambondromifehy's postrush abnormality featured a broader cast of apparently flawed, irresponsible protagonists. These were stories of people "burning" or conning those to whom they would be most obligated under normal circumstances—miners cheating pit-mates they called "brothers" out of profits that should have been shared, newly arrived prospectors reneging on promises made to longtime residents they called "grandparents," women fleecing and fleeing men they called "husbands," and so on (Walsh 2009). Once again, though, underlying such apparent abnormality were familiar patterns of reciprocal exchange and their associated anxieties, processes, and possibilities that prevailed just as well elsewhere as here.

To other, differently positioned, observers of the rush, it wasn't Ambondromifehy's residents' behavior toward one another that was deemed most problematic, but their apparent disregard for the environmental consequences of their work. Ambondromifehy sits alongside Ankarana National Park, one of Madagascar's best-known and most visited protected conservation areas. For reasons to be discussed further shortly, miners had begun prospecting and mining within the park in late 1996, and by the time I arrived in 1997, the national conservation agency responsible for managing the park had lost control of the place. As what Sodikoff might term "low-wage conservationists" (2009), park guards had neither the incentive nor the means to keep thousands of miners out of the park and away from the sapphire veins underlying its famed limestone massifs. In reports that circulated well beyond the region, Ambondromifehy's miners came to be portrayed as shortsighted ravagers, bent on destroying Ankarana's delicate ecosystems and threatening the region's burgeoning, and purportedly sustainable, ecotourist trade. What such portrayals missed, however, is that miners were certainly not alone in their willingness to defy conservation policies that appeared to privilege foreign interests, or to test and cross the boundaries of supposedly "taboo" places in pursuit of their livelihoods (Walsh 2005, 2006).

In introducing Ambondromifehy as I have here, I do not intend to present it as just another Malagasy community in which young men behave irresponsibly, brothers turn on brothers, grandparents are disappointed, spouses leave one another, and people have complex relationships with local landscapes and the authorities who govern access to them. As I had been warned before I ever saw it, Ambondromifehy was and remains unmistakably different than other communities. And yet, as hinted at in the examples just offered, a number of the most distinctive features of life in this place also spoke to certain broader realities facing all people in Madagascar—people who make lives alongside one another amid complex networks of mutual responsibility that knot them up not just with the elders, neighbors, workmates, patrons, siblings, spouses, children, and landscapes, but also with politicians, police, soldiers, conservation workers, state officials, ancestors, land spirits, and other, often distant, authorities that claim and/or are attributed the power to exert influence over what goes on in their lives. In my experience, what makes Ambondromifehy such a noteworthy place is not, as other observers often stress, that it is a place of marginal actors whose transgressions suggest abnormalities that need righting, but that it is a place in which people are negotiating new norms to fit the distinctive uncertainties that are forever ahead of them. In abiding Ambondromifehy's uncertainties, the community's postboom residents have established new normals through engagements with and reflections on the ambiguities of the norms and centers in relation to which others so commonly reckon them abnormal or marginal. In keeping with the central themes of this book, in the next two sections I focus especially on how this process is apparent in how Malagasy state policies, projects, and representatives have figured in Ambondromifehy's supposedly abnormal development over the past 20 years.

THE RUSH

Madagascar is often characterized as one of the world's remaining frontiers of mineral wealth, and the country has not surprisingly become an important target for transnational mining investment and large-scale project development. That noted, the majority of people currently involved in Madagascar's mining sector, including the residents of Ambondromifehy, are occupied with what it commonly termed "informal" or "artisanal/small-scale mining." While each of these labels carries meanings of its own, they share in being most commonly invoked in contrast with what they are *not*, that is, informal mining is *not* formalized mining (regulated, structured, and monitored according to established standards), and artisanal/small-scale mining is *not* industrial and/or large in scale. A preference for formalized, large-scale mining is generally implied in such contrasts, the thinking being that corporations and state partner-regulators can do a better job of squeezing sustainable development from the fundamentally unsustainable work of mining. In Madagascar, as Remy Canavesio has recently noted, successive governments over the past several decades have tended to favor mining codes that have enabled "foreign stakeholders to gain access to Malagasy mining resources," ensuring the success of "many investment projects in the formal mining sector" (2014:147). However, this same period has also seen rapid growth in the country's informal mining sector, growth driven not by policy but by the adaptive reactions of Malagasy people themselves to the country's profound economic and political uncertainties.

The account of northern Madagascar's sapphire rush offered here is drawn largely from a 1999 interview I conducted with Rejean, a man in his 30s who was, at the time of our conversation, the president of an association of independent miners. Rejean was among the first prospectors to arrive in the region in 1996, and like other early arrivals he entered the rush with extensive experience of the informality of artisanal mining, having lived and worked previously in a gold-mining region nearly 50 kilometers south of Ambondromifehy. Knowing nothing of sapphires (and all that made them different from gold) at the time, what brought him to the region were not just rumors of the great value of this heretofore unknown stone, but a good indication of that value in the form of a newly established mining project in the hilly terrain east of Ambondromifehy—a project overseen by a small company that had, after months of surveying, secured claims to several large tracts of gem-rich land in the region. "At first it was just eight of us who had come from mining gold," Rejean explained at the start of his account, "After about a week, as word got out, there were 40 of us, and we decided to propose to work together with the company that was already there." The company wasn't receptive to these miners' requests, however, and after several months of tense relations, the fast-growing community of informal miners working on the fringes of the company claim selected a group of men (including Rejean) as representatives to act in the manner of "parents," that is, as representatives responsible to and for their fellow miners. While Rejean and others sought claims to land on which *they* could legally mine for sapphires, however, the company made repeated complaints about them to the nearest police post, located more than 30 kilometers away, and the police and military eventually entered the scene and forced miners out. It was only then, Rejean specified, in October 1996, that prospectors moved their efforts to the other side of the national highway running through the middle of Ambondromifehy, and into what conservationists labeled the "taboo forest" of Ankarana National Park (see Figure 7.1)—an area that, due to its long-standing "protected" status, had not yet been surveyed for possible gem deposits. Miners entered the park en masse on a Saturday, Rejean explained. "Sunday they looked. Monday they looked. On Tuesday [sapphires were found and] it cracked open, and many more followed."

The advent of mining inside Ankarana National Park coincided with the rapid development of Ambondromifehy itself. As any unpermitted entry into the park was illegal, there were no impromptu settlements of miners, buyers, and entrepreneurs like the ones to be found at the sites of mining rushes elsewhere in the region. Instead, miners traveled into the park under cover of darkness, mined covertly over several days (often hidden from sight within the caves for which the park is well known), and then returned to Ambondromifehy to sell what they had found and stock up on provisions. And as the town and trade grew, sapphire prices rose and accompanying stories of conspicuous consumption spread. It was around this time, Rejean noted, that a stone first sold for a million Malagasy francs (around US$65).

Then one sold for 5 million, then 12 million, and so on, opening new opportunities for speculation among fast-learning Malagasy traders with money to invest, and setting off a period of great diversification in the local trade.

Although working inside the "taboo forest" of Ankarana National Park freed miners like Rejean from conflicts with the company and the state representatives (police and military, as well as representatives of the ministry

Figure 7.1 A Tree Marking the Boundary of Ankarana National Park That Warns Artisanal Miners to Keep Out of the "taboo forest" (*ala fady*). *Source*: Photo by Andrew Walsh.

of mines) who supported its claims, this move necessitated new negotiations with the national conservation agency and still more state officials. "It was not our intention to mess up the 'taboo forest,'" Rejean assured me as he had assured the conservation workers and other concerned parties with whom he met at the time. "It's that [they] haven't given us any land on which we can mine, from which we can make our living." Miners' demands were eventually met with the promise of access to land on the outskirts of the park, but this promise never materialized. As the months went on, many more thousands of fortune hunters arrived, and the informal workings of the local sapphire trade became further embedded in Ambondromifehy. By the time I arrived to live in the community in 1999, conservation workers could do little but watch as thousands entered Ankarana National Park. Police and military took over the job of trying to keep people out of the park, but many of them reportedly became involved in the trade as well, fostering a climate in which people like Rejean had good reason to distrust anyone involved in state efforts at regulating their access to mining sites. At times, such distrust extended to foreigners as well, as many speculated as to the *real* motivations of the foreign conservationists and ecotourists who were being welcomed into the very forests from which miners were being restricted (Walsh 2005).

Listening to Rejean's words more than 15 years after I recorded them, I am especially struck by his insistence on referring to the people he represented in various negotiations with the company, the conservation agency, and various state officials not as *mpitandraka* or *mineurs*—that is, as miners—but as *vahoaka*—"the people," citizens, or, most broadly, subjects of a polity—the implication being that he represented those with political rights that ought to be acknowledged, even if they were mining illegally on claims titled to a company or within the bounds of a protected area. The point became especially clear as he described the electoral campaign of a fellow leader of the miners' rights movement in 1998. The candidate's populist platform was simple—his election to the National Assembly, he promised, would support the interests of the thousands of miners and others in the region whose visions of development clashed with those of an existing government that so clearly privileged the interests of private mining companies and international conservation organizations. It wasn't meant to be, however. Although the candidate's name was eventually put on the ballot, the vast majority of adults in Ambondromifehy (new arrivals with good reason to favor this candidate) were not allowed to vote. "We weren't given electoral cards," Rejean exclaimed,

> They didn't let "the people" [*vahoaka*] vote. We didn't have the right. Why is it that all the people [in other communities] around Ambondromifehy were allowed to vote, but we in Ambondromifehy couldn't vote even though we are

> children of Madagascar? They said we were "visitors" [*vahiny*], but if you are born in Madagascar you aren't a visitor! Even a foreigner with Malagasy citizenship is not a visitor. It should be that when a person comes to a community and lives more than three months, they are no longer a visitor but a person "responsible for the community" [*tompontanana*, a term most reserved for longtime residents of Ambondromifehy]. It's already three years now that we've been living here. And we cannot vote. That's why I say that we don't have the rights that make us humans.

By the late 1990s, the Malagasy state had been implementing structural adjustment policies (with advice and support from the International Monetary Fund and The World Bank) intended to liberalize the economy for some time already, fostering a political-economic environment favoring market-driven growth, foreign investment, land privatization, strict natural resource management, and the interests of international conservation organizations (Corson 2016)—an environment, in other words, in which independent miners like Rejean struggled to find a viable footing. As noted earlier, this was a period in which the state was promoting the country's mineral resources as important assets that could be harnessed in order to serve the public good. And yet, as Rejean and others in Ambondromifehy experienced it, state engagement with "the people" around these resources left much to be desired. In the month following the election of 1998, he joined almost a thousand others in a massive, weeklong protest in the nearby provincial capital city of Antsiranana. "We didn't go to make trouble," he explained, "We had one question: What is there to do?"

As Rejean described them, the proposals forwarded by the miners' movement on this and other occasions invariably included provisions for the formalization of their work—miners and collectors would have photo-ID "badges," he assured me, to ensure that their comings and goings from regulated areas could be tracked, and that all of the people making money from sapphires would pay taxes. But these proposals were continually turned away, as were any requests for the funding of even the most basic public services (schools, wells, medical clinics, and the like) for the residents of Ambondromifehy. Not even emergencies threatening 'the people' of the community inspired much of a response. In the two months prior to my discussion with Rejean, Ambondromifehy's residents had been struck by a massive fire and an outbreak of cholera, neither of which elicited any substantial assistance. "What does this mean?" Rejean asked toward the end of our discussion, commenting further on the fact that none of six recent requests for governmental assistance had received a response. "We don't know, I can tell you."

There is little question that, as far as many were concerned, the simplest solution to the headache posed by Ambondromifehy would have been for the rush to end and the thousands of "visitors" who had descended on the region to move on and elsewhere. Indeed, hope came to some critical observers of Ambondromifehy's abnormal development in the form of a new, and even larger, sapphire rush in southern Madagascar that had already drawn many of Ambondromifehy's most daring prospectors away by the time I spoke with Rejean in 1999. I asked Rejean about this (then) new rush and the associated assurances I had heard from some that Ambondromifehy's sapphire trade would soon collapse. "I can't imagine Ambondromifehy without people," he said, "people will come and go. New rushes will crack open and people will go to them. But so long as there are sapphires here, there will be people." Rejean was right. The year 2016 marked the twentieth anniversary of the rush, and as of 2019 Ambondromifehy remains a sapphire mining and trading town—albeit of a different sort to the one in which I had first met Rejean.

BACK TO NORMAL?

Over the decade following my conversation with Rejean, indicators of the predicted decline of Ambondromifehy were easy to observe. Most obvious to me when I returned for an extended visit in 2003 was the fact that many of the houses of the miners and traders with whom I had spent time previously—houses that, in other communities, would have indicated people's investment and long-term intentions in a place—had been abandoned. Not just abandoned, though, but abandoned in an especially irresponsible way, without any notice given to neighbors left behind. In the densely packed maze that Ambondromifehy had become during the rush, abandoned houses were dangerous in that they provided fuel for quick-spreading fires. In response to this clear sign of decline and shallow social relations among neighbors, however, another trend emerged: those who had stayed behind had begun meeting to deliberate over and address the problem posed by these abandoned houses. And so, by communal decision, abandoned houses were being systematically dismantled, even without the permission of those who had built them—something that, in other communities, would have never been considered. The lots that opened up were taken over by longtime residents or those relative newcomers who intended to stay on longer, transformed into larger courtyards, gardens for manioc and greens, or planted with trees that wouldn't bear fruit or give shade for several years. Although Ambondromifehy was unquestionably the site of many shallow passages through its earliest boomtime years, over the decades of apparent decline that followed, it has become a place of deepening engagements and increasingly normal uncertainties (Walsh 2012, 2015; see Figure 7.2).

Figure 7.2 A One-Time Sapphire Trading Stand in Ambondromifehy That Had, by 2013, Been Converted to a Stand for Selling Squashes. *Source*: Photo by Andrew Walsh.

Luc, a one-time miner turned collector, is one of a number of postboom settlers I make a point of visiting whenever I'm back in Ambondromifehy—we first met in 2003, and I saw him most recently in 2018. In 2010, I asked Luc about whether he ever intended to *hody* or "return home" to the region on Madagascar's northeast coast from which he had emigrated. He corrected me, explaining that it was (by then) Ambondromifehy to which he "returns home" following visits elsewhere on the island. This was a home of a different kind, however. As embedded as he had become in this community by the time of that conversation, he has always been (and remains) on the lookout for new opportunities elsewhere. He will leave for good eventually, he told me in 2017, reminding me that, as he had explained years earlier, "Ambondromifehy is an easy place to live in, but it is an easy place to leave."

Although Luc, like Rejean, claimed to have become *tompontanana*—someone "responsible for the community" in Ambondromifehy—he was clearly a very different sort of resident than the *tompontanana* who have been farming, raising cattle, tending ancestral tombs, and invoking land spirits in the region for generations. Where longtime resident *tompontanana* seek prosperity through, and are in many ways constituted by, processes and responsible relationships intended to ensure various sorts of continuity, productivity, and growth, Luc's strategy for making a living here, and thus one of the main sources of his social being, was fundamentally different in being extractive and temporary.

That Luc's priorities and interests were quite different from those of Ambondromifehy's longtime residents does not make him abnormal, however. Like other postboom inhabitants of Ambondromifehy I have met over the years, he might well be classified among the millions of others for whom, as Abdou Maliq Simone has put it, "movement" has become "an increasingly 'normalized' social practice" (2003:8) that is especially well suited to the uncertain economic and political circumstances with which they live. As suggested in the previous section, and as Simone suggests has been the case more broadly, Luc and others are no strangers to "popular disillusionment with [the state], labor-intensive demands of securing basic needs, an entrenched 'negotiability' of justice, and [the] deleterious effects of internationally mandated and supervised economic reform processes" (2003:1). Not that such conditions preclude the "persistence of stable moral economies, viable livelihoods and production systems" that keep people in place, however. As Simone specifies, sources of stability and certainty that have traditionally kept people in place continue to "survive," but they do so "within a context where their capacity to socialize and to be an authoritative structuring of people's practices, anticipations, and loyalties must increasingly co-exist with more 'grab what one can however one can' economies" (2003: 2). And as indicated in Luc's reflections on the developing history of Ambondromifehy, the role of the state in such contexts seems destined to remain an ambiguous one.

Where Rejean decried the state's apparent lack of interest in seeing Ambondromifehy develop like other communities during the early years of the rush, by 2006 Luc was in a good position to argue that the withdrawal of state institutions and oversight had actually improved the lot of people like him. Perhaps the most dramatic shift came in 2002 with the destruction of the town's newly built police post amid a national political crisis. Although rumors circulated that the post's destruction was the work of disgruntled miners who were fed up after years of shoddy treatment by the police, Luc avoided such a simple version, suggesting that the equally corrupt and untrustworthy military had played a role as well. Regardless, the effects of post's destruction were profound. As early as 2004, miners who had once feared being raided, shaken down, and potentially jailed and/or fined by local police had moved into Ankarana National Park, occupying mining sites within the protected area in ways that, while still not legal, were no longer covert. With this occupation of the park came the relative normalization of miners' relations with their mining sites and with one another, as mechanisms for regulating disputes among claimants to particular pits or sapphire veins took shape. In town too, a diminishing population and the absence of the police coincided with a return to relatively normal, safer, communal life. By 2006, for example, Luc kept money in his house without fear of being robbed. The town's once notorious thieves were no longer a threat, he reported. Besides, he added, whatever threat they posed was less than that posed by governmental workers and bankers who would surely "eat" away at his earnings if he ever declared and tried to save them.

From the earliest years of the rush, the most powerful civic associations in Ambondromifehy were those that linked newcomers from the same home region. These associations, common in other ethnically heterogeneous communities in Madagascar, offered members aid in times of crisis, ensuring, for example, that members who died while away would be able to have their bodies transported home. Indeed, the local candidate in the election discussed in the previous section was put forward not by a political party, but by the membership of one such regional association. As Luc noted in both 2006 and 2008, other kinds of association were hard to manage here. No matter how close residents of the town had become through common participation in the sapphire trade, they have also "met when grown"—an expression I often heard in explanations of why it is that people in Ambondromifehy so often seem to distrust one another. Meeting when grown means *not* sharing a sense of shared responsibility to/for elders, ancestors, land spirits, and other authorities to whom people who grow up and make lives together might hold one another accountable. What made regional associations different, Luc suggested, was their role in transporting bodies to the "ancestral lands" to which they were meant to return. Only a fool, he said, would steal money that had been set aside for such a purpose. Funds raised through dues paid to associations of miners or collectors, or by the parents of schoolchildren intent on building a new room for a schoolhouse, or even by members of a religious congregation were less dangerous, in his estimation, and it wasn't unusual for such money to be "eaten" by those entrusted with it.

Although Ambondromifehy's population had fallen considerably since the height of the boom (from over 15,000 to around 3,000), by 2010 the community was unquestionably big and well established enough to warrant the services and attention that other, much smaller, communities in the region took for granted. None of the public projects proposed by Rejean and other local leaders in 1999—an expanded state school, a health clinic, and a water tower, for example—had been carried out, however. While some residents suggested the possibility that, given its size and importance to the local economy, Ambondromifehy ought to have an electrical generator and grid, this notion seemed far-fetched and inadvisable to Luc. As he saw it, although Ambondromifehy could certainly do with more services, these services would only come with costs and oversight that he was happy to live without. A water system would mean having to pay for water; an electrical grid would mean having to pay for electricity. What made Ambondromifehy such an appealing place to wait out his next move was its low cost of living, he explained, and more state services would likely make the place more expensive. What's more, he worried that more state involvement might mean renewed efforts at formalizing the region's sapphire trade. By 2006, the police were coming to town only rarely, usually to support conservation agents concerned with loggers and charcoal producers operating within Ankarana National Park. Although still numerous, miners were apparently no longer a concern. This, Luc specified, was not a product of a change in state policy regarding Ambondromifehy and the activities of its residents, however. Rather, the opening up of the "taboo forest" to miners was a sign of just how "disorderly" and/or "unstable" (*tsy milamina*) the Malagasy government had become.

The fact that Ambondromifehy has remained underserved by the state over the past 20 years is undoubtedly related in part to the political turmoil of this period. The effects of two successive national political crises (in 2001–2002 and 2009–2011) are, in the wake of yet another disputed election in late 2018, still being felt throughout the island. That all crises involved rumors of corrupt politicians and public officials as well as related concerns over the (mis)management of Madagascar's land and mineral resources only supports local miners' and traders' sense that the interests of state representatives and officials in the local sapphire trade are competing with their own. The lack of attention paid to Ambondromifehy during its postboom years indicated more than just ineffective governance, however. There was something deliberate to it as well, as indicated by the fact that over the same period other communities in the region did receive state support for the kinds of projects that Rejean had promoted. For example, the nearby community of Mahamasina, located at the main entrance to Ankarana National Park, received considerable assistance for water and education projects from both governmental and international nongovernmental sources, even despite its relatively small population. But this is not surprising. As the burgeoning center of the region's ecotourist trade, Mahamasina promises the sort of sustainable development that international advisers, conservationists, and the Malagasy state recommend. Ambondromifehy, on the other hand, has never shaken its reputation as a place to avoid. Although no longer home to the thievery, conspicuous consumption, and chaos for which it was known in the early years of the rush, it remains abnormal in appearing fundamentally *un*sustainable—always "near dead" as outsiders have often told me.

On return visits to Ambondromifehy in 2004, 2006, 2008, 2010, 2013, 2015, 2017, and 2018, I have been assured repeatedly (as I had been as early as 1999) that the sapphire trade would soon collapse entirely. And there has been no shortage of departures of miners and traders to cite as evidence of the coming end. First, in 1998, it was the major sapphire rush in southern

Madagascar that drew so many away. Then a ruby rush in the southeast. And then a gold rush in the very region from which the community's earliest prospecting newcomers had come. Between our 2008 and 2010 conversations, Luc had joined thousands of others in leaving town for a demantoid (green garnet) rush several hundred kilometers to the south. His and others' stories of that rush echoed those I had recorded about life in Ambondromifehy just a decade earlier. Luc and others returned home to Ambondromifehy put off not just by the uncertainties of dealing in a new sort of gemstone, but the discomforts and insecurity of the rush itself. "There's too much mafia," Luc recounted in describing the place in 2010,

> "Too many criminals. They spray people in the eyes [with aerosol mace] and then rob them. Those of us who had come from [Ambondromifehy] weren't comfortable there. It isn't stable/orderly [*tsy milamina*]. Here it is. Do you notice that even the [Thai gem buyers] sleep here [in Ambondromifehy]? There is no mafia here. There!? A foreigner wouldn't dare sleep there. They'd come into your room with a machine gun. Here [i.e., Ambondromifehy] is a place that makes one comfortable [mahatamana]."

In contrasting Ambondromifehy's orderliness/stability with the chaos of the demantoid rush, Luc used the same expression—*tsy milamina*—that he had earlier used to describe the disorder and instability of the Malagasy government. In retrospect, it seems clear that whatever order or stability Ambondromifehy has achieved over the past 20 years has come not just in the absence of orderly state governance or the formalization of a chaotic trade or the effective regulation of access to Ankarana National Park but as a partial result of these absences. As Simone might predict, Luc and others who have been left to their own devices in Ambondromifehy may not be reproducing the "moral economies, viable livelihoods and production systems" of their parents, but much as the mobility that has brought them to this place has become normalized, so too have the profound uncertainties that come with their work in this place.

REFERENCES

Canavesio, Remy. "Formal Mining Investments and Artisanal Mining in Southern Madagascar: Effects of Spontaneous Reactions and Adjustment Policies on Poverty Alleviation." *Land Use Policy* 36 (2014): 145–154.

Corson, Catherine. *Corridors of Power: The Politics of Environmental Aid to Madagascar*. New Haven: Yale University Press, 2016.

Simone, Abdou Maliq. "Moving Towards Uncertainty: Migration and the Turbulence of African Urban Life." *Conference on African Migration in Comparative Perspective, Johannesburg, South Africa*, 2003.

Sodikoff, Genese. "The Low-Wage Conservationist: Biodiversity and Perversities of Value in Madagascar." *American Anthropologist* 111, no. 4 (2009): 443–455.

Walsh, Andrew. "Lost and/or Left Behind in a Malagasy Outpost of the 'Underworld of Gemstones.'" *Critique of Anthropology* 35, no. 1 (2015): 30–46.

Walsh, Andrew. "After the Rush: Living with Uncertainty in a Malagasy Mining Town." *Africa: The Journal of the International African Institute* 82, no. 2 (2012): 235–251.

Walsh, Andrew. "The Grift: Getting Burned in the Northern Malagasy Sapphire Trade." In *Economics and Morality: Anthropological Approaches*, edited by Katherine E. Browne and B. Lynne Milgram, 59–76. Lanham: Altamira Press, 2009.

Walsh, Andrew. "'Nobody has a Money Taboo': Situating Ethics in a Northern Malagasy Sapphire Mining Town." *Anthropology Today* 22, no. 4 (2006): 4–8.

Walsh, Andrew. "The Obvious Aspects of Ecological Underprivilege in Ankarana, Northern Madagascar." *American Anthropologist* 107, no. 4 (2005): 654–665.

Walsh, Andrew. "In the Wake of Things: Speculating in and about Sapphires in Northern Madagascar." *American Anthropologist* 106, no. 2 (2004): 225–237.

Walsh, Andrew. "'Hot Money' and Daring Consumption in a Northern Malagasy Sapphire-mining Town." *American Ethnologist* 30, no. 2 (2003): 290–305.

Chapter 8

To Legally Beg or Illegally Work?

Norms and Illegality among Asylum Seekers in Hong Kong

Gordon Mathews

Hong Kong at present has some 12,000 asylum seekers from countries around the world.[1] The Hong Kong government readily takes in most of those who claim to be asylum seekers, but only very rarely deems them refugees: those whose claims are seen as legitimate. Asylum seekers receive a minimal Hong Kong government subsidy and are strictly prohibited from working. However, it is extremely difficult to live on this subsidy in Hong Kong, and so many of them work anyway, risking the possibility of two years in jail. Asylum seekers may stay in Hong Kong waiting for many years while their claims are evaluated and, typically, eventually rejected. In Hong Kong, more than in many other societies, work is the raison d'etre of adults; one in the prime of life who does not work is not seen as a full human being. Not allowing asylum seekers to work is a way of denying their full humanity, a government strategy in a society increasingly pushed to be Chinese, and that does not want developing-world foreigners in its midst, unless they are female maids.[2] However, Hong Kong also requires the illegal labor of asylum seekers, and asylum seekers themselves seek to work.

In this chapter, based on interactions with asylum seekers in a class I have taught weekly at Hong Kong's Chungking Mansions (see Figure 8.1) for the past 15 years, as well as interviews with 120 asylum seekers, with government-employed interpreters for asylum seekers, and with police and a few immigration officials (see Mathews 2011, 2012, 2014, 2018), I explore how asylum seekers are forced by government policy into a situation in which they can either be legal and live off government subsidies as, in effect, beggars in violation of Hong Kong social norms; or they can be illegal and live off the wages of work, conforming to Hong Kong social norms, but, if they are unlucky, winding up in jail. For these asylum seekers, norms and legality are in direct contradiction in Hong Kong, a situation used by the Hong Kong government as a means of keeping asylum seekers apart from Hong Kong life. I first discuss in the pages that follow the basic situation of asylum seekers in Hong Kong. I then examine the issue asylum seekers face of whether or not to work, and how asylum seekers go about working while avoiding getting caught and jailed. I then examine work as a means to finding a marriage

Figure 8.1 Entrance to Chungking Mansions, Hong Kong. *Source*: Photo by Gordon Mathews.

partner and earning a Hong Kong ID card. Finally, I examine the larger implications of the Hong Kong government's policy toward asylum seekers, in placing them in an untenable situation in following either Hong Kong norms or Hong Kong laws:[3] there is a reasonable solution to the problem of asylum seekers in Hong Kong today, but it is one that will probably never be enacted.

THE SITUATION OF ASYLUM SEEKERS IN HONG KONG

Asylum seekers are those who have fled their countries but have not yet been legally recognized as refugees by the United Nations High Commissioner for Refugees (UNHCR) or by host governments. Up until 2014, Hong Kong relied on the UNHCR for the determination of who was valid as a refugee; alternatively, asylum seekers turned to the Convention Against Torture (CAT) to make their claims, as decided by the Hong Kong government. Only a very small number of asylum seekers were granted refugee status, enabling them to be resettled in the United States or Canada: the UNHCR accepted less than 10% of claimants (Chen 2013); through CAT, under 1% were accepted: only 77 claimants of 3,000 who applied (Justice Centre Hong Kong 2014: 5). In 2014, the Hong Kong government began a Unified Screening Mechanism, taking over the determination of refugee status from the UNHCR. Since the Unified Screening Mechanism was adopted, of 23,184 claims, only 77 have been substantiated, an acceptance rate of well under 1% (Legislative Council, Hong Kong. 2019). This is a far lower rate of acceptance of asylum seekers than other societies in the developed world. But while some asylum seekers have been deported to their home countries after their claims and appeals have been rejected several thousand face deportation (Leung 2018), most wait many years in a Hong Kong limbo: some members of the class of asylum seekers I teach have been in Hong Kong 13 years or more.

The large majority of asylum seekers in Hong Kong are from South Asia, with some 10% from sub-Saharan Africa, and increasing numbers from Southeast Asia; most asylum seekers are male between the ages of 20 and 40, with less than 25% female. One reason why most are young and male is that young men are more likely to be politically active, but also, young men may feel the burden to economically support their birth or marital families, and may feel economically and socially stymied within their developing-world home countries. The biggest reason for this national distribution of asylum seekers is geographic: while asylum seekers in Africa, Syria, and Afghanistan seek to go to Europe, those from India, Pakistan, and to an extent East Africa, as well as Indonesia and the Philippines, may seek to come to Hong Kong. Hong Kong's population is largely made up of those whose families fled

China at some point over the past 60 years. Nonetheless, Hong Kong has long suffered from panics over illegal immigrants, from the outcries over Vietnamese boat people in the 1980s and 1990s (McCalmon 1994; Chan 2003), to worries in the 2000s over mainland women seeking to deliver their babies in Hong Kong.

The current wave of South Asian and African asylum seekers began coming to Hong Kong in the wake of 9/11 and the tightening of visa restrictions in other developed countries. The Hong Kong government has since the early 2000s provided a stipend to asylum seekers, at present HK$2,700 of rent assistance and food rations (with no cash ever entering asylum seekers' own hands). This sum—some US$348—is sufficient to stave off destitution, the Hong Kong government claims, while avoiding "a magnet effect" of asylum seekers flocking to Hong Kong (W. Chan 2013); but asylum seekers say that this is insufficient, and so they have no choice but to work. In 2014, a protest by asylum seekers took place, in this case against an NGO contracted by the government to provide assistance to asylum seekers (Vecchio and Beatson 2014). Although articles in the English language press remain generally favorable to the situation of asylum seekers in Hong Kong, newspapers in the Hong Kong Chinese language press have become increasingly critical (see, e.g., *Oriental Daily* 2015), and some politicians have begun to inveigh against asylum seekers, such as the email I received recently from a Hong Kong political candidate: "Expeditiously Formulating Measures to Combat BOGUS REFUGEES."

Hong Kong is different from many other developed-world societies in several respects. First, it has a relatively liberal immigration policy. If people from Tanzania or India or a number of other developing-world countries fly to New York or Tokyo without a visa, they will be returned to their home countries. However, in Hong Kong, they will be admitted on a tourist permit issued at the Hong Kong airport. Not all developing-world countries have easy admission: Pakistanis and Nigerians require visas. But the general ease of admission to Hong Kong makes the issue of asylum seekers an acute problem, and makes Hong Kong a destination of choice for some savvy asylum seekers. (Other asylum seekers, however, particularly those who entrust their journey to an agent, may have been promised passage to the United States, Canada, or Europe, and may rub their eyes in shock when they find themselves in Hong Kong.) Second, unlike most developed countries, Hong Kong accepts almost no asylum seekers as refugees in its own territory. Those accepted as refugees stay in Hong Kong only pending their resettlement elsewhere. Virtually the only way that an asylum seeker can remain in Hong Kong permanently is to marry a Hong Kong resident, and through this means obtain a Hong Kong ID card.

Despite these differences, Hong Kong adopts some of the same rhetoric as elsewhere in the developed world. Asylum seekers are typically seen as legitimate if they are fleeing political, ethnic, or religious persecution, but illegitimate if they are seeking better economic prospects. In fact, the situation of asylum seekers is more complex than this, and the personal, political, and economic are often inextricably woven together in their accounts and lives. A newspaper editorial (*South China Morning Post* 2010) criticized the Hong Kong government for dragging its feet in creating a comprehensive policy toward asylum seekers, saying that "either claimants are genuine and their lives are at risk, or they are merely economic migrants whose claims should be quickly disposed of." However, as Marfleet notes, "increasingly, both pure refugees and purely economic migrants are ideal constructs rarely found in real life" (2006: 310), a statement which applies to Hong Kong as much as anywhere else in the world. In Hong Kong just as in the world at large there is vast disagreement over asylum seekers, with some saying they are innocent victims subjected to forced marginalization, and others claiming that they are cheaters and criminals. As should be apparent from the pages that follow, asylum seekers are in the middle, no worse or no better than any other group of human beings. But if I myself were a young person in Lagos or Karachi or Kolkata with no prospects at home, I would certainly consider becoming an asylum seeker in Hong Kong, as a potential path to a better life.[4]

TO WORK OR NOT TO WORK

Asylum seekers everywhere, unless they are fortunate enough to be well provided for within the society they have wound up in, need to work (Jacobsen 2005). In many European societies, under at least some conditions, such as if their cases remain undecided after 6 months, or after 12 months (Migration Watch UK 2013), asylum seekers may indeed work. In Hong Kong, it is absolutely forbidden, on penalty of jail. Nonetheless, most asylum seekers work.

Those who do not work are often Somali. This is because Somali asylum seekers have accurately gauged that their chance of obtaining refugee status and going to the United States (at least up until 2017) or Canada to live has been high. This is true of no other nationality among asylum seekers in Hong Kong (as of this writing, there are almost no Syrian or Afghan asylum seekers in the territory): for an Indian or Pakistani or Nigerian or Ghanaian or Kenyan or Vietnamese or Indonesian, the chance of obtaining refugee status is all but nonexistent. This difference in acceptance rates is apparently due to the fact that Somalia, with a barely functioning government, has been deemed dangerous, whereas all the other societies mentioned above are deemed peaceful enough to make asylum seekers' claims seem dubious.[5]

This has a very significant effect on the decision of whether or not to work. For Somalis, working in Hong Kong would be extremely risky. All work by asylum seekers is illegal, but getting caught working is quite unusual. Nonetheless, if a Somali asylum seeker were to get caught and be prosecuted and jailed for two years, then the opportunity to be accepted as a refugee overseas may be denied: they have, after all, been convicted of a felony. I know of several Somali asylum seekers who have worked—they have decided that the possibilities of getting caught are low enough that they chanced it—but most Somalis will not do this: why should they risk losing their one great opportunity to obtain a new life in the developed world?

There are a few others who do not work. In several cases I know of, this is because the asylum seeker has been tortured, or suffered persecution, and trusts that the screening system, despite all the odds indicating otherwise, will comprehend this. I have twice visited the home countries of asylum seekers in Africa or South Asia and met with their families, and have come away convinced that they have indeed been tortured or threatened—both of these men refused to work, believing that because they had come to Hong Kong as asylum seekers, they should follow Hong Kong laws (one of these men eventually obtained refugee status and now lives in Canada; the other still waits in Hong Kong). In several other cases I know of, the asylum seeker does not work because he or she would rather scrimp by on next to nothing—or live off the earnings of a girlfriend—than work.

However, the vast majority of asylum seekers do work at a range of different jobs. Some asylum seekers work in e-waste, dismantling electronic appliances for their parts; others dismantle used cars, a common enterprise in more isolated areas of Hong Kong's New Territories. At these sites, lookouts survey the surrounding areas for police raids. Other asylum seekers work in South Asian restaurants. Other asylum seekers engage in off-the-books construction or other forms of work at which they have skill, or at trade in electronic or other goods sent back to their home countries.[6] There are some 63,000 South Asians in Hong Kong, close to 1% of Hong Kong's population (Erni and Leung 2014: 5), and so the South Asians who are asylum seekers can blend in relatively easily with those who are not asylum seekers, not attracting attention, as a sub-Saharan African might, since there are few sub-Saharan Africans in Hong Kong other than asylum seekers.[7] Many asylum seekers work in Chungking Mansions (Mathews 2011), where, due to the ethnic population in the building as well as the architecture (police can't quickly get to the upper floors, and so working asylum seekers can be easily tipped off in advance as to their presence), it is relatively easy to work without much danger of getting caught.

Some of these jobs are more vulnerable than others to getting caught by police; but in any case, police cannot easily catch those asylum seekers who work. Any time police stop someone behind the counter in Chungking Mansions and ask to see a Hong Kong ID card, that person can always say, "I don't have a Hong Kong I.D. I'm an asylum seeker—here are my papers. I'm just here for a few minutes filling in for my uncle, who had to leave," and police cannot easily prosecute the person. I have often encountered undercover police in Chungking Mansions, and can readily recognize them, as can any savvy asylum seeker. (I confess to having occasionally enjoyed introducing myself to undercover police in Chungking Mansions: "Hi, I'm an anthropologist doing research in Chungking Mansions. And you must be a policeman! Glad to meet you!") Undercover police have a typical mode of dress and demeanor, and anyone with a bit of practice can identify them from 100 yards away.

I have, on several occasions, witnessed how hard it is, given Hong Kong's stringent rights-protecting laws, for police to catch working asylum seekers. On one occasion, two undercover police in Chungking Mansions were in an Indian restaurant seeking to catch an Indian waiter, whom they believed to be an asylum seeker illegally working; if he would serve their orders, he could indeed be caught. But upon seeing them, he merely stepped outside the restaurant to mingle with the crowd of passersby; the undercover policeman and policewoman repeatedly asked for *biryani*, but no one in the restaurant paid them any attention, until they eventually departed, frustrated. I have also seen an African phone-store clerk confidently fend off the queries of undercover police ("That phone? No, I don't know the price. Let me call the guy who runs this shop. No, it's not my shop. No, I don't work here! I'm just sitting here for a while") until they left. Some asylum seekers do get caught working by undercover police—sex workers soliciting customers are an easy target, since as soon as a price is mentioned, they can get arrested for working illegally (as opposed to merely seeking sex without mention of money, which cannot be prosecuted), as are sellers of copy watches, and of course drug dealers—but by and large, an asylum seeker must be unlucky as well as careless in order to get caught working. Asylum seekers remain extremely nervous about police, simply because getting arrested and convicted would be catastrophic; but this happens only rarely.

Given this situation, it makes sense for most asylum seekers—all but those who feel that they have a strong chance of obtaining refugee status—to work. Most important is the fact that the sustenance provided to asylum seekers is not enough to live in—a few live off charity, often provided by Christian churches or by NGOs; some also are supported by Indonesian or Filipina domestic helper girlfriends (Vecchio 2015: 145), who may provide financial as well as emotional sustenance. But most work, at laboring jobs that are readily available in a Hong Kong where labor is insufficient, as numerous reports have testified (Lee 2015; Siu 2015). Even if wages in Hong Kong for undocumented workers are meager, they nonetheless far exceed the wages of the developing-world societies that asylum seekers come from. One Indian asylum seeker I know spends his days touting for customers for a Chungking Mansions restaurant; at this job he makes far more money from his work than does his wife, a teacher back in Kolkata. For asylum seekers like him, Hong Kong is a paradise in the sense that it provides developed-world wages. The wages he gets are small—Hong Kong $3,500 per month, around US$480, in a society where the legal minimum wage is the equivalent of about HK$5,200 per month—but represent a windfall as far as he is concerned. I went back to Kolkata with him to visit his family, and saw that he is his three-generation family's major breadwinner because of the money he can make in Hong Kong.

Indeed, if an asylum seeker can work for a few years and send money back home, then he or she can do very well once returning home. A Kenyan sex worker in Chungking Mansions made this very clear to me when she said that if she could practice her trade for four years in one of Hong Kong's bar districts, Wan Chai, then she would have enough money to send her son through school to university back in Nairobi, and then start her own restaurant. Asylum seekers in less lucrative professions said the same thing: a few years of working in Hong Kong could—if they carefully sent their money back home, and if their money was not spent back home, but indeed saved—then their lives could be very good indeed. This is always dangerous, because the temptation for family back home will be to spend rather than save the money earned overseas, as several asylum seekers have bitterly recounted to me; but if the money is indeed saved, then it may be a life-altering windfall once the asylum seeker returns home.

Some asylum seekers—for example, Filipina and Indonesian domestic helpers who declare that they are asylum seekers after their contracts have ended—are often deported after a year or two by the Hong Kong government, but asylum seekers from elsewhere, whose claims are not so easy to refute, are often not deported for an extended period: the Hong Kong government jails them but does not deport them unless they themselves sign forms testifying that they agree to be deported. A prominent Hong Kong lawyer has declared to asylum seekers—at least so it was reported to me by asylum seekers who were there—that "you will never be deported. The system of appeals in Hong Kong courts means that you can stay for as long as you want." This statement is not entirely true—lawyers accept cases on the basis of whether or not those cases are winnable, and asylum seeker without a solid case may have trouble obtaining representation other than the duty lawyers assigned to them after they are charged with a crime, who may or may not conscientiously represent them—but does indicate that those asylum seekers who come to Hong Kong specifically to work may have a considerable degree of leeway. If they have enough savvy to tell a plausible story, then their stay in Hong Kong may be indefinite. It is sometimes surprisingly difficult to arrive at a plausible story—there are standard stories swapped among some asylum seekers that rapidly lose credibility since they are so often repeated, and so some asylum seekers are always on the lookout for the right story to tell—but for those who can relate such a narrative, their time in Hong Kong may be long.

A question that may have occurred to readers of this chapter is that of veracity. What percentage of Hong Kong asylum seekers are lying in their accounts? I have heard claims ranging from 60% to 99%. My sense is that many asylum seekers lie on details, in accordance with what the forms they must fill out upon declaring themselves as asylum seekers seem to require, but most are in that gray area between lies and truth: they have a solid reason to leave their own countries, but because that reason may not exactly fit what they are required to state, they must lie. As one asylum seeker told me, "We tell one thing to the lawyers, another thing to government officials, another thing to NGOs, and other things to you. Who knows what is true? Even we don't know." My own sense is that most asylum seekers have very good reason to leave their own countries, whether to earn more money for a family in need, or because an employer or colleague or family member threatened them with death, and they felt no choice but to flee, but these reasons generally will not fit the quite narrow grounds of the forms that asylum seekers are required to fill out, attesting that they are have been victims of or have been threatened with torture, or that they are facing specific political, religious, or ethnic persecution. Facing such forms, of course they lie: no one in their right mind would not, unless their actual stories fit the requisite forms as they typically do not.

For those asylum seekers who come to Hong Kong overtly to work, the best course of action is clear: find a good story, and work as long as you can. Eventually, after many appeals of your case, you will perhaps be jailed and deported. But if you can extend your case for as long as possible, and work hard and save up your money, you will have supported your family back home, earning your family's gratitude and respect, and may also have a sizeable nest egg once you return. This is the situation for a number of the South Asian asylum seekers in Hong Kong whom I know. They know very well what the situation in Hong Kong is, and seek to tell their stories and maximize their stay in Hong Kong in order to work for as long as possible. However, other asylum seekers I know seem to have reasons to flee home and make their lives in Hong Kong, beyond the lure of higher wages alone. These asylum seekers also typically work, because they feel they must work to survive, and also because they have families and relatives back home they must support; but work isn't their primary motivation. They have come to Hong Kong to make a new life for themselves. This, however, may be extraordinarily difficult.

Laws versus Norms in Hong Kong

Except in extraordinary cases, the only way an asylum seeker can permanently stay in Hong Kong is through marriage to a person with a Hong Kong ID card. For Somalis, at least up until recently, there has been no need to seriously consider this, since the odds of obtaining refugee status and making a new life in the United States or Canada are high, or at least were in the United States until Donald Trump became president and blocked Somali refugees. This is not to say that Somalis and Hong Kong residents do not fall in love with each other—I have seen this happen—but simply that this is typically a distraction rather than a means to obtaining the rights to a new legal status, nationality, and home. South Asian asylum seekers too have romantic relations with Hongkongers, but for those who are intent on working, these too are sometimes more a diversion than a path to a new life. Most South Asian asylum seekers in Hong Kong form relationships—if they form any romantic relationships at all—with Filipina and Indonesian domestic helpers in Hong Kong.

It is, among the asylum seekers I know well, not the Somalis or South Asians, but other Africans, as well as the Middle Easterners and Russians, for whom ongoing relations with Hong Kong residents are sought after. This is because, more than many Somalis up until recently, they cannot realistically hope to attain refugee status to go to the United States or Canada (although a few do attain this), and more than some South Asians, they do not simply view Hong Kong as a place to make money and then return home. Most of these people feel that they cannot go home again—the circumstances that led them to leave their home country, whether political, religious, ethnic, or economic (or whatever combination of these) are such that this is impossible, they feel. At the same time, the odds of another country taking them as refugees are extremely low. For these people, Hong Kong beckons as home—there is no other home for many of them.[8] And again, the one obvious way that Hong Kong can indeed become their home is through marriage to a Hongkonger. Marriage to a domestic helper will not help (and indeed, may cost the domestic helper her job); it must be to a resident of Hong Kong holding a Hong Kong ID card. Once this marriage has taken place and been investigated by immigration authorities, then a Hong Kong ID card will eventually be granted to the asylum seeker; after seven years, the asylum seeker can become a permanent resident of Hong Kong.

But typically, relationships with Hongkongers—and particularly asylum seeker men involved with Hong Kong women—are difficult, because, I am told, "once the woman knows you are an asylum seeker, you'll never see her again."[9] This is not because asylum seekers have a particularly bad reputation in Hong Kong: while conservative political parties fulminate against "fake asylum seekers," and while newspaper stories about asylum seekers engaging in crimes are often to be found, asylum seekers in Hong Kong are generally supported by pro-democratic groups championing ethnic diversity; at least among some segments of Hong Kong university students, having asylum seeker friends is a mark of status. Rather, the disdain of Hong Kong women is because asylum seekers are known to have very little money, and in materialistic Hong Kong, a man without money is not to be taken seriously.

Even dating requires this—an asylum seeker whose Hong Kong girlfriend pays for him all the time is unlikely to be accepted, both within the cultural contexts that asylum seekers come from, and also within the Hong Kong cultural context, where men and women can share expenses of dates, but where the woman cannot consistently pay. On a number of occasions, male asylum seekers have come to me to ask, abashedly, for several hundred Hong Kong dollars. I ask why they need the money. They say, "I have a date, and I can't let her know that I'm an asylum seeker." I generally refuse these requests, not least because the asylum seeker cannot maintain this fiction forever—at some point, he will have to tell the truth. When this truth is told, it most typically prevents the relation from continuing. An Indian asylum seeker whom I know discussed with me how his romantic relationship with a young Hong Kong woman came to naught: one night he discussed the possibility of marriage with her, and she promptly broke up with him: "I'm just with you to have fun, not to get married!" Asylum seekers can often pretend not to be asylum seekers for a while, and can in some cases "have fun," but eventually they cannot sustain the illusion that they are marriageable material unless they work.

For all asylum seekers, work—or perhaps university study or some other legitimate social role in Hong Kong society—is their only path to meet Hong Kong women and to perhaps eventually marry.[10] I earlier noted how in Hong Kong work is the raison d'etre of adults; one in the prime of life who does not work is not seen as a full human being. Vecchio notes (2015: 55) that work, for many asylum seekers, is not only a matter of earning money, but of also gaining a sense of achievement; as an asylum seeker told me, "When I work, I'm not a beggar. I'm earning the money for my life." Those who work fit the norms of society, not just in Hong Kong but in the societies from which asylum seekers come. There are also gender norms—most asylum seekers in Hong Kong are male, and work is what defines them as men. To fit their norms of maleness and of usefulness, they must work. I have consistently seen, in my 15 years of interaction with asylum seekers, that those who do not work are more likely to be afflicted with sleep disorders and psychological problems, and are more likely to require medical intervention; those who do work are more likely to lead stable lives, not simply in a financial sense but in a psychological sense as well. This is not always the case, but very often is indeed the case.

I know one Indian asylum seeker well, a man who works as a clothing seller in Chungking Mansions. After being in love with an Indonesian domestic helper who eventually spurned him since their marriage was impossible (she would lose her job if they married), he then married an emotionally unstable Hong Kong woman whom he had met in Chungking Mansions,[11] gambling that through such a means he could eventually earn his Hong Kong ID card. He suffered through nights of waking up at 3 a.m. to find her absent (off gambling? engaged in prostitution? taking drugs? He did not know). Because, as an asylum seeker, he could not have a bank account in Hong Kong, he had to rely on her bank account, but she would on occasion take much of his money for her own uses. Despite all these difficulties, he carefully trained her as to what she should tell immigration officials when they make their unannounced visit to check on asylum seeker marriages to see if they are valid, by interviewing wife and husband separately about their common activities. Somehow, despite their somewhat discrepant stories, they passed the test, and today he is the proud owner of a Hong Kong ID card, legally working and speculating on getting a divorce once he has his permanent Hong Kong ID card, issued after seven years.[12]

I know of five marriages between asylum seekers and Hongkongers that have apparently been successful, at least so far, with, to my knowledge, no rumblings of divorce, so this is not impossible. In these cases, it is asylum seeker men who are older and are sophisticated about the world, marrying Hong Kong women who are not in their early 20s but rather in their 30s, who know something about relationships and who can discern what they seek in a husband. In several cases I know of, the Hong Kong wife has provided the initial financing for a business in Hong Kong or in Guangzhou that the husband then operates, enabling the husband to become, to at least some extent, a family breadwinner. The husband may not make as much money as his wife does—these women may have university degrees in Hong Kong: before the man becomes economically self-sufficient, he must accept his wife's economic superiority, something quite difficult for most of the African, Middle Eastern, and South Asian men I know. These men have in their asylum seeker years in Hong Kong typically violated Hong Kong law by working, and obtained enough money to woo a Hong Kong woman. Eventually, through marriage and the eventual attainment of a Hong Kong ID card, they can come to work legally, and the contradiction in their lives between norms and laws can end.

But tragedy may also result from these marriages, beyond that of merely divorce. Seven years ago, the Hong Kong wife of an African asylum seeker, pregnant with his child, killed herself and her unborn child. This was because the husband had spent his evenings hanging out with his African friends in Chungking Mansions rather than staying at home with his wife, as is the

Hong Kong norm, and she was convinced that he was seeing other women (as apparently he was not). This was not norms versus law, but norms versus norms, ending in catastrophe.

Despite this, it is clear that for a lucky few asylum seekers, they can indeed work, make money, marry, become legal, and then work at more lucrative pursuits. The norm is for a man to work. The law says that an asylum seeker can't work. This contradiction can only be solved if an asylum seeker gains refugee status or a new passport and settles in another country, or if the asylum seeker can successfully marry a Hong Kong woman and become, eventually, a permanent Hong Kong resident. If either of these happen, then the contradiction between norms and laws can be overcome. If neither of these happen, then the contradiction between norms and laws leads most asylum seekers to choose the norm of work over staying legal. This renders the asylum seeker illegal, a criminal under Hong Kong law, justifying the Hong Kong government's poor treatment of asylum seekers, since "they are all criminals, only coming here to work," as I have sometimes been told by Hong Kong Chinese. But it also may be the asylum seeker's best chance not only to make a survivable wage for the time being, but also to marry and stay in Hong Kong permanently. This is the dream motivating at least some Hong Kong asylum seekers.

IMPLICATIONS

The Hong Kong government's treatment of asylum seekers, despite what some NGO commentators maintain (see, e.g., some of the posts on Vision First 2016), is not as severe as that of many other developed countries. Asylum seekers can enter Hong Kong relatively easily, can obtain very minimal subsistence, and can move freely in Hong Kong without being imprisoned, although they cannot legally work. Nonetheless, the government's policy has fundamental problems: it requires asylum seekers to wait an extremely long time for a decision, and it eventually rejects virtually all asylum seekers, an outcome at odds with that of most other developed societies. The practical outcome of this is that asylum seekers, unable to survive on the minimal welfare allowance they receive, are often forced to work illegally, something that benefits economic asylum seekers, who may save up a considerable sum of money before their claims are eventually rejected, but that harms "genuine" asylum seekers who may be afraid to work because if they are caught, their refugee claims may be denied, and they may be deported back to their home countries.

The effect of the policy is to separate laws and norms for asylum seekers in Hong Kong. If asylum seekers feel that they have a good chance of being deemed "genuine," then it makes most sense for them to follow the law and ignore the Hong Kong norm that a man should work. But for everyone else, the norm of work wins out over the law. Asylum seekers' motivations for working are clear, from what I have thus far written. But what is the motivation of the Hong Kong government in pursuing this policy?

Hong Kong, like most other developed-world societies, seeks to keep asylum seekers at arm's length because they are from the developing world: government officials have told me informally that the government's biggest concern is that if word gets out that Hong Kong is a good place for asylum seekers, every plane from Lagos and Karachi and Kolkata to Hong Kong will become filled with asylum seekers. At the same time, however, it is widely acknowledged that a chronic labor shortage threatens Hong Kong's construction industry, restaurant sector, and other areas of business. Asylum seekers form an informal labor source that can be illegally hired and paid far below the minimum wage, and that supports Hong Kong small businesses that otherwise would go bankrupt. These include many of the businesses in Chungking Mansions that rely on cheap prices, and some of the industries in Hong Kong's New Territories that are dirty, dangerous, and otherwise unprofitable, such as dismantling used cars for their parts. These businesses survive through illegal labor.

The government does occasionally send out police raids, and does occasionally prosecute; but it by and large turns a blind eye to illegal labor. I think that this is practically inevitable, given the strictures of Hong Kong law, but also intentional. By using a screening system that requires asylum seekers to wait for many years, and by providing asylum seekers with insufficient support to live on, it ensures their availability as illegal labor, and supports Hong Kong small businesses that otherwise might go under. Rather than legally recognize foreign laborers, which would entail greater responsibility, the government would rather keep them illegal and thus deportable, but at the same time keep them in situations where they are extremely difficult to catch and prosecute. The Hong Kong government prefers to use asylum seekers as an illegal labor source because it can then meet the needs of some Hong Kong low-end employers without having to acknowledge the existence of these foreign workers except as illegals.

I cannot prove that this is the case, but the government's refusal to implement an obvious commonsensical solution suggests that it may indeed be. The obvious solution to the problem of asylum seekers, and one that would largely solve the problem of asylum seekers, would be to offer a limited three-year or four-year nonrenewable work visa, somewhat similar to that which is offered to domestic helpers (although that is typically renewable). This would serve to separate those asylum seekers who come to Hong Kong specifically to work from those fleeing political, religious, or ethnic persecution; those who come to Hong Kong as asylum seekers would then greatly decrease in number, since many would choose a limited work visa instead. This would make the government's judgments concerning asylum seekers' claims far easier, but the government apparently does not want to consider this solution. Indeed, when I have discussed this solution in public forums, and in media outlets such as *The South China Morning Post* (Mathews and Vecchio 2011) I heard from NGOs but never a word from anyone in the Hong Kong government. Partly this may be because the government ignores academics in general except for those who toe its line, but more, I think, it is because the government prefers this labor force to remain illegal and unacknowledged.

If this solution were adopted, it would have the effect of legitimizing those asylum seekers who work in Hong Kong: they would be legal, although temporary, and so norms and laws would not be in such direct contradiction in their lives. It would also have the effect of legitimizing those who do not work, those who choose laws over norms, because they would come to be seen as legitimate asylum seekers rather than liars, as is often the case in Hong Kong at present. Hong Kong's norms may well broaden to accept such people: work might come to be seen as not the only path by which men may become normatively acceptable. The contradiction of laws and norms would thus perhaps diminish. And of course, beyond this the Hong Kong government would solve the problem of so many asylum seekers working illegally.

However, it seems that both the Hong Kong government and asylum seekers themselves don't want to solve this problem. The Hong Kong government may prefer to keep working illegal for asylum seekers, so that if the unemployment rate increases, it can inveigh against illegal asylum seekers and deport many more of them. The illegality of work for asylum seekers gives them a convenient cover. The views of asylum seekers themselves seem to have little impact on government policies, but most working asylum seekers I know prefer the current situation, because they can typically work indefinitely as illegal workers rather than being limited by fixed-term contracts. They complain about the Hong Kong government's unjust policies, but benefit from those policies. Let norms and laws remain separate, they might say if they were anthropologists, for they are savvy enough to navigate between them. The current situation in Hong Kong—the gap between norms and laws in the lives of asylum seekers—is obviously the result of a deeply flawed government policy, but one that benefits both the government and many asylum seekers themselves. And so, it will probably remain.

NOTES

1. I use the term "asylum seekers" rather than the more politically correct term "refugees" in this chapter because the overwhelming majority of asylum seekers in Hong Kong will never attain refugee status, given the fact that the Hong Kong government rejects virtually all claims.

2. Hong Kong has some 390,000 domestic helpers, largely Filipina and Indonesian. See Constable (2007, 2014) for a detailed glimpse of their lives.

3. For a dated but excellent analysis of the legal situation of Hong Kong asylum seekers, see Loper (2010). Dauvergne's account of the relation of law to migration around the world (2008) is key in considering the travails of Hong Kong asylum seekers within a global legal perspective, although for reasons of space, I cannot pursue this line of inquiry here.

4. In the pages that follow, the asylum seekers I discuss are all male. This is partly because asylum seekers in Hong Kong tend to be predominantly male, as earlier noted, but also because the majority are Muslim, involving comparatively greater gender segregation: Muslim women tend not to work among the asylum seekers I know. All marriages between asylum seekers and Hongkongers that I know of involve a male asylum seeker and a female Hongkonger.

5. A question that Hong Kong Immigration investigators often ask of asylum seekers is, "If you have the problem that you've described, why can't you simply go off to a city in your home country where no one knows you and make a new life for yourself? Why did you have to come to Hong Kong?" Asylum seekers typically say that the ethnic, religious, or political problem they face is of such magnitude that there is nowhere in their own country that is safe for them to go; but in politically more-or-less stable countries, this may not seem believable to investigators.

6. See Vecchio (2015: 165–93) for a more detailed discussion of asylum seeker work in Hong Kong than I have provided here.

7. See, for an extended account of South Asian asylum seekers in Hong Kong, Murgai (2013), and Erni and Leung (2014) for an account of South Asians at large in Hong Kong.

8. A tactic that some asylum seekers have begun using since 2019 is to obtain a new passport from their country of origin and then to use it, along with the educational qualifications they earned in Hong Kong through distance learning, to find employment in developing-world societies. Two of my former students have sent me pictures of themselves in suits, proudly proclaiming their new professional status as ESL teachers in countries such as Vietnam or Indonesia.

9. African asylum seekers I know sometimes assert that this is because of racial discrimination: "Hongkongers are incredibly racist towards Africans," I have often heard, not least when one's daughter is dating an African—although these racial attitudes seem very much to be changing among the more liberal younger generation in Hong Kong (Mathews 2018). However, the Central Asian and Middle Eastern asylum seekers I know—who indeed may look "white"—also have trouble finding Hong Kong spouses. My sense is that while racism is certainly real in Hong Kong, the most pivotal reason why these men have trouble marrying is because they are asylum seekers.

10. University study is generally off-limits for asylum seekers, because they cannot pay the fees—although a few NGOs have recently emerged in Hong Kong to help asylum seekers pay tuition. Many asylum seekers, encouraged by university teachers, take classes informally. Aside from campuses, Christian churches—unlike mosques in Hong Kong, which are gender segregated—are also suitable places to meet potential partners, but from the stories I've heard, Hong Kong women met in church may sometimes be too demanding and rigid for such relationships to be successful.

11. Chungking Mansions is *terra incognita* for almost all Hong Kong Chinese. The female Hongkongers to be found in Chungking Mansions are likely to have considerably less social and cultural capital than most Hongkongers.

12. As I was making the final revisions to this chapter in fall 2020, this man phoned me from Pakistan to invite me to his upcoming wedding to a Pakistani woman—having obtained his Hong Kong identity documents, he can take her with him back to Hong Kong.

REFERENCES

Chan, Wai-kwong. "From Refugee Camp to City Streets: The Different Lives of Young Vietnamese in Hong Kong." M. Phil. Thesis, Dept. of Anthropology, Chinese University of Hong Kong, 2003.

Chan, Wilfred. "Hong Kong's 'Shameful' Treatment of Asylum Seekers Exposed." *CNN*, July 18, 2013. http://edition.cnn.com/2013/07/18/world/asia/hong-kong-refugees-exposed/, accessed November 29, 2020.

Chen, Te-ping. "Hong Kong Changing the Way It Handles Refugees." *Wall Street Journal*, July 16, 2013. https://www.wsj.com/articles/SB10001424127887324694904578601171702287356, accessed November 29, 2020.

Constable, Nicole. *Maid to Order in Hong Kong: Stories of Migrant Workers*. 2nd edition. Ithaca: Cornell University Press, 2007.

Constable, Nicole. *Born Out of Place: Migrant Mothers and the Politics of International Labor Law*. Berkeley: University of California Press, 2014.

Dauvergne, Catherine. *Making People Illegal: What Globalization Means for Migration and Law*. Cambridge: Cambridge University Press, 2008.

Erni, John Nguyet, and Lisa Yuk-ming Leung. *Understanding South Asian Minorities in Hong Kong*. Hong Kong: Hong Kong University Press, 2014.

Jacobsen, Karen. *The Economic Life of Refugees*. Bloomfield, CT: Kumarian Press, 2005.

Justice Centre Hong Kong. "Meeting the Bare Minimum: Hong Kong's New Screening Process for Protection." 2014. http://www.justicecentre.org.hk/framework/uploads/2014/03/USM-Briefing-Meeting-the-Bare-Minimum-HK-New-Screening-Process-for-Protection.pdf, accessed November 29, 2020.

Lee, Eddie. "Chronic Labour Shortages Threaten Hong Kong's Infrastructure Building Boom." *South China Morning Post*, April 15, 2015. https://www.scmp.com/news/hong-kong/economy/article/1766598/chronic-labour-shortages-threaten-hong-kongs-infrastructure, accessed November 29, 2020.

Legislative Council, Hong Kong. Paper for the House Committee meeting on March 1, 2019. https://www.legco.gov.hk/yr18-19/english/hc/papers/hc20190301cb2-874-e.pdf, accessed November 29, 2020.

Leung, Christy. "Failed Asylum Seekers Left in Limbo as Countries Drag their Feet on Helping Hong Kong Deport 2,000." *South China Morning Post*, August 7, 2018. https://www.scmp.com/news/hong-kong/hong-kong-law-and-crime/article/2158595/failed-asylum-seekers-left-limbo-countries, accessed November 29, 2020.

Loper, Kelley. "Human Rights, *Non-refoulement* and the Protection of Refugees in Hong Kong." *International Journal of Refugee Law* 22, no. 3 (2010): 404–439.

Marfleet, Philip. *Refugees in a Global Era*. New York: Palgrave Macmillan, 2006.

Mathews, Gordon. *Ghetto at the Center of the World: Chungking Mansions, Hong Kong*. Chicago: University of Chicago Press, 2011.

Mathews, Gordon. "Arguing, Learning, Waiting." Op-ed column, *New York Times*, June 27, 2012. https://www.nytimes.com/2012/06/28/opinion/asylum-seekers-wait-and-learn-in-hong-kong.html, accessed November 29, 2020.

Mathews, Gordon. "Asylum Seekers in Hong Kong: The Paradoxes of Lives Lived on Hold." In *Migration in China and Asia: Experience and Policy*, edited by Jijiao Zhang, and Howard Duncan, 73–85. New York: Springer, 2014.

Mathews, Gordon "Asylum Seekers as Symbols of Hong Kong's Non-Chineseness." *China Perspectives* 3 (2018): 51–58.

Mathews, Gordon, and Francesco Vecchio. "Open and Shut Cases." Op-ed Column, *The South China Morning Post*, January 14, 2011. https://www.scmp.com/article/735588/open-and-shut-cases, accessed November 29, 2020.

McCalmon, Brian. "Winding It Up in Hong Kong: The Increasing Impatience with Vietnamese Asylum Seekers." *Georgetown Immigration Law Journal* 8, no. 2 (1994): 333–342.

Migration Watch UK. "Asylum Seekers and the Right to Work in the European Economic Area." 2013. http://www.migrationwatchuk.org/briefing-paper/316, accessed November 29, 2020.

Murgai, Gaurav. "Hunting Mirages of Success: Dreams of Extralegal South Asians in Hong Kong." M.Phil. thesis, Dept. of Anthropology, Chinese University of Hong Kong, 2013.

Ngo, Jennifer. "Six Asylum Seekers Claim Protection in Hong Kong in a Week—But NGOs Say Officials are Turning More Hostile." *South China Morning Post*, September 22, 2015. https://www.scmp.com/news/hong-kong/education-community/article/1860289/six-asylum-seekers-claim-protection-hong-kong, accessed November 29, 2020.

Oriental Daily. (in Chinese) "Torture Claimants Cost HK Government HK$600,000,000 Annually and Only 0.4% Are Real." March 28, 2015. http://hk.on.cc/hk/bkn/cnt/news/20150328/bkn-20150328222614750-0328_00822_001.html, accessed November 29, 2020.

Siu, Phila. "Hong Kong Restaurant Sector Faces Serious Labour Shortage." *South China Morning Post*, November 22, 2015. https://www.scmp.com/news/hong-kong/economy/article/1881637/hong-kong-restaurant-sector-faces-serious-labour-shortage, accessed November 29, 2020.

South China Morning Post. "Loopholes Mean Genuine Asylum Seekers Suffer." *Editorial*, November 28, 2010. https://www.scmp.com/article/731851/loopholes-mean-genuine-asylum-seekers-suffer, accessed November 29, 2020.

Vecchio, Francesco. *Asylum Seeking and the Global City*. London: Routledge, 2015.

Vecchio, Francesco, and Cosmo Beatson. "Asylum Seekers' Occupy Movement in Hong Kong." *Race & Class* 56, no. 2 (2014): 96–104.

Vision First. 2016. http://www.vfnow.org/, accessed November 29, 2020.

Afterword

Florence E. Babb and Rudi Colloredo-Mansfeld

As this book makes admirably clear, street economies have long been beset by polarized thinking, whether from their researchers or their publics. The theorizations and case studies brought together by coeditors Cristiana Panella and Walter E. Little reveal that most street economies are small-scale, urban, and extensions of informal trade networks of hard-working individuals on the social margins. Notwithstanding their economic precarity, these operators are often socially and politically potent. On the one hand are those observers proclaiming the essential criminality of those individuals who use illicit means to act in their self-interest, and who clutter the sidewalks and threaten the progress of modernizing urban areas. On the other hand are those, like Peruvian neoliberal economist Hernando de Soto, who see impoverished urban entrepreneurs, not criminals, who when freed from extensive municipal red tape, will successfully advance as formal sector workers. Amid such dualist views, a host of overdetermined symbols comes into play. The informal versus formal distinction maps readily onto other modernist binaries: underdeveloped versus developed, socially embedded versus market-mediated, individual versus firm, off-the-books versus regulated.

The contributors to *Norms and Illegality* make both conceptual and ethnographic interventions to unsettle such binary notions. Conceptually, they underscore the fluidity of informal/formal activity and what the binaries often overlook, pointing instead to the ubiquity of *gray* transactions (Smart) in social and economic lives. This complex, ambiguous deal-making exists in physical places made difficult by an only sporadically present and frequently absent state. Indeed, in the human careers that are presented here, grayness emerges recurringly, such that trades and jobs that were once resolved as either properly legal or illegal, white or black, once again go gray and need to call forth tactics to settle their new ambiguities.

Ethnographically, these writers tighten the analysis of grayness through the central focus of this book: the specificities of "illegality." The phrases that follow—"not-yet-legal" (Smart), "illegal values" (Panella), "official illegality" (Little), and "extralegality" (Smart)—map the contours of this terrain. Illegality at times can be a transient collective moment, such as an informal market poised to be recognized by municipal authorities. Illegality may be an obdurate feature of a trade, as in the traffic in Malian antiquities. Or illegality may be existential as with the case of the Roma, an aspect of collective origins that a people do not seek to resolve, to avoid censure and to placate the state. Attending to illegality, the writers do not simplify the grayness of so-called informal work, but instead give us subjectively valid terms for understanding the pressures of state action (and, sometimes, inaction) in daily work life.

What is most innovative in this project is the attention to corporeal agency (Panella) and to the enactment of cultural intimacy (Herzfeld) that underlies the everyday struggles to negotiate what is and is not allowed in public spaces, that is, the authors' interest in discerning how practices that may better be termed "extralegal" come to be tolerated, and sometimes even encouraged, in urban contexts. The analysis in these pieces tacks back and forth between the givenness and materiality of bodies and the abstractions of state and market. The specificity of men and women in their physical presence, their dress, their inventories of goods, and mode of transport through the city index cultural categories that agents of the state—police, market commissaries, tax authorities, immigration officers—appropriate toward political ends. Whether these agents sanction, accommodate, harass, instruct, or ignore embodied women and men plying trades in the streets signals the everyday praxis of legality in face-to-face confrontations. Abstractions of law become resolved in the dialectic and deference of a street encounter.

We have the case of Antigua, Guatemala's street economy with its male shoe shiners and photographers and female food and handicrafts sellers, catering to the public and to tourists coming to the UNESCO cultural heritage site (Little). While there is a concern to "clean up" the city for tourism, authorities tolerate the informal street trade because of the practical needs it serves and its popularity among residents and visitors. Likewise, informal migrant workers in Rome, here focusing on Roma and Senegalese traders, meet racism and social exclusion as illegal subjects (Clough Marinaro and Panella)—though in different ways, relating to their social and racial identities. Tellingly, these resistant bodies must aim to become "less illegal" and show themselves to be "deserving" in order to escape capture and deportation. And in the case of the market traders in the Northern Philippines, those who might be evicted for not fitting in with the image of the gentrified, modern city struggle for inclusion through negotiating for their right to a livelihood and access to urban resources (Milgram and Mendoza). In the case of asylum seekers in Hong Kong, we see that two migrant groups, from South Asia and sub-Saharan Africa, are viewed as suspect and are put in the untenable position of either complying with the law, which demands that they must rely on state stipends and not seek employment, or earning a precarious living illegally and embracing the social norms expected of these male migrants (Mathews).

The liminality of living with uncertainty in contested urban spaces not only challenges norms but often becomes the new normal in places with expansive street economies. It is not only street vendors and other service workers living on the margins who sense this, but so do state interests and policymakers who recognize the long-term prospects of the urban informal sector, whether illegal or legal. Officials make their peace with conditions as they exist by managing to find the advantages that may be wrung from the persistent bodies filling the urban space over prolonged periods of time. Spatiality and temporality work together in the contexts examined in *Norms and Illegality*, so that mobilities over the course of time reveal whose right to the city and its resources may win out in the long run. De Soto (1989) famously suggested over three decades ago that impoverished urban entrepreneurs could be liberated from informal, illegal status if the government were to cut the extensive red tape that kept them from successfully building their businesses and contributing to the formal economy. The authors in this book, in contrast, have a more critical approach to the dim prospects of such change under conditions of neoliberal capitalism, and also a more nuanced recognition of the ways that states and extralegal subjects are in constant negotiation over the terms of the latter's participation in urban political economies.

One significant realm of inquiry we would have liked to see explored further in this collection is that of the intersectionality of gender, race, and other forms of social difference that can be vitally important in differentiating the experiences of marginalized bodies in informal and extralegal settings. The authors have a sharper perception of social class and national identity differences, but offer fairly fleeting attention to the impact of gender and race as analytics for understanding the complex gray areas under consideration. We usefully learn that the Guatemalan street economy is marked by a certain gender division of labor in relation to goods and services on offer, and that indigenous Maya women in traditional dress hold a certain cultural capital, yet this does not guarantee them a place to sell items on the street; these insightful gendered observations could be explored further. We also glean from the chapter on artisanal mining in Madagascar that young men's bravado as "ravagers" seeking their fortune is at odds with the town's ecotourism aspirations; this brief attention to gender and masculinity is fascinating and could shed more light on the postboom settlers and clashing visions of development. We only learn from the endnotes to the illuminating Hong Kong study that all the interviewees were men and that the African asylum seekers among them disclosed the enormous racism they had experienced in the city: this is worth more prominent consideration. The study of Roma and Senegalese migrants in Rome comments on the increasing racism the migrants have faced, yet this too could be productively brought into the discussion of shifting perceptions of illegality and marginality as well as outright discrimination in the street economy.

We would propose that it is often among those gendered and racialized bodies marked as most vulnerable that we see these constructions of the *other* in sharpest relief. For the alterity of these trades draws from its varied transgressions, not merely of legal codes or of social conventions but of the laws of capital, labor, and profit. The Roma pluck from dumpsters discarded objects, deemed useless by previous owners to sell anew. Miners in Ambondromifehy rely on gemstone booms and rushes, on a time horizon that has no dependable future. These economic elements and actors are far from the commodity of Marx or the rationality of Weber, and gendering, racializing, and elevating of ethnic boundaries become tactics covering the capriciousness of capitalism. Moreover, objectifying the bodies populating street economies also allows for persistent *non*economic injustices to flourish in the intimacies of cultural lives.

Related to these identity-based forms of difference and inequality, we discover in these contributions evidence of the daily struggles and small triumphs of those populating street economies in diverse settings. Indeed, the authors reference the hope and resilience found in marginalized sectors of informalized and often criminalized economies. This book whets our appetite to know whether there is political activism in the settings discussed that might be brought to light, whether pressure is placed on the state to grant urban space and the basic right to work for a living. Or, alternatively, whether the need to keep a low profile and avoid negative attention as *informals* and *illegals* mitigates against such outspokenness and public protest.

Over our years of research in the Andean region, Babb in Peru and Colloredo-Mansfeld in Ecuador, we have considered local political economies bearing considerable resemblance to the cases elaborated in this book. Babb (2018) has followed the lives and work of market and street sellers, artisans, and service providers—often regarded as informal even if they pay city fees and are subject to official restrictions over the use of public space. A number of these individuals have played an active part in market unions and other organizations fighting to expand their legal rights. Moreover, their efforts to press for more just legislation and treatment affecting their work lives are frequently coupled with their cultural and political struggles not only as impoverished bodies but as indigenous women, highland migrant men, and, in short, as deeply gendered and racialized subjects. Their efforts to be regarded as *worthy* contributing members of a society that often abhors them, to gain inclusion and recognition for the vital needs they meet and services they provide, and for the cultural rights they are entitled to, are often on prominent display. In some cases, their simple act of showing up and making collective claims for urban space has met success.

Yet, the fight for regulatory authority based on cultural grounds can be unpredictable. Colloredo-Mansfeld (2008) has tracked the efforts of an indigenous artisan union in Ecuador to exempt its members from child labor laws when merchants travelled abroad to sell their wares. In 2001, national headlines proclaimed 12 indigenous boys and girls were working as virtual slaves, selling artisan textiles in the streets in Uruguay, watched over by an experienced craft dealer. While the union leadership supported the repatriation of the youths, freeing them from their circumstances, they noted they had all begun their working lives in a similar fashion. They used the authority of the union to limit future state surveillance of its traders. Cecilie Ødegaard's (2008) research on the law, state and local norms, and contraband trade between Peru and Bolivia similarly discovered that traders justified their extralegal activity in terms of long-standing cultural exchange practices. In the current book, the antiquities looters of Mali (Panella) and the sapphire mine-rush workers in Madagascar (Walsh) reveal a widespread urban distrust and criticism of what are perceived as unsavory individuals who ply these trades; yet the authors tell a different story of more ambivalent if still troubling practices, and of a concern with research ethics in documenting them.

We have found in our own research that struggles over economic, political, and intercultural rights are generally closely intertwined in the lives of those engaged in urban street economies. Contested forms of exclusion and inequality are nearly always differentiated by corporeal racial and gender as well as socioeconomic circumstances. These forms can be observed across scales, running the gamut from the very local and culturally intimate to state-level regimes of authority and enforcement, or abandonment. In some cases, coming together as street vendors, petty manufacturers and artisans, informal miners, and service workers making collective claims for the right to a viable livelihood has resulted in a measure of success. Even in less successful cases, the alterity of their work is nonetheless defended by these marginalized workers and occasionally by those who patronize their services. Is such mobilization occurring among those we have read about in these pages? And if not, what obstacles may keep them from leveraging their collective power as vital workers in urban street economies? It is a testament to this thoughtful and generative book that we are left with ample questions to explore in future research.

REFERENCES

Babb, Florence E. *Women's Place in the Andes: Engaging Decolonial Feminist Anthropology*. Berkeley: University of California Press, 2018.

Colloredo-Mansfeld, Rudi. "Globalization from Below and the Political Turn among Otavalo's Merchant Artisans." In *The Ecuador Reader*, edited by C. de la Torre and S. Striffler, 377–384. Durham, NC: Duke University Press, 2008.

de Soto, Hernando. *The Other Path: The Invisible Revolution in the Third World.* New York: Harper & Row, 1989.

Ødegaard, Cecilie. "Informal Trade, *Contrabando* and Prosperous Socialities in Arequipa, Peru." *Ethnos* 73, no. 2 (2008): 241–266.

Index

About the Editors

Cristiana Panella is senior researcher in Social and Cultural Anthropology at the Royal Museum for Central Africa (Tervuren, Belgium). Her research has focused on heritage theory and in-depth fieldwork in informal/illegal circulation of antiquities and gold in Mali and counterfeits in Italy. In particular, she is interested in corporeality issues of marginal and illegal practices, and to the interrelation between heterogeneous systems of value. Currently, she is working on an interdisciplinary approach to the relationship between ethics, heritage, and corporeality with regard to Motion, Life Styles, and Health issues. She is preparing a book on an emic perspective of heritage theory through the ethnography of the clandestine trade in Malian ancient terracotta.

Walter E. Little is a full professor of Anthropology at the University at Albany, SUNY with a PhD from the University of Illinois at Urbana-Champaign. He studies the social and political economies of Latin American indigenous peoples, particularly in Guatemala, Mexico, and in the Albany, NY region. His multisited ethnographic research combines political economy and interpretive perspectives in order to better understand the politics of identity, economic development, cultural heritage and tourism in urban places, and the everyday practices of handicrafts production and marketplace interactions. He is the author of numerous articles, books, and reviews, including *Mayas in the Marketplace: Tourism, Globalization, and Cultural Identity* (2004), which won Best Book of 2005 from the New England Council for Latin American Studies, and *Street Economies in the Urban Global South* (2013), coedited with Karen Tranberg Hansen and B. Lynne Milgram, which won the Society for the Anthropology of Work Book Prize in 2014.

About the Contributors

Florence E. Babb (University of North Carolina at Chapel Hill) is the Anthony Harrington Distinguished Professor of Anthropology. She is the author of *Between Field and Cooking Pot: The Political Economy of Marketwomen in Peru* (1998[1989]); *After Revolution: Mapping Gender and Cultural Politics in Neoliberal Nicaragua* (2001); *The Tourism Encounter: Fashioning Latin American Nations and Histories* (2011); and *Women's Place in the Andes: Engaging Decolonial Feminist Anthropology* (2018). She collaborated in the School for Advanced Research seminar that resulted in the volume *Street Economies in the Urban Global South* (Hansen, Little, and Milgram, eds.).

Isabella Clough Marinaro (John Cabot University in Rome) has a Ph.D. from the University of Bath. She has worked for many years on the political and social conditions of Roma communities in Italy and the policy processes affecting them. Her current research focuses on urban development and its social consequences in Rome, as well as changing forms of crime and the informal economy in Italy. She has co-edited two books: *Italian Mafias Today: Territory, Business and Politics* (in press) and *Global Rome: Changing Faces of the Eternal City* (2014). She is now working on various articles and a single-authored book exploring multidimensional informalities in contemporary Rome.

Rudi Colloredo-Mansfeld (University of North Carolina at Chapel Hill) is Senior Associate Dean for Social Sciences and Global Programs and Professor of Anthropology. Since 1991, he has written and taught about community economies, artisan production, indigenous movements and cultural change in the context of globalization. His publications include the books, *The Native Leisure Class: Consumption and Cultural Creativity in the Andes*,

(Chicago 1999) *Fighting Like a Community: Andean Civil Society in an Era of Indigenous Uprisings* (Chicago 2009) and *Fast, Easy and In Cash: Artisan Hardship and Hope in the Global Economy* (with Jason Antrosio, Chicago 2015).

Michael Herzfeld (Harvard University, Leiden University, and Shanghai International Studies University) has a DPhil in Social Anthropology from Oxford University. His twelve monographs include *A Place in History: Social and Monumental Time in a Cretan Town* (1991), *The Social Production of Indifference: The Symbolic Roots of Western Bureaucracy* (1992, *The Body Impolitic: Artisans and Artifice in the Global Hierarchy of Value* (2004), *Evicted from Eternity: The Restructuring of Modern Rome* (2009), *Cultural Intimacy: Social Poetics and the Real Life of States, Societies, and Institutions* (2016, revised edition), *Siege of the Spirits: Community and Polity in Bangkok* (2016), and *Subversive Archaism: Troubling Traditionalists and the Politics of National Heritage* (2021).

Gordon Mathews (The Chinese University of Hong Kong) has a Ph.D. in Anthropology from Cornell University. He is the author of *The World in Guangzhou* with Linessa Dan Lin and Yang Yang (2017), *Ghetto at the Center of the World* (2011), *Hong Kong, China: Learning to Belong to a Nation*, with Eric Kit-wai Ma and Tai-lok Lui (2008), *Global Culture/Individual Identity: Searching for Home in the Cultural Supermarket* (2000), and *What Makes Life Worth Living? How Japanese and Americans Make Sense of Their Worlds* (1996)

Lorelei C. Mendoza (University of the Philippines Baguio) has a Ph.D. from the Catholic University of Leuven. Her research focuses on gender and household economics and local natural resource management. She is author of "Bargaining in rural households: a study of decisions on labor market participation in the Cordillera Region," *Philippine Review of Economics* (2006); "Policy Innovations and Effective Local Management of Forests in the Philippine Cordillera Region," *The Cordillera Review*(2009); and "Local Policy and Water Access in Baguio City, Philippines," *International Journal of Social Ecology and Sustainable Development* (2020).

B. Lynne Milgram (OCAD University) has a Ph.D. in Anthropology from York University. Her research in the Philippines analyzes alternative economies, informality/extralegality, and gendered work regarding crafts, the used clothing trade, food provisioning, and public market redevelopment. She is the co-editor of *Street Economies in the Urban Global South*, co-edited with Karen Tranberg Hansen and Walter E. Little (2013), *Economics and*

Morality: Anthropological Approaches, co-edited with Katherine E. Browne (2009), *Material Choices: Refashioning Bast and Leaf Fibers in Asia and the Pacific* co-edited with Roy W. Hamilton (2007), and *Artisans and Cooperatives: Developing Alternative Trade for the Global Economy*, co-edited with Kimberly M. Grimes (2000).

Alan Smart (University of Calgary) has a Ph.D. in Anthropology from the University of Toronto, Ontario. He has conducted research in Hong Kong since 1982. He is the author of *Posthumanism: Anthropological Insights* (2017), *The Shek Kip Myth: Squatters, Fires, and Colonial Rule* (2006), and *Making Room: Squatter Clearance in Hong Kong* (1992).

Andrew Walsh (University of Western Ontario) Ph.D. in Anthropology from the University of Toronto. His research focuses on artisanal sapphire mining, conservation, ecotourism, and small-scale development projects. He co-editor of *The Anthropology of Precious Minerals* (2020), with Elizabeth Ferry and Annabel Vallard, and is the author of "The ordinary ethics of charcoal in northern Madagascar," *Journal of the Royal Anthropological Institute 25 (2019)* and *Made in Madagascar: Sapphires, Ecotourism and the Global Bazaar (2012).*

www.ingramcontent.com/pod-product-compliance
Ingram Content Group UK Ltd.
Pitfield, Milton Keynes, MK11 3LW, UK
UKHW021904150926
475560UK00004B/331

9 781793 646309